Fire Your Stock Analyst!

FT Prentice Hall
FINANCIAL TIMES

In an increasingly competitive world, it is quality
of thinking that gives an edge—an idea that opens new
doors, a technique that solves a problem, or an insight
that simply helps make sense of it all.

We work with leading authors in the various arenas
of business and finance to bring cutting-edge thinking
and best-learning practices to a global market.

It is our goal to create world-class print publications
and electronic products that give readers
knowledge and understanding that can then be
applied, whether studying or at work.

To find out more about our business
products, you can visit us at www.ft-ph.com.

Pearson
Education

Fire Your Stock Analyst!

Analyzing Stocks on Your Own

Harry Domash

An imprint of PEARSON EDUCATION
Upper Saddle River, NJ • New York • London • San Francisco
Toronto • Sydney• Tokyo • Singapore • Hong Kong
• Cape Town • Madrid
Paris • Milan • Munich • Amsterdam

www.ft-ph.com

Library of Congress Cataloging-in-Publication Data

Domash, Harry
    Fire your stock analyst! : analyzing stocks on your own / by Harry Domash
      p. cm.
   Includes index.
   ISBN 0-13-035332-9 (alk. paper)
     1. Investment analysis. I. Title: Analyzing stocks on your own. II. Title.

HG4529 .D566 2002
332.63`2042--dc21

200227871

Hardcover Edition
Production Supervisor: Wil Mara
Acquisitions Editor: Jim Boyd
Developmental Editor: Jennifer Blackwell
Editorial Assistant: Allyson Kloss
Marketing Manager: Bryan Gambrel
Manufacturing Manager: Alexis Heydt-Long
Buyer: Maura Zaldivar

Paperback Edition
Vice President, Editor-in-Chief: Tim Moore
Executive Editor: Jim Boyd
Editorial Assistant: Susan Abraham
Development Editor: Jennifer Blackwell
Associate Editor-in-Chief and Director of Marketing: Amy Neidlinger
Cover Designer: Sandra Schroeder
Managing Editor: Gina Kanouse
Senior Project Editor: Lori Lyons
Senior Indexer: Cheryl Lenser
Senior Compositor: Gloria Schurick
Manufacturing Buyer: Dan Uhrig

 © 2006 by Financial Times Prentice Hall
An imprint of Pearson Education, Inc.
Upper Saddle River, New Jersey 07458

First Printing February 2006

ISBN 0-13-226038-7

Pearson Education LTD.
Pearson Education Australia PTY, Limited
Pearson Education Singapore, Pte. Ltd
Pearson Education North Asia Ltd
Pearson Education Canada, Ltd.
Pearson Educación de Mexico, S.A. de C.V.
Pearson Education—Japan
Pearson Education Malaysia, Pte. Ltd
Pearson Education, Upper Saddle River, New Jersey

FINANCIAL TIMES PRENTICE HALL BOOKS

For more information, please go to www.ft-ph.com

Kenneth R. Ferris and Barbara S. Pécherot Petitt
Valuation: Avoiding the Winner's Curse

International Business and Globalization

Robert A. Isaak
The Globalization Gap: How the Rich Get Richer and the Poor Get Left Further Behind

Johny K. Johansson
In Your Face: How American Marketing Excess Fuels Anti-Americanism

Peter Marber
Money Changes Everything: How Global Prosperity Is Reshaping Our Needs, Values, and Lifestyles

Fernando Robles, Françoise Simon, and Jerry Haar
Winning Strategies for the New Latin Markets

Investments

Gerald Appel
Technical Analysis

Guy Cohen
The Bible of Options Strategies: The Definitive Guide for Practical Trading Strategies

Guy Cohen
Options Made Easy, Second Edition

Michael Covel
Trend Following: How Great Traders Make Millions in Up or Down Markets

Aswath Damodaran
Investment Fables: Exposing the Myths of "Can't Miss" Investment Strategies

Harry Domash
Fire Your Stock Analyst! Analyzing Stocks on Your Own

David Gladstone and Laura Gladstone
Venture Capital Investing: The Complete Handbook for Investing in Businesses for Outstanding Profits

George Kleinman
Trading Commodities and Financial Futures, Third Edition

Michael J. Panzner
The New Laws of the Stock Market Jungle: An Insider's Guide to Successful Investing in a Changing World

Peter Rosenstreich
Forex Revolution

Michael C. Thomsett
Options Trading for the Conservative Investor

Michael Thomsett
Stock Profits: Getting to the Core—New Fundamentals for a New Age

Leadership

Jim Despain and Jane Bodman Converse
And Dignity for All: Unlocking Greatness through Values-Based Leadership

Marshall Goldsmith, Cathy Greenberg, Alastair Robertson, and Maya Hu-Chan
Global Leadership: The Next Generation

Marshall Goldsmith, Vijay Govindarajan, Beverly Kaye, and Albert A. Vicere
The Many Facets of Leadership

Theodore Kinni and Donna Kinni
No Substitute for Victory

Management

Rob Austin and Lee Devin
Artful Making: What Managers Need to Know About How Artists Work

Thomas L. Barton, WIlliam G. Shenkir, and Paul L. Walker
Making Enterprise Risk Management Pay Off

J. Stewart Black and Hal B. Gregersen
Leading Strategic Change: Breaking Through the Brain Barrier

William C. Byham, Audrey B. Smith, and Matthew J. Paese
Grow Your Own Leaders

Subir Chowdhury
Organization 21C

Nicholas D. Evans
Business Agility

Charles J. Fombrun and Cees B.M. Van Riel
Fame and Fortune: How Successful Companies Build Winning Reputations

Robert B. Handfield and Ernest L. Nichols, Jr.
Supply Chain Redesign

Amir Hartman
Ruthless Execution: What Business Leaders Do When Their Companies Hit the Wall

Faisal Hoque
The Alignment Effect

Kevin Kennedy and Mary Moore
Going the Distance: Why Some Companies Dominate and Others Fail

Steven R. Kursh
Minding the Corporate Checkbook: A Manager's Guide to Executing Successful Business Investments

Roy H. Lubit
Coping with Toxic Managers, Subordinates…and Other Difficult People

Tom Osenton
The Death of Demand: The Search for Growth in a Saturated Global Economy

Stephen P. Robbins
The Truth About Managing People…And Nothing but the Truth

Ronald Snee and Roger Hoerl
Leading Six Sigma: A Step-by-Step Guide Based on Experience with GE and Other Six Sigma Companies

Susan E. Squires, Cynthia J. Smith, Lorna McDougall, and William R. Yeack
Inside Arthur Andersen: Shifting Values, Unexpected Consequences

Jerry Weissman
Presenting to Win: The Art of Telling Your Story

Marketing

David Arnold
The Mirage of Global Markets: How Globalizing Companies Can Succeed as Markets Localize

To my loving wife Norma,
who read every word of this book more than once.

FIGURE CREDITS

The author gratefully acknowledges permission to use the following—

- Figures 2-1, 6-1, 7-1, 10-2, 12-1, and 14-1-14-4: MSN Money.
- Figure 7-2: Courtesy of Hoover's, Inc.
- Figures 9-1, 9-2, 13-1, and 15-1: Reuters.com.
- Figures 10-1 and 13-2: Chicago-based Morningstar, Inc. is a leading provider of investment information, research, and analysis. For more information about Morningstar, visit www.morningstar.com or call 800-735-0700.
- Figures 10-10 and 10-11: ValuBond, Inc.
- Figure 14-5: BigCharts.
- Figure 15-2: *Financial Times*

TABLE OF CONTENTS

PART FOUR MORE TOOLS 321

Chapter 18 Earnings Reports & Conference Calls 323

Chapter 19 Detecting Scams, Frauds, and Pump & Dump 327

Appendix A How to Read Financial Statements 333

INTRODUCTION

*"Not everything that can be counted counts,
and not everything that counts can be counted."*

—*Albert Einstein*

This is a book about analyzing stocks.

The process of writing this book turned out to be a huge educational experience for me. I thought that I knew something about the subject when I started. After all, I'd been teaching it, writing about it, and doing it for years.

I had pored over scores of investing how-to books by famous and not so famous gurus and studied their teachings. I meticulously researched how I would have fared if I had followed their strategies in the past. Based on their work, I synthesized and tested my own strategies.

In the process of researching this book I interviewed 15 professional money managers and market analysts. I had never met any of them when I started. I found some because they managed best-in-class mutual funds with solid long-term market-beating performance records. Others were market analysts or private money managers practicing innovative strategies that I'd heard about from other professionals or through their own writings. About half of those I contacted graciously agreed to talk to me.

In truth, I may have misled them. They probably thought I was writing one of those books that features a single guru per chapter, a sort of minibiography describing their childhood, working style, office environment, as well as their investing methods.

I didn't do any of that. I focused our conversations on just three areas: (1) how do they identify investment candidates, (2) how do they analyze them, and (3) how do they decide when to sell.

I had interviewed money managers before, but not at that level, and not in this context. It was an on-the-job learning experience, and I flubbed the first couple, in terms of asking the right questions. But after a while, I got the hang of it.

Interviewing a money manager is a lot different from reading a book they've written, or hearing them speak. For starters, you don't have to go over the same ground if you've already read their works, or heard descriptions of their methods. Instead, you can zero in on the details, asking questions like: How do you define overvalued? How do you identify good management? How do you pinpoint an industry's strongest player? What are your sell signals?

Often the conversations took me to unexpected places. For instance, I was unaware of Porter's Five Forces Model before Nicholas Gerber gently brought it to my attention (by the time Ken Shea mentioned it a week or so later, I responded as though it were old hat). The Porter model inspired the business plan evaluation strategy that became Tool #5.

Some interviews led me to academic research that I'd always assumed was just too, well, academic, to be of interest. That's how I discovered the work of University of Chicago Business School professor Joseph Piotroski, whose research inspired the fiscal health exam featured in Chapter 10.

Perhaps my biggest surprise concerned value investing. I could never figure it out before. I'd read books packed with data proving that low P/E stocks outperform glamour stocks, but I could never make it work. The turkey P/Es just kept getting lower after I bought them. After interviewing several money managers, it hit me that what they did bore little resemblance to what I'd read about value investing. They weren't buying low P/E stocks. They were buying great companies that had stumbled! There's a world of difference between those two approaches.

The wealth of information that these market experts and researchers so kindly shared with me forms the basis for what follows. But being an ungrateful sort, I didn't give them their deserved recognition by describing each of their strategies separately. Rather, I distilled them into the combined analysis tools and strategies that make up this book.

Who Should Read This Book

This is not a get-rich-easy kind of book. There are no magic formulas revealed. I wrote it for people who know that making money in the stock market takes more than running a screen or watching CNBC. I wrote this book for investors willing to put in the time and effort it takes to find and research profitable stock investments.

What's in This Book

I've read many investing books filled with great concepts and strategies that left me feeling unfulfilled, because they didn't tell me how to put those wonderful ideas into practice. This book describes practical step-by-step strategies for finding, researching, and evaluating investment candidates. Equally important, it also tells you when to sell.

I describe two step-by-step strategies, one for growth stocks, and the other for value investors. Some experts advise that both are, in fact, similar strategies. While it's true that you can have a value-priced growth stock, the two analyses processes are very different. When value investors are selling, growth investors are buying. So it's unlikely that the value and growth investors would own the same stock at the same time. While the two strategies are different, they draw on a common set of analysis tools.

What's Different?

This isn't a rehash of conventional wisdom and familiar strategies. The methods described make use of information readily available to anyone connected to the Internet, but in new ways, including:

How to Gauge the Risk of Owning a Specific Stock

Typically, investors rely mostly on past performance to determine the risk of owning a stock. But in the end, stocks move in response to changes in a company's earnings prospects. A price chart shows you history; analyzing fundamentals can help you see the future. You'll discover how to use those fundamentals to evaluate the risks specific to each stock.

Analyzing the Analysts

Recent events demonstrate that you can't depend on analysts' recommendations to make money in the market. But there's still much to be learned from their ratings and forecasts.

What a Stock's Valuation Tells You

Knowing the expectations implied in a stock's valuation tells you much about the rewards versus risks of owning the stock.

How to Set Target Prices

Something that the pros always do, but nobody ever told you.

Industry Analysis

Has your candidate picked a market worth pursuing? If so, are you riding the winning horse?

Business Plan Analysis

Is your candidate more like Wal-Mart or Kmart? Analyzing its business plan will help you find out.

Financial Fitness Evaluator

Bankruptcies are bad news for stockholders, but nobody ever told you how to find out if your stock is a bankruptcy candidate.

How to Use Sale Forecasts

Analysts' consensus sales forecasts have only recently become available. Here's how to use them to identify companies likely to come up short at earnings report time.

Analyze Profitability

Profitability is more than earnings per share. Here's how to find out if your candidate is really making money.

Detect Accounting Shenanigans

Some executives will do whatever it takes to meet earnings forecasts. Here's how to find out if they're cooking the books to do it.

When to Sell

Specific rules for selling, depending on whether you're a growth or value investor.

Notes on Examples

Most of the examples used to illustrate the recommended analyses strategies draw on data that was available on a particular historical date. However, many of the strategies developed out of interviews and research conducted specifically for the book. Consequently, the examples demonstrate what could have been done, but not necessarily what I did on those dates.

Many examples compare annual operating characteristics of firms that have different fiscal year-end dates. For the sake of clarity, I used the closest calendar year for the comparisons. For instance, if one company's fiscal year ended November 30, 1999, and another on January 31, 2000, I labeled the annual data for both as calendar year 1999. So while the figures shown may be technically inaccurate, they're close enough to support the point made by the examples.

Accounting Shortcuts

Certain accounting formulas such as return on assets call for determining the average asset totals over the course of a year. Instead, I use the year-end figures because you can pick them directly off of the balance sheet instead of having to calculate them. Consistently applying such shortcuts simplifies the calculations and won't materially affect your results.

Frequently Mentioned Websites

These Websites are the primary resources necessary to implement the analysis described in this book. Most are referenced throughout the book, so I've listed their Web addresses (URLs) here rather than everywhere that they appear.

The addresses of additional Websites required only for specific analysis strategies are included where they're referenced.

SEC Info (www.secinfo.com): All firms' SEC reports are posted on the SEC's own EDGAR database (www.sec.gov), but most reports are lengthy and it's difficult to locate specific information. SEC Info and a number of other sites provide a table of contents for most reports so that you can locate and download specific sections such as the management's discussion, the statement of cash flows, and so forth. Most of these sites require a subscription; however, SEC Info, as of July 2005, was still free.

Hoover's (www.hoovers.com): A good source for an easy-to-understand company description, and best of all, a usually accurate list of a firm's top three competitors.

Morningstar (www.morningstar.com): Morningstar's Financials report saves you the trouble of computing trailing 12 months' operating cash flow, a data item required in the Busted Cash Burner analysis (Chapter 10). Morningstar's Stock Valuation report listing historical price/earnings, price/sale, price/book and price/cash flow ratios for the trailing twelve months as well as each of the past 10 years is also unique.

MSN Money (money.msn.com): One of only two sites I've found that provides detailed financial statement data in user friendly format. MSN Money's 10-Year Financial Summary reports are the mainstay of the target price strategy (Chapter 6). MSN Money is the only site I've found that lists EBITDA, a data item required to assess financial strength (Chapter 10), on its income statements.

Reuters Investing (www.reuters.com/investing): In my view, the best source for viewing financial statements. Reuters statements are updated faster, are more accurate, and provide more detail than any other source I've found. Reuters powerful Ratio Comparison report enables you to compare a company's valuation ratios, performance measures, and much more, to its market sector, industry, and to all the firms making up the S&P 500 Index.

Yahoo (finance.yahoo.com): My favorite resource for analysts' buy/sell ratings and forecasts because it shows you analysts' sales (revenue) as well as earnings forecasts. Yahoo's insider trading report is easy to interpret and is the only such report I know of that lists trades going back two years. While you're there, click on Major Holders to see the names of all significant insiders, plus the major institutional and mutual fund holders.

ACKNOWLEDGMENTS

Guru Acknowledgments

I want to thank each of these professionals for sharing their time and insights with me. The strategies described in this book were inspired by their comments and strategies. As you read the book, you'll recognize their ideas in every chapter. Our conversations were quite lengthy and each could fill a chapter. Here is a very condensed abstract. These are in no way a complete representation of their strategies, they're merely interesting tidbits that came out of the conversations.

John Buckingham
Al Frank Asset Management
Laguna Beach, California
John Buckingham is president and chief portfolio manager of money manger Al Frank Asset Management and editor of the *Prudent*

Speculator newsletter. Buckingham follows classic investment strategies, buying underpriced firms with long-term track records and holding them as long as it takes. Buckingham views everything in terms of cycles, and likens value investing to farming in that "you plant the seeds, and then wait for them to blossom." Buckingham relies on a firm's historical performance as a guide to the future. He prefers firms with plenty of cash in the bank, strong cash flow, and low debt. Buckingham favors the price/sales ratio to measure value.

Jim Chanos
Kynikos Associates
New York, New York

Jim Chanos is the famous short seller who was the first to blow the whistle on Enron in January 2001. Short sellers are ardent fundamental analysts and Chanos ranks among the best. Chanos spends most of his efforts analyzing the balance sheet instead of the income statement. He compares capital expenditures to depreciation charges to see if a company is adequately replenishing its assets. He sees receivables and/or inventories growing faster than sales a red flag. Chanos considers the frequent occurrence of nonrecurring charges an indicator of poor management quality.

Michelle Clayman
New Amsterdam Partners
New York, New York

Michelle Clayman founded and runs private money management firm New Amsterdam Partners. Clayman has a strong quantitative bent—she derives her analysis criteria by studying historical data. Clayman considers multiple instances of nonrecurring charges, and receivables or inventories increasing faster than sales as red flags. She requires high return on equity of her candidates.

Jim Collins
Insight Capital Management
Walnut Creek, California

Jim Collins runs investment management firm Insight Capital Management and publishes *OTC Insight*, a top-rated investment newsletter.

Collins employs a quantitative screen comparing stock performance to volatility to define an initial list of candidates, and then picks the fundamentally strongest from that group. Collins emphasized that sales, not earnings, are the best measure of growth. Collins looks to the stock charts, specifically weakening relative strength, for his sell signals. He also considers high valuations compared to the company's own historical values as a red flag.

David Edwards
Heron Capital Management
New York, New York

David Edwards is president and primary portfolio manager of private money management firm Heron Capital Management. Edwards, a growth investor, relies mostly on fundamental analysis, but also watches the price charts to help with the timing of his buy and sell decisions. Edwards emphasized the importance of picking the leading companies in growing market sectors, and his thoughts on how to do that inspired much of what you'll find in Tool #4, Industry Analysis. Edwards looks to a firm's own historical ratios to establish valuation, rather than to the overall market or to its industry. Edwards prefers firms with strong operating cash flow, and high return on equity. He believes that for proper diversification, portfolios should contain a least 32 stocks, with no more than 25 percent in any one sector. Edwards follows a strict selling discipline and my "when to sell" sections reflect many of his ideas.

Nicholas Gerber
Ameristock Funds
Moraga, California

Nicholas Gerber is manager and founder of the Ameristock Fund. Gerber is primarily a large-cap investor with a bent toward value. Gerber introduced two important concepts to me. One, the Porter Five Factor Model, was the inspiration for Tool #5, Business Plan Analysis. Gerber's concept of gauging the growth rate inferred by a stock's valuation inspired the implied growth analysis strategy featured in Tool #2, Valuation. Gerber uses return on equity to measure profitability, but double checks it by requiring book value to grow at the same rate.

Louis Navellier
Navellier Associates
Reno, Nevada

Louis Navellier, founder and president of the firm bearing his name, publishes several newsletters, runs mutual funds, and manages money. Navellier selects stocks by first running a screen that compares stock performance to volatility, and then picks the fundamentally strongest from that list. Navellier bases his fundamental analysis on computer run analysis of his database to determine the factors that are the best stock selectors in the current market. He shared his recent research with me, and that information helped to form the strategies described in this book.

Paul Rabbitt
Rabbitt Analytics
Hermosa Beach, California

Paul Rabbitt is president of stock analysis firm Rabbitt Analytics. Rabbitt uses a computerized database to rank companies, giving them what he terms a Q-Rank. The highest scoring Q-Rank companies show strong relative strength, recent positive earnings surprises, and strong and accelerating earnings growth. Rabbitt was one of the only market experts that I interviewed who doesn't use return of equity as a selection criterion. In fact, Rabbitt mentioned that he had recently removed ROE from his criteria list because he found that it didn't help.

Peter Schliemann
Rutabaga Capital Management
Boston, Massachusetts

Peter Schliemann founded private money manager Rutabaga Capital Management. A value manager, Schliemann looks for unloved, underfollowed companies in run-of-the-mill businesses that are going through a rough patch. Schliemann believes in the regression to the mean concept, and seeks out companies with below normal profit margins. He focuses on return on capital as a profitability measure, and seeks out firms with the biggest difference between ROC and cost of capital. Schliemann looks for positive cash flow, and avoids companies that are growing by acquisition. He prefers firms where insiders are buying the company's stock with their own money. Schliemann compares a stock to its own history to gauge when it's overvalued or undervalued. He prefers low expectation stocks meaning that they have low institutional ownership, few analysts covering the stock, and even fewer buy recommendations. He sees rising receivables, increasing provisions for bad debt, deteriorating cash flow, and increased borrowings as sell signals.

Susan Schottenfeld
TCW Asset Management Company
Los Angeles, California

Susan Schottenfeld, co-manager of the TCW Galileo Value Opportunities Fund, introduced me to the concept of "looking through the valley to the next peak," the foundation of value investing, at least the interpretation that I've adopted for this book. Schottenfeld seeks out companies selling at low end of their historical P/E range based on normalized earnings. She attempts to discover if the company is different now, than it was two years ago; that is, is the problem temporary? She looks for catalysts such as new management, better capacity utilization, divesture of bad units, and so forth, and prefers candidates with strong free cash flow. She sells when a firm's stock price reaches fair value, or if she notices a big jump in receivables, inventories, or accounts payables. She'll also sell if a competitor is having trouble or if she notes significant insider selling.

Ken Shea
Standard & Poor's
New York, New York

Ken Shea is director of equity research at Standard & Poors. Shea, mostly growth stock oriented, believes that you have to apply different rules depending on where a firm is in its cycle. For instance, though a believer in the importance of free cash flow, he doesn't apply that requirement to fast growers. Shea also considers it important to understand a candidate's business model. Shea considers management quality an important factor and is wary of companies growing by acquisition. Shea looks for companies with low margins that can improve, and sees slowing revenue growth, as well as big nonrecurring charges, as red flags.

Nancy Tengler
Fremont Funds
San Francisco, California

At the time I interviewed her, Nancy Tengler was president and chief executive officer of Fremont Investment Advisors, and co-portfolio manager of Fremont's New Era Value Fund. Though a value manager, Tengler doesn't mind taking some pages out of the growth manager's playbook. For instance, she prefers stocks with analyst coverage and strong operating margins. Tengler's favored valuation ratio is price/sales ratio, not by itself, but compared to the S&P's price/sales ratio, which she calls the relative price/sales ratio. She compares her relative price/sales ratio to historical values and uses it as her primary buy/sell signal. Tengler tracks capital spending to assure that a company is replenishing its assets. Tengler's somewhat offhand comment that "when value investors sell, they sell to growth investors," gave me tremendous insight into the relationship between the value and growth styles.

John C. Thompson
Thomson Plumb
Madison, Wisconsin

John C. Thompson, comanages the Thompson Plumb Growth Fund. Thompson mixes growth and value strategies. He believes that every company has some years that are better than others, and looks for firms currently growing slower than their historic rate. Thompson introduced me to the concept of earnings leverage, meaning that a small increase in revenues can lead to a big improvement in profits when a company is operating close to its breakeven point.

Thompson looks for firms with no debt and lots of cash. He's a big believer in what he terms free cash flow, but he defines cash flow as excluding changes in working capital, along the lines of EBITDA. Thompson places great importance on understanding a firm's business model.

Thatcher Thompson
Merrill Lynch
New York, New York

Thatcher Thompson is a Merrill Lynch analyst specializing in the business services sector. Factors he considers important are revenue visibility, a company's position vis a vis the competition, sales growth and earnings growth, margins, cash flow versus net income, and low debt. Thompson's red flags include negative earnings surprises and/or reduction in guidance, departure of the CFO, growth by acquisition combined with declining margins, or declining cash flow combined with rising receivables.

Geraldine Weiss
Investment Quality Trends
La Jolla, California
Geraldine Weiss, now retired, published her *Investment Quality Trends* newsletter for more than 30 years. Weiss' strategy hinges on tracking blue-chip stock's dividend yields. It's an effective method and Quicken.com implemented a version her strategy in its One-Click Scorecard. I tracked the performance of Quicken's four Scorecard stock-picking models and Weiss' was the hands-down winner. In our interview, Weiss stressed the importance of strong institutional sponsorship; in fact if my notes are correct, she said that "there is never too much institutional ownership."

Academic Acknowledgments

A brief review of academic research that contributed to the strategies in this book.

- "Earnings Quality and Stock Returns: The Evidence from Accruals," Konan Chan, Louis K.C. Chan, Narasimhan Jegadeesh and Josef Lakonishok. Working Paper, January 2001.

  Accruals result from increases in inventory and accounts receivable levels and from decreases in accounts payables. The study found that firms showing an increase in earnings accompanied by a large increase in accruals underperform in the three years following the high-accrual year compared to the previous three years. The study found changes in inventory to be the most important accrual factor for predicting future returns.

  The study noted that since accrual increases are accompanied by corresponding cash flow decreases, the increase in accruals could be detected by comparing cash flow to earnings. That is, earnings increase, but cash flow doesn't.

■ "Value Investing: The Use of Historical Financial Statement Information to Separate Winners from Losers," Joseph D. Piotroski, *Journal of Accounting Research*, Vol. 38, No. 3 Supplement 2000.

Piotroski found that applying simple financial health tests using financial statement data to eliminate weak companies can significantly improve the performance of value portfolios.

■ "Earnings Surprises, Growth Expectations, and Stock Returns, or Don't Let an Earnings Torpedo Sink Your Portfolio," Douglas J. Skinner and Richard G. Sloan. Working paper, April 2001.

Found that growth stocks exhibit a much larger negative response to negative earnings surprises than value stocks. The study found that "it is the disappointment per se and not its magnitude that is important to stock market participants." The authors say, "when earnings news is positive, growth stocks outperform value stocks, but that when growth stocks disappoint, they underperform value stocks by substantially more than they outperform when the news is good."

■ "Characteristics of Price Informative Analyst Forecasts," Cristi A. Gleason and Charles M. C. Lee. Working Paper, September 23, 2000

Found that stocks with analyst forecast revisions move in the direction of the revisions, but only if, in the case of positive changes, the revised forecasts are also above the consensus forecast. The study found the effect also worked the opposite; that is, negative forecast revisions sink the stock price if the revised forecasts are below the consensus. The study found that the "magnitude of the revision is relatively unimportant."

■ "Cash Flow is King: Cognitive Errors by Investors," Todd Houge and Tim Loughran, *Journal of Psychology and Financial Markets,* Vol. 1, No. 3 and No. 4, 2000.

Found that high cash flow firms significantly outperform low cash flow firms.

Special Acknowledgment

I would like to thank Standard & Poor's Institutional Market Services unit, particularly J.P. Tremblay, Director, Investment Products, and analyst Jerome Blanchette for providing me with historical data derived from S&P's COMPUSTAT database. S&P's data very much facilitated my research.

PART ONE

—————— **GETTING STARTED**

1

THE ANALYSIS PROCESS

Experts tell us that investment success requires a disciplined approach for finding, researching, and analyzing potential investments. This chapter describes one such approach, and the ensuing chapters fill in the details. It's based on sound principles that are practiced by market-beating money managers. It's certainly not the only way, and it may not be the best way. But it's a place to start, and following it will make you a better investor. After you've mastered these strategies, you can modify them to suit your needs.

The process involves finding investment candidates, weeding out the obvious misfits, researching and analyzing the survivors, picking the best candidates, and equally important, applying a clear-cut set of selling rules.

Finding Candidates

Finding stocks to analyze can be as easy as going to your hair salon, talking to your neighbors, picking up a magazine, surfing the Internet, or turning on the TV. You'll find no shortage of tips, and you'll welcome them once you've gained confidence in your analysis skills, because you'll be able to weed out the bad ideas quickly.

As your experience grows, you'll get a feel for what discriminates strong candidates, and you'll find yourself increasingly taking advantage of screening to uncover investment ideas. *Screening* is a technique for scanning the entire market for stocks meeting your criteria. It's a powerful tool, but to use it effectively, you have to first understand how to identify the best candidates. That will come with time, and in the meantime, I've provided a few sample screens in Chapter 3 to get you started.

Treat all names you get, whether from your own screens, friends, TV gurus, or even Warren Buffett, as tips to analyze using the techniques you are about to learn.

Analyzing Stocks

Remember COSC:
Concentrate On the Strongest Candidates

Our analysis techniques follow a survival-of-the-fittest approach, where you're constantly weeding out the weakest contenders. These techniques work best if you start with a large group of candidates, say 10 to 20, instead of just a few. Researching stocks takes time and effort, so eliminate weak contenders as soon as you discover them. That way you can concentrate your research on the strongest candidates. Be ruthless. There is no point in wasting time researching stupid ideas.

Quick Prequalify

Use the quick prequalify test to identify the obvious misfits. These may be stocks that would be bad news for any investor. Perhaps they're firms with businesses based more on hype than reality with little or no sales or earnings. Or they could be stocks that simply don't fit your investing style; e.g., maybe they're value stocks, and you're a growth investor.

Use the quick prequalify test to check:

- **Company and industry overview:** Find out something about the company's business and its industry. It may be in a business or market sector that you favor or that you want to avoid. For instance, the home building industry usually prospers when interest rates drop and suffers in a rising interest rate environment. So your take on the future direction of interest rates would influence how you view homebuilders.

- **Market capitalization:** Market capitalization defines a company's total value (share price multiplied by number of shares). The biggest firms are designated large-caps, and progressively smaller firms are termed mid-caps, small-caps, and micro-caps.

  There is no good or bad market capitalization, but each size has its own pluses and minuses in terms of potential risks and rewards. Generally, larger companies are considered safer, and smaller firms offer more growth potential. However, even these generalities vary with current market conditions.

  You may decide that a particular company size range best suits your needs or, conversely, that you're open to all possibilities. Whatever you conclude, eliminate candidates in this step that don't fit your requirements.

- **Valuation ratios:** Valuation ratios such as price to earnings (P/E) or price to sales (P/S) define how market participants view your candidate's earnings growth prospects. High valuations reflect in-favor stocks, that is, those seen having strong growth prospects, and thus appeal to growth investors. Conversely, value players look for stocks with low valuation ratios, indicating that most market players (growth investors) view them as losers.

  Any given candidate will fit into either the growth or value categories, but not both. The valuation ratios give you a quick read as to whether you have a value or growth candidate on your hands.

- **Trading volume:** Trading volume is the average number of shares traded daily. Low trading volume stocks spell trouble because they're subject to price manipulation and mutual funds can't buy them. Here's where you'll toss these bad ideas.

- **Float:** Corporate insiders such as key executives and board members are restricted as to when and how often they can buy and sell their company's shares. So insider-owned shares are not considered available for trading. The float is the number of outstanding shares not owned by insiders, and thus available for daily trading.

Acceptable float values depend on your investing style. Large firms typically have floats running from a few hundred million shares into the billions. However some investors seek out firms with much smaller floats, typically below 25 million shares. Since the float represents the supply of shares available for trading, these small floats mean that the share price could take off like a rocket if the company hits the news and the demand for shares overwhelms the available supply.

- **Cash flow:** Where reported earnings reflect myriad accounting decisions, cash flow is the amount of cash that actually flowed into, or out of, a company's bank accounts as a result of its operations. Consequently, cash flow is the best measure of profits.

Except for the fastest growers, viable growth candidates should be reporting positive cash flow. Here's where growth investors should eliminate cash burners from consideration. On the other hand, viable value candidates may very well be reporting negative cash flow resulting from the problems that caused their fall from grace.

- **Historical sales and earnings growth:** Whether you're seeking out-of-favor value prospects or hot growth candidates, your best prospects are firms with a long history of solid long-term sales and earnings growth. In this step, you'll dispose of stocks that don't meet this basic requirement.

■ **Check the buzz:** There's no point wasting time researching a stock if the company's main product has just been rendered obsolete by the competition. At this point, get up to speed on the buzz surrounding your candidate. Negative buzz is bad news for growth stocks, and you should disqualify such growth candidates. It's a different story for value prospects, however. The negative buzz is part and parcel of the market's disenchantment with the stock, and is contributing to making it a value candidate.

You will eliminate many of your bad ideas during the quick prequalify check, most in less than five minutes once you get the hang of it. Take your survivors on to the detailed analysis.

Detailed Analysis

The COSC (concentrate on the strongest candidates) analysis process is described in Chapter 16 and Chapter 17. Although describing two very different selection strategies, both employ the same analysis tools detailed in Part 2.

The COSC process consists of 11 steps, each using a corresponding analysis tool. For instance, Step 7 involves analyzing a candidate's financial health, and employs Tool #7, Financial Strength Analysis. The analysis tool chapters describe step-by-step procedures for performing each analysis, while "COSC Growth" and "COSC Value" describe how to apply the results to each investing style.

Obviously, you'll need to be familiar with the appropriate analysis tool to perform the corresponding analysis step.

Eliminate a candidate when it fails any step. For example, don't carry a candidate to Step 2 if it failed Step 1.

Step 1: Analyzing Analysts' Data

Market analysts are employed by brokerages and other firms to evaluate and rate publicly traded corporations. Start your detailed analysis by reviewing market analysts' buy/sell recommendations and earnings and revenue forecasts to determine the level of market enthusiasm for your candidate. The best value candidates are the ones that analysts don't like. Conversely, growth investors need to see some, but not too much, enthusiasm for their candidates. The Sentiment Index, described in Chapter 4, is a useful gauge of analysts' enthusiasm.

Analysts' earnings growth forecasts are another measure of a stock's suitability as a growth or value candidate. Strong forecast earnings growth disqualifies value candidates but identifies strong growth prospects.

Step 2: Valuation

Would you buy a stock if you knew that the company would have to grow its earnings 75 percent every year merely to justify its current stock price? In this section, you'll determine the earnings growth implied by your candidate's current stock price. This will help you gauge whether there's sufficient upside stock price potential to justify further research.

Step 3: Establishing Target Prices

Many value investors use target prices to establish buy and sell points for otherwise-qualified stocks. For instance, a stock may be an attractive candidate, but its current stock price is too high to provide the needed margin of safety. So the value investor will wait for the stock to come down to the preestablished target price before buying. It isn't bought if it doesn't reach the buy target. Once purchased, the stock is sold when it reaches its predetermined sell target price.

Although setting buy and sell targets is a linchpin of the value strategy, growth investors would benefit by following the same procedure. Doing that would have helped investors avoid many of the disasters that marked 2000 and 2001. Tool #3, "Setting Target Prices," makes it easy.

Step 4: Industry Analysis

Companies are more likely to achieve success and make money for their shareholders if they're selling into fast-growing market sectors than if they're mired in a slow growth or stagnant industry. You'll analyze your candidate's industry growth prospects and other factors that affect industry player's success prospects in this step. Pinpointing attractive industries is all for naught if you pick the wrong companies. Thus, your analysis will also include identifying the strongest players in each industry.

Step 5: Business Plan Analysis

Microsoft is one of the world's more profitable companies, while Gateway Computer struggles. The difference is in the business models. In this step, you'll determine if your candidate is more like a Microsoft or a Gateway.

Step 6: Assess Management Quality

Many money managers consider gauging management quality an important part of the analysis process. You don't have time to visit candidate's plants and schmooze with key executives, and you don't have to. You can evaluate management quality from the comfort of your own home by reviewing the résumés of key executives and directors, measuring the firm's accounting quality, and completing other easily accomplished checks.

Step 7: Financial Strength Analysis

You lose big if one of your holdings files bankruptcy. But a firm doesn't have to go bankrupt to ruin your day. Just the rumors that it might are enough to sink its stock price. Market analysts typically don't bother to check a firm's financial strength before recommending a stock. That's why so many advised buying Enron, Kmart, Global Crossing, and other recent bankruptcies just months before they failed.

You don't have to be a victim. You can measure any public corporation's financial health using the strategies described in this section.

Step 8: Profitability & Growth Analysis

In the end, stock prices follow earnings. In this step you'll analyze sales and profitability trends to determine whether your candidate's earnings are more likely heading up or heading down. You'll also find out if your candidate is really profitable, or just gives the appearance of making money.

Step 9: Detecting Red Flags

It's a disaster when you learn that your stock just dropped 40 percent because it reported disappointing earnings, or management cut future growth forecasts. These disasters usually don't come without warning. In this step, you'll check for red flags signaling future disappointments before they sink the stock price.

Step 10: Ownership Considerations

Despite the advantages of the Internet, mutual funds and other institutional investors have access to better information about stocks than individual investors. Therefore, analyzing institutional ownership data can help you decide whether you're on the right track.

Insiders are directors, key officers, and large investors. Naturally, you'd like to see that key officers own their company's stock, but too much insider ownership signals danger.

This is where you'll sort out institutional and insider ownership data to determine if it's favorable or unfavorable.

Step 11: Price Charts

Believe it or not, occasionally knowledgeable insiders withhold important information that would affect your investment decision until they've had a chance to act by dumping or loading up on the stock. In these instances, the stock's price action is your only clue that something is going on.

That's why it's important to check a stock's price chart before buying. In this step, you'll ascertain whether the stock chart is signaling that it's okay to buy.

Analysis Scorecards

You'll find separate scorecards in Appendix B for the growth and value analysis strategies. Make copies and fill out the appropriate scorecard when you analyze a stock. You'll be amazed how just filling out the scorecard will improve your analysis.

When to Sell

For me, selling a stock is often more difficult than buying it. If I've made money, I enjoyed the experience and I don't want to leave the party when there's still money to be made. It's even harder to sell if I'm behind. The game isn't over as long as I hold onto the stock, and there's always hope that it will go back up. But once sold, the loss goes on my permanent record.

It's easy to delay selling by saying "Let's wait and see what it does tomorrow." All too often putting off selling turns profits into losses and turns small losses into bigger losses.

Establishing a strict sell discipline is an effective antidote for seller's procrastination. The "COSC Growth" and "COSC Value" analysis chapters each provide detailed instructions for deciding when to sell.

In many instances, a condition triggering a sell signal for a growth investor wouldn't provoke the same response from a value investor. For example, a significant reduction in earnings forecasts usually triggers an automatic sell for growth investors, but wouldn't faze a value player. Conversely, a strong uptrending price chart often tells a value investor that it's time to sell, but the same event would signal to a growth type that the party is just beginning.

However certain events such as deteriorating fundamentals, significant earnings restatements, and announcements of large acquisitions warn all players that it's time to sell.

Summary

Following an organized approach to finding, researching, buying, and selling stocks will make you a better investor. Now that you know where we're heading, read on to get started.

2

EVALUATING RISK

Risk is the probability of losing money. All stocks are risky compared to government-insured savings accounts; but some stocks are a lot riskier than others. Yet investors rarely evaluate the inherent risks when contemplating buying a stock. But it makes sense to do so. For instance, suppose that you were considering two stocks, and your analysis showed that both had the possibility of doubling in price over the next two years, but Company A's stock was twice as risky as Company B's. Knowing that, the choice between Company A and Company B becomes obvious.

Portfolio Risk

You can reduce your overall risk by diversifying your investments over a variety of stocks in diverse industries.

The airline and oil industries provide a classic example. Increasing oil prices translate to high profits for the oil industry, but the resulting increases in fuel costs depress airline profits, and hence their stock prices. Conversely, airlines tend to prosper when fuel prices drop, and the oil industry is suffering.

Opinions vary on the number of different holdings required for adequate diversification. Some say that you can achieve adequate diversification with as few as 12 stocks, while others say as many as 40 or 50 different holdings are required. Diversify as much as possible, and above all, avoid investing more than 25 percent of your funds in any one sector, e.g., technology, health, financial, and so forth.

Does Low Valuation Equal Low Risk?

Several academic studies found that portfolios made up of low valuation stocks, say those with low P/E ratios, outperformed high valuation portfolios over various time frames. In other words, value-priced stocks outperform growth stocks. That sounds like news that you can use, but when you delve into the details, you'll find that just a few stocks account for the value portfolio's outperformance. It turns out that most stocks making up those portfolios actually lost money.

To illustrate that phenomenon, I made up a portfolio of deep-value stocks. These were stocks that as of February 2001 had price/book ratios between 0.1 and 0.5. I call them deep-value stocks because usually a price/book ratio below 1.0 is enough to qualify a stock as value-priced. A total of 501 stocks met my deep-value requirements.

I measured the performance of my deep-value portfolio between February 2001 and February 2002. It returned 3 percent over the 52 weeks. That was a good return considering that the market as measured by the S&P 500 dropped around 12 percent during the period.

But when I looked at the results in detail, I found that a few outsized performers skewed the returns. For example, excluding just the top 10 performers would have turned the 3 percent gain into a 6 percent loss.

The same effect worked in reverse. Removing the ten biggest losers increased the portfolio return to 5.1 percent. Unless you bought all 501 stocks, you could have made money, or you could have lost money, depending on the particular stocks you picked.

I've done many similar tests in my search for the magic formula that would routinely turn up a list of market-beating stocks at the push of a button. Whenever I thought I'd uncovered the Holy Grail, it always turned out that a few stocks powered the portfolio's returns.

So What?

Here's the point! It doesn't matter if value-priced stocks are more or less risky than growth stocks if you're only buying 5, 10, or 20 stocks. Your risk hinges on only three issues:

1. Overall market risk
2. Industry risk
3. Risks specific to your stocks

We'll examine overall market and industry risks, then move on to evaluate the risks specific to individual stocks.

Market Risk

Even if you're a great stock picker, it's tough making money holding stocks in a bear, or downtrending, market. On the other hand, you can make lots of mistakes and still rake in profits in strong markets. That's where the market expression: "Don't mistake a bull market for brains," came from. Consequently, overall market risk is an important factor in the risk equation.

Of course, predicting future stock market direction requires knowing which way interest rates, inflation, and a host of additional economic factors are heading. Economists spend their careers trying to discover the answers to these questions, usually without much success.

Instead of pondering these unanswerable questions, we'll gauge market risk by looking at two easily determined factors: is the market currently undervalued or overvalued and is the market currently moving up, or moving down?

Market Valuation

Several studies show a relationship between market risk and the difference between the market's valuation and prevailing interest rates. It's an inverse relationship, meaning low prevailing interest rates support higher market valuations. The S&P 500 Index is usually used as a proxy for the entire market, and most experts express the market's valuation in terms of the S&P 500's price to earnings (P/E) ratio. This P/E ratio is simply the market-weighted average P/E of the stocks making up the index. Market-weighted means the bigger the firm in terms of market-capitalization, the more weight given to its P/E in the calculation.

One way to determine where we are in terms of valuation is to invert the market's P/E to get earnings yield. For instance, the yield is 5 percent if the P/E is 20 (1/20 = 0.05 or 5%). Then compare the market yield to prevailing interest rates, typically the three-month U.S. Treasury bill rate.

Usually the market yield is higher than the T-bill rate. What's important is the spread (difference) between the two rates. The market is considered high risk when the spread is low or negative.

Table 2-1 compares market yields, the three-month T-bill rate, and the spread between the two, as of December 31, going back to 1984. The table also shows the following year's S&P 500 index returns.

For example, Table 2-1 shows that as of December 1994, the market yield was 1.0 percent higher than the T-bill rate, and the S&P 500 moved up 34 percent in the next 12 months.

As the case with most market indicators, comparing the market earnings yield to the T-bill rates doesn't always work, but it's clear that negative spreads signal higher risk than positive spreads. That makes sense since negative spreads result from low market yields, which correspond to high market valuations (high P/Es).

TABLE 2-1   Market yields, T-bill interest rates, the spread between
the two, and the following year's S&P 500 index return.

Date	Market Yield (E/P)	3-Month T-Bill	Spread	Following Year's S & P Return
12/00	4.2%	6.3%	-2.1%	-13%
12/99	3.1%	5.3%	-2.2%	-10%
12/98	3.6%	4.5%	-1.4%	20%
12/97	4.5%	5.4%	-0.9%	27%
12/96	5.3%	5.1%	0.2%	31%
12/95	5.9%	5.2%	0.7%	20%
12/94	6.7%	5.7%	1.0%	34%
12/93	5.6%	3.1%	2.5%	-2%
12/92	5.3%	3.3%	2.0%	7%
12/91	5.6%	3.9%	1.7%	5%
12/90	7.1%	6.7%	0.4%	26%
12/89	7.7%	7.9%	-0.2%	-7%
12/88	9.1%	8.5%	0.6%	27%
12/87	7.7%	6.0%	1.7%	13%
12/86	7.7%	5.7%	2.0%	2%
12/85	8.3%	7.3%	1.0%	15%
12/84	11.1%	7.9%	3.2%	26%

Market Direction

Sizing up the current market direction gives you a heads-up as to whether it makes sense to invest new money or stay on the sidelines. A strong uptrend gives you a green light to add to positions, while a strong downtrend advises caution.

Since many investors rely on the S&P 500 to represent the market, the easiest way to gauge market direction is to compare the index to its 200-day moving average (MA) (see Figure 2-1). If the S&P is above its 200-day MA, it's probably in an uptrend, and vice versa. The distance between the index and its moving average reflects the trend strength. The trend is strong if the index is far above or below its moving average. It indicates a trendless or consolidating market if the index is hovering near, or crisscrossing, its moving average.

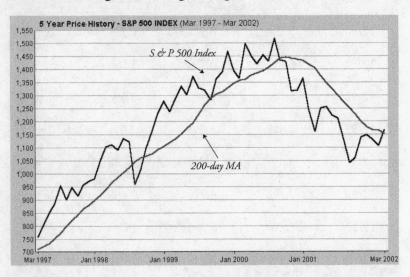

FIGURE 2-1   Use MSN Money to display a chart of the S&P 500 Index and its 200-day moving average. Consider the market in an uptrend when the index is above its moving average.

The S&P 500 Index reflects the action of large-cap stocks in a wide variety of industries. Other indexes may provide better indications depending on the particular market sector that you're considering. For instance, the Nasdaq reflects the action of tech stocks, and the Russell 2000 index better shows how small-caps are faring.

There are a variety of other indexes available to show the action of mid-caps, value or growth stocks, or of individual industries. Stock-Charts (www.stockcharts.com) is a good place to find these indexes. Click on Market Summary to see the complete list.

It's best to avoid buying stocks in a downtrending market unless it belongs to an industry sector showing strength despite the weak overall market.

Spotting Strong Industries in a Weak Market

No matter how weak the market, stocks in some industries will do fine. You can still make money if you spot those strong industries. You can use BigCharts' Industries report (Figure 2-2) to identify strong industries. BigCharts (www.bigcharts.com) displays lists showing the 10 best and 10 worst performing industries for periods ranging from one week to five years. The default is three months, and that's a good starting point. But things change quickly, so check the one-month listings to make sure that a hot industry on the three-month chart isn't fading. Once you've spotted an industry of interest, you can click on the industry name to see a list of the 10 best and 10 worst performing stocks within that industry for the selected period.

You take on additional risks when you buy stocks in underperforming industries, even in strong overall markets. So it pays to see how your candidate's industry is faring anytime that you're considering a purchase.

Company-Specific Risks

Company-specific risks relate to a firm's business plan, stock valuation, profitability, accounting practices, growth strategy, and other factors particular to the company, rather than to the overall market.

Some of the risks listed in the following pages are serious enough to disqualify a candidate from further consideration and are identified as such in the description. Others are less severe and by themselves would not disqualify the stock. However, in the end you'll do best by picking the candidates with the fewest risk factors.

10 Best Performing Industries

Industry Name	Percent Change (over time selected)
DJ Mining Index (US)	25.03%
DJ Nonferrous Metals Index (US)	22.71%
DJ Lodging Index (US)	22.59%
DJ Auto Parts Index (US)	22.27%
DJ Aerospace Index (US)	22.14%
DJ Containers & Packaging Index (US...	20.80%
DJ Forest Products Index (US)	20.44%
DJ Consumer Electronics Index (US)	19.38%
DJ Tires Index (US)	19.18%
DJ Heavy Machinery Index (US)	19.18%

FIGURE 2-2 BigCharts 10 best performing industries over the past three months, as of March 17, 2002. Start by selecting Industries on BigChart's home page (www.bigcharts.com). You can click on an industry name to see a list of the 10 best and 10 worst performing stocks in the industry.

Products on Allocation

Companies selling products into markets where demand exceeds supply can only fill a proportion of each customer's order until the firm is able to ramp up its production. Customers soon figure out that they must order two or three times what they really need to get sufficient product. They often stockpile inventory to make sure that they don't run short. The resulting exaggerated order rate causes analysts, investors, and company officials to overestimate demand.

Eventually production catches up with demand and customers begin receiving full, instead of partial orders. Since they overordered, they find themselves overstocked, and start canceling orders. This scenario invariably plays out faster than everyone expects. Trex Company's experience illustrates the phenomenon.

Trex makes fake wood decking material. It pioneered and dominates the fast-growing field. In early 2000, Trex couldn't keep up with demand and had to put its customers on allocation even though it had ramped up production by more than 70 percent. Trex continued to add production lines and in August told customers that shipments would soon catch up with orders. Customers adjusted quickly by reducing orders down to the levels they really needed. As a result, instead of the expected increase, Trex's September quarter sales dropped to $25 million, compared to June's $36 million.

Litigation

Large corporations are almost always being sued–sometimes by disgruntled employees or customers, sometimes by other corporations over patents or other issues, or sometimes by shareholders upset because they lost money on the stock. These lawsuits are part of the costs of doing business and usually would not affect your analysis. However sometimes a company is involved in a lawsuit that could materially affect its business prospects, or even threaten its survival.

Companies such as MP3.com and Napster were almost driven out of business by lawsuits brought by music publishers and recording companies in 2001, contending that MP3 and Napster were distributing copyrighted songs without paying. Asbestos-related litigation has driven several large firms into bankruptcy. Just the threat of a large lawsuit can weigh heavily on a company's stock price.

Corporations must disclose all significant lawsuits in their quarterly and annual reports. Management, of course, routinely says that all such claims are without merit. Nobody, certainly not company management or stock analysts, can predict the outcome of a lawsuit. Avoid all stocks facing litigation with a potentially costly outcome.

Restates Earnings

A company usually restates earnings when its auditor or the Securities and Exchange Commission (SEC) finds that its earlier reported earnings were too high. Any significant downward earnings restatement is a red flag signaling that the company had been practicing creative accounting to enhance its reported earnings. Circumstances vary, but just because it was caught once doesn't mean management has changed its ways. Avoid firms that significantly restated earnings downward unless new management is now in charge.

Sector Outlook Diminishes

Earnings disappointments or reduced guidance from one company in a market sector warns that all companies in the same market face similar problems.

The contract manufacturing industry affords a good illustration. On September 13, 2000, SCI Systems, one of the industry's major players, said that it wasn't going to meet its September quarter forecasts. The company blamed the shortfall on slower than expected sales and on component shortages. You'd think that those same issues would apply to all players, but analysts didn't see the connection. According to one analyst, SCI's woes were a "temporary problem" caused by a "design flaw in one of its customer's products."

SCI's competitors Solectron, Jabil Circuits, and Flextronics took the news in stride, taking just small hits to their share prices at the time. However investors in those stocks would have been well advised to heed SCI's warning. A month later all three began death slides that eventually led them to lose more than 60 percent of their value. Avoid stocks in industries where competitors have recently reduced earnings guidance, or have reported negative surprises.

Interest Rate Risk

Interest rate changes, or even the prospect of changes in rates, usually move the market. Rising interest rates are perceived as bad for stocks in general and pressure the entire market. Interest sensitive industries such as homebuilders, utilities, and all companies carrying high debt can be especially hard-hit when rates rise. Banks and others in the financial sector suffer when the spread between short- and long-term interest rates narrows.

Conversely, energy, healthcare, and technology stocks often outperform the market in rising interest rate environments.

Interest rate changes, actual or prospective, in the direction that works against a particular company's industry sector add risk but are not necessary a disqualifying factor per se.

Company-Specific Risks Described in Subsequent Chapters

Here are company-specific risk factors described in more detail in Part 2.

Financial Health

Company failure is the most disastrous stock ownership risk that you face. Shareholders typically lose their entire investment when a company files bankruptcy. Don't even think about buying a stock without first checking its financial health to make sure that it's not a bankruptcy candidate. You will learn how in Chapter 10.

Business Plan/Growth by Acquisition

Some companies are better investment prospects than others because they have superior business plans. They may address markets with little competition, produce products seen as superior by consumers, have better distribution methods, and so on.

You can't assume that a firm has a viable business plan just because it's publicly traded and analysts are recommending buying its stock. The dot-com bust illustrated that given the right circumstances, firms with little chance of success can raise billions of dollars from gullible investors, both amateur and professional.

An especially important factor of a company's business plan is its growth strategy. Most firms grow by developing new products, opening new stores, and so forth. However some resort to an acquisition strategy to maintain growth after they've saturated their original markets. Early successes implementing this strategy lead to overconfidence. Eventually the company makes a bad acquisition, its results fall short of expectations, and the shortfall sinks its share price. Since it was issuing shares to pay for the acquisitions, the lower stock price devalues its acquisition currency, further slowing growth which puts more pressure on the share price.

Chapter 8 describes how to evaluate a business plan, including how to spot companies growing mainly by acquisition. The chapter includes a scorecard for evaluating business plans. Possible scores range from −11 to +11. Candidates with negative scores are riskier than those scoring positive, but a negative score is not by itself a disqualifying factor.

Valuation

The market often bids up profitable companies with intriguing business plans to unrealistic valuations, making them risky investments, despite their strong prospects. Eventually most firms trade at prices reflecting their long-term growth prospects. You can determine the annual earnings growth rate implied by a stock's current valuation using the methods described in Chapter 5. Few firms grow earnings as much as 40 percent annually for sustained periods, and most don't achieve anywhere near that rate. Consider stocks with implied earnings growth of 30 percent or higher as risky bets, but high valuation by itself is not necessarily a disqualifying factor.

Faltering Growth/Creative Accounting

Young companies exploiting emerging market opportunities often experience explosive growth in their early years. The market expects that growth to continue indefinitely and prices the firm's shares accordingly. Those early growth rates are unsustainable, and company management sometimes resorts to accounting shenanigans to maintain the illusion of growth when real growth slows. Eventually the house of cards collapses, earnings fall short of expectations, and the stock price crumples. Chapter 12 describes how to spot red flags signaling slowing growth and the accounting shenanigans that frequently mask faltering growth. Avoid stocks showing any red flags.

High Expectations

Unmet expectations lead to disappointment, and the market reacts by hammering the offending company's stock price. The higher the expectations, the more chance of disappointment. Consequently, high expectations equate to high risk. Chapter 4 describes how to calculate a Sentiment Index score based on analysts' buy/sell recommendations. Sentiment Index values of 9 or higher indicate risk, but high Sentiment Index scores alone are not a disqualifying factor.

Summary

Professionals always evaluate the risks intrinsic to a prospective stock purchase, and you should too. Be wary of investing in overvalued markets or in downtrending markets or sectors. There are thousands to choose from, so disqualify stocks with product allocation, litigation, earnings restatement, sector outlook, financial health, or creative accounting risks. The existence of any of the less serious risk factors makes a stock less desirable, so in terms of risk, "less is more."

3

SCREENING

Screening is the most efficient way to find stock candidates because you can tailor the screens to filter out undesirable stocks, permitting you to focus your research on worthwhile candidates. Screening is an art that requires some practice to get it right. When you first try a new screen, it will turn up too many or too few candidates. When you get the right number, say 20 or so, you'll find that you don't like most of them. Eventually you'll devise a set of screening parameters that gives you a manageable list of candidates worth researching.

Back in the Internet heydays, you had a choice of a dozen or so powerful search programs. But at this writing, the choice has narrowed down to only four screeners worth talking about:

- AOL
- MSN Money
- Reuters
- Business Week

AOL's Stock Search (www.aol.com) is the least powerful of the group in terms of screening parameters, but it has one big advantage: ease of use. You can learn how to use it in a flash and run a quick screen whenever you get a hot idea. (AOL now offers its investing tools to non-members at no charge.)

Reuters Investor PowerScreener (reuters.com/investing) is in the same league as MSN's Deluxe Screener, both in terms of power and ease of use. I haven't counted, but PowerScreener probably offers fewer screening parameters than MSN Money, but it's also a little easer to use. Also, Reuters provides a tutorial that MSN doesn't.

Business Week's Advanced Stock Search (www.businessweek. com) is almost as easy to use as AOL's screener, and it offers more screening parameters. Business Week's search offers a feature that I haven't seen anywhere else. After you run a screen, you can see how much money you would have made or lost by running the screen up to 12 months before and buying all the stocks that the screen turned up at that time. On the downside, it's a pain to use. Once you run a screen, you can't simply modify a parameter and re-run the screen. You have to enter everything again, and that gets old pretty fast.

You'll probably come up with plenty of your own screens after you've read this book. But here are a few samples to give you some ideas. The first two samples can be run on most screeners, although you may have to modify them somewhat depending on which screener you've selected. However, the third search (Down & Out Value Stock Finder) is designed specifically for MSN's Deluxe Screener and includes a brief rundown on how to program the screener. Similarly, the fourth sample screen (Bulletproof Stocks) is tailored specifically for Reuters PowerScreener and includes hints on how to set up the screen.

Sample Growth Screen

This section contains suggested screening parameters for finding fast growing, but reasonably priced and profitable, growth candidates. The screen requires 20 percent recent annual revenue growth and at least 18 percent forecast average annual earnings growth. An 8 percent minimum return on assets requirement assures that passing candidates reported recent profits.

All the screeners described here allow you to limit your search to specific industries or to stocks listed on specific exchanges such as the New York Stock Exchange or Nasdaq. Business Week's screener lets you specify minimum and maximum values for each search parameter on a single line (it ignores values left blank). The other screeners require two entries, one for the minimum and the other for the maximum.

Here are the suggested search parameters along with the rationale for the selected values and suggestions for modifying the specified values to better suit your needs.

Market Capitalization

Specify $150 million minimum market capitalization.

Once below $500 million or so, the lower the market capitalization, the higher the risk. I set the minimum at $150 million, but risk-averse investors should change the setting to $500 million. It's somewhat academic, because I only turned up one company below $500 million when I ran the screen, and that was TTI Team Telecom, which had a $320 million market cap.

Price to Sales Ratio

Specify a minimum P/S ratio of 2, and a maximum of 9.

P/S ratios below 2 usually signal value-priced stocks, and this is a growth screen. Supermarket chains and other low-margin businesses may flunk this requirement because they often sport P/S ratios below 2. Change the minimum P/S requirement to 1 if you want to see those stocks. Nothing new showed up in the results when I tried eliminating the minimum altogether. It's a good idea to specify some positive number, say 0.1, for the minimum; otherwise you'll occasionally turn up oddball companies with negative P/S ratios.

The 9 P/S maximum is an arbitrary limit I set to preclude overpriced stocks. Since it is an arbitrary limit, you may want to fiddle with it to see what turns up if you set it higher or lower.

Revenue Growth

Specify minimum 15 percent 5-year revenue growth, 20 percent 3-year revenue growth, and 20 percent 1-year revenue growth (revenue means the same thing as sales).

I set the 5-year growth figure lower to pick up companies showing recent sales growth acceleration. The 20 percent recent minimums are aggressive and may eliminate blue-chip medium growers. Lowering the bar to 15 percent for all 3 periods added 6 more stocks to the 14 turned up by the original revenue growth requirements, including Home Depot and sunglass maker Oakley.

Analysts Consensus Ratings

Specify 2 maximum.

Consensus ratings in this instance means the average of all analysts' buy, hold, and sell ratings. Strong buy ratings equate to a consensus value of 1 and hold ratings (meaning sell) are worth 3. My 2 maximum value equates to a weak buy. The only growth stocks you'll find with ratings worse than weak buys are "busted" growth stocks.

Latest Quarter Earnings Surprise

Require a 0 percent minimum surprise.

Setting the requirement to 0 eliminates companies that reported earnings below analysts' forecasts (negative surprise) in their most recent quarterly report. Many professionals believe that negative surprises foretell more negative surprises. You are sure to lose money when a stock you own reports a negative surprise.

Next 5 Years Estimated Earnings Growth

Specify 18 percent minimum.

This setting requires that the analysts consensus 5-year average annual growth forecast must be at least 18 percent. Earnings growth is what growth investing is all about. The 18 percent minimum may be too aggressive for your taste, but I wouldn't reduce it to anything lower than 14 percent.

Current Ratio

Require a 1.5 minimum current ratio.

The current ratio is the company's current assets (cash, inventories, and receivables) divided by its current liabilities. Current ratios below 1 indicate that a company's short-term debts exceed its assets. The higher the ratio, the stronger the company's finances, at least on a short-term basis. The 1.5 minimum is arbitrary. You can lower it if you promise to religiously do the appropriate financial health analysis.

Long-Term Debt/Equity

Specify a 0.5 maximum long-term debt to equity ratio.

The long-term D/E ratio compares the long-term debt to stockholders' equity (book value). The higher the ratio, the higher the debt. The 0.5 maximum D/E value screens out firms that are susceptible to debt-induced failure. But it also eliminates most firms in the financials sector that typically operate with high debt levels. As the case with current ratio, you can raise the D/E maximum to 1.5 if you don't skimp on the financial health analysis.

Revenue

Require annual revenue of $50 million minimum

$50 million in annual revenues isn't much for a publicly traded corporation. You're asking for trouble if you significantly reduce this requirement.

Return on Assets

Specify a minimum 8 percent ROA

ROA measures profitability. The higher the ROA, the better, but you'll turn up more candidates by reducing the minimum required ROA. I wouldn't go below 5 percent. Increase your minimum ROA requirement if your screen turns up too many candidates.

Share Price

Require a $5 minimum share price

Share prices below $5 say there's a lot not to like about the stock, and that implies more risk than you need.

Percent Institutional Ownership

Specify 30 percent minimum institutional ownership

Mutual funds and other institutional buyers prefer growth stocks. Lack of institutional ownership probably means these pros don't think that they can make money owning the stock.

Results

This screen should turn up 15 or 20 strong growth candidates. If it doesn't, modify the parameter values as suggested to increase or decrease the number of hits.

Value Screen

The basis of value investing is finding good companies that are currently on the outs with most market players. This screen looks for value-priced stocks that are out-of-favor with analysts and mutual funds. The search verifies that passing candidates are indeed out-of-favor by requiring a weak stock chart.

Market Capitalization

Specify a minimum $250 million market capitalization.

Value strategies usually lead you to mid- and large-cap prospects. It's unlikely that companies smaller than $250 million market-cap would qualify; so don't waste time analyzing them.

Price to Sales Ratio

Specify 3.0 maximum P/S

You'll probably find that most of your viable candidates will have P/S ratios below 2, so this requirement eliminates just the obvious misfits. Try reducing the maximum if you're getting too many hits.

Analysts Consensus Ratings

Specify 2.2 minimum

Analysts consensus rating values are: strong buy (1), buy (2), hold (3), weak sell (4), and strong sell (5). A 1 consensus rating means that every analyst covering the stock rates it a strong buy, and 3 translates to hold (meaning sell). The 2.2 minimum limits your selection to stocks rated between weak buy and hold, or worse. Since analysts rate most stocks at buy, or better, this requirement limits the results to firms out of favor with most analysts.

Current Ratio

Specify 1.5 minimum

Current ratio is the company's current assets divided by its current liabilities. Value strategies require financially strong firms. Candidates with lower current ratios are unlikely to pass your financial strength tests.

Long-Term Debt/Equity

Require 0.4 maximum

The long-term D/E ratio compares a company's long-term debt to stockholders' equity (book value). The higher the ratio, the higher the debt. Low debt firms are your best bets. Try increasing the maximum if you don't get enough hits.

Revenue

Specify $50 million minimum TTM revenue.

You'll often find companies showing up in your screening results that aren't real companies, or at least they don't have real businesses. Sales of $50 million over the last four quarters (trailing twelve months [TTM]) isn't much for a public corporation, so this requirement keeps you from wasting time on companies with no sales.

Share Price

Require a minimum $5 share price.

Real cheap stocks usually aren't worth evaluating. What constitutes "real cheap" varies with market conditions and your own views. Many mutual funds won't buy stocks trading below $5, so that's a reasonable minimum.

Relative Strength

Specify a maximum value of 60 for relative strength.

Relative strength compares each stock's price performance to the performance of all stocks over the past 12 months. A relative strength value of 90 means the stock outperformed 90 percent of all listed stocks. The recommended 60 maximum prevents the screen from turning up strong stocks. You want to find underperforming stocks that will become strong stocks after you buy them.

Percent Held by Institutions

Specify 5 percent minimum, and 60 percent maximum.

Most mutual funds and other institutional buyers prefer growth stocks. Typically institutional ownership ranges between 40 percent and 95 percent for in-favor stocks. However, institutional owners are only required to report their holdings quarterly, and even then, with a two month delay, so ownership data could be out of date. That would be especially significant if the subject company's fall from grace happened recently. Although you're looking for out of favor stocks, you don't want them so far out of favor that no institutions own them, and the 5 percent minimum precludes such stocks. Try increasing the maximum if you don't get enough hits, and reducing it if you get too many.

Results

I turned up 57 candidates when I ran the screen during a weak market when analyst ratings were unusually pessimistic. Changing the maximum relative strength to 50 and the maximum P/S ratio to 2.5 reduced the number of hits to 33.

"MSN Money" Down & Out Value Stock Finder

This screen uses MSN Money's Deluxe Screener's unique capabilities to find those companies with strong historical sales growth and profitability histories that have recently stumbled.

MSN Money offers one of the Web's most powerful and flexible screening programs. Unfortunately it is also one of the most challenging to learn, especially since MSN Money offers only limited instructions.

It's worth learning if you have the time and the inclination. There is too much information to cover here, but here's a brief rundown—go to MSN Money's Stocks page (moneycentral.msn.com/investor) and select Stock Screener. The screener looks something like a spreadsheet with rows and columns. The rows are initially blank, and you fill them in as needed. Each row holds one search specification and three columns: Field Name, Operator, and Value.

Place your cursor in the Field Name area of the first row and click to bring up the screening parameter menu. Pick a parameter, and then move your cursor to the Operator column and choose one. Choices are arithmetic symbols such as the "equal sign" or the "less than or equal to" symbol, and the like. Then move to the Value field where you can enter a custom value or pick another parameter.

MSN Money provides no list of available parameters. So you'll have to browse through the various categories to find out what's available and where to find it.

I'll explain the process in more detail as I describe the screening parameters. For clarity, I've listed each search term in MSN Money's Deluxe Screener row format.

Return on Assets

Operator: <=

Value: 0.7*ROA: 5-year Avg.

Specifies companies with ROA (based on the last four quarters' earnings) no greater than 70 percent of the firm's five-year average ROA. This term finds companies with depressed ROA compared to its historical averages, a desirable trait for a value candidate. Entering the "0.7*" part of the value parameter is tricky. Select Custom Value. Type 0.7* and click the down arrow on the right side of the Custom Value box and select the Five-Year Average ROA parameter.

ROA: 5-Year Avg.

Operator: >=

Value: 10

Specifies that qualifying companies have five-year average ROAs of 10 percent or higher. This term ensures that companies passing the screen possess a history of above-average profitability.

Price/Sales Ratio

Operator: <=

Value: 2.5

Requires a P/S ratio no higher than 2.5, ensuring that the screen finds only value-priced stocks.

Debt/Equity Ratio

Operator: <=

Value: 0.5

Screens out debt-heavy companies.

Current Ratio

Operator: >=

Value: 1.1

Screens out firms facing a short-term cash crunch.

Avg. Daily Vol. Last Qtr.

Operator: >=

Value: 50,000

Specifies 50,000 share average daily volume to screen out stocks with insufficient trading volume (liquidity).

12-Month Revenue

Operator: >=

Value: 50,000,000

Requires a minimum of $50 million annual sales during the last four quarters to weed out firms without substantial sales.

Rev. Growth Qtr vs. Qtr

Operator: <=

*Value: 0.5*5-Year Revenue Growth*

Requires that the last quarter's year-over-year sales growth be no more than 50 percent of the company's five-year average annual sales growth. This condition identifies companies with recent sales growth below long-term trends, a hallmark of promising value stock candidates.

5-Year Revenue Growth

Operator: >=

Value: 10

Requires that passing stocks must show 10 percent minimum long-term sales growth. This term, combined with the previous test, insures that although currently down and out, qualifying firms have a reasonably strong historical sales growth history.

Mean Recommendation

Operator: <=

Value: Moderate Buy

Requires that passing stocks have average analysts' recommendations of "moderate buy" or worse. Analysts' moderate buy ratings (buy) are between real buys (strong buy) and sells (hold), and indicate ambivalence at best, a desirable quality for value candidates.

Results

I turned up 29 candidates in a variety of different industries when I ran the screen in March 2002. Try increasing the minimum ROA and reducing the maximum price/sales ratio if you get too many hits. Reduce the minimum ROA and the minimum current ratio (to 0.9) if you get too few.

Reuters Investor Bulletproof Stocks

This screen finds candidates unlikely to be bankruptcy candidates any time soon.

Except for firms filing bankruptcy to avoid big lawsuits, companies usually fail for only one reason: they run out of cash. Some are recent startups that never reached profitability and folded when they used up their initial public offering (IPO) stash and couldn't raise more. Others are formerly successful firms that ran into tough times when their earnings slumped to a level where they could no longer make interest payments.

Both categories share similar symptoms. They're either burning cash—that is, more cash is flowing out than in—or their cash flow isn't sufficient to service their debt. Avoiding bankruptcy candidates boils down to developing a set of requirements that cash-starved companies can't possibly meet. That's the goal of this screen. I call the survivors "bulletproof stocks."

Here are the bulletproof stock qualifications:

- Positive operating cash flow
- Positive net income
- Sales at least $50 million
- Current ratio of 1.5 or higher
- Total D/E ratio less than 0.4

The operating cash flow, net income, and sales requirements all refer to each company's TTM results.

The positive operating cash flow requirement, in theory, eliminates cash burners. But it's not foolproof, and insisting on positive earnings helps to assure that the company is, in fact, profitable. Requiring sales of at least $50 million filters out companies that look good on paper but, in reality, have no substantial business.

Insisting on positive income and cash flow doesn't assure that those inflows are sufficient to service the firm's debt. The current ratio compares a firm's current assets to its short-term debts. Requiring a current ratio of at least 1.5 assures that current assets exceed short-term debts by a 50 percent margin, screening out companies that are cash flow positive now but weighed down by previously built-up short-term debts.

The total D/E ratio compares the total of short- and long-term debt to the firm's shareholder's equity or book value. Total D/E ratios of 0.5 or less usually define low debt companies. Requiring ratios below 0.4 provides an extra margin of safety.

You program the screener by adding screening parameters one at a time by clicking on "Add a Criterion" and then selecting the desired parameter from a list.

I've included an English language description and Reuters's abbreviation in parenthesis for each screening term.

Price to Cash Flow Greater than Zero

{Pr2CashFlTTM} > 0

The bulletproof formula requires positive cash flow. By definition, the cash flow is positive when the price/cash flow ratio is positive.

Current Ratio Greater than 1.5

{CurRatioQ} > 1.5

The current ratio compares current assets, specifically cash, inventories, and accounts receivables, to short-term debt.

Total Debt to Equity Ratio Less than 0.4

{Dbt2EqQ} < 0.4

NetScreen is the only screener I've found that provides the total D/E ratio search parameter required by the bulletproof formula. Total D/E includes both long- and short-term debt which differentiates it from the long-term D/E parameter provided by most screening programs.

TTM Sales Greater than $50 Million

{SalesTTM} > 50

Requiring $50 million sales during the last 12 months filters out companies that aren't real businesses.

Net Profit Margin Greater than Zero

{NPMgn%TTM} > 0

The bulletproof formula requires positive net income of any amount for the last four quarters. The net profit margin is the net income divided by sales. The profit margin can't be a positive number unless the net income is also positive.

Results

The screen should show about 800 bulletproof stocks. You can print the list in groups of 100, or you can download it into a spreadsheet.

The Zen of Screening

It takes some practice to become proficient at screening. When you run your first screens you'll probably come up with no hits because you've specified too many parameters and/or made your requirements too tight. It's hard to determine which requirements are causing the problem when that happens. It's easier to go the other way. That is, start with just a few parameters and relatively loose requirements so that you get too many hits. Then add parameters and tighten requirements one-by-one until your screen comes up with a reasonable number of candidates to research, say 15 to 30 stocks.

After you've done some preliminary research, you probably won't be happy with many of the stocks in your first group of candidates. If that's the case, modify your screening parameters to disqualify the offending stocks. Repeat the process until your screens produce reasonably sized lists of qualified stocks.

If you come up with especially good screens, send them to me at hdomash@winninginvesting.com, and I'll post them on my Website.

Premade Screens

Some sites offer ready-to-use or premade screens. The advantage of premade screens is you don't have to come up with your own search parameters. Someone else has done that, so all you have to do is push a button to get the results.

One problem with premade screens is that you don't have much of a feel for the quality of the screening strategy.

There is an exception. The American Association of Individual Investors (AAII) site offers a large variety of premade screens and tracks their performance over time. AAII, a not-for-profit organization, provides education in the area of stock and mutual fund investing. You have to be a member to access the screening area. Membership is $49 a year and includes a monthly investing magazine that by itself is worth the price. The magazine doesn't tout stocks; instead it's educational in content and describes stock and mutual fund selection strategies followed by well-known money managers.

When I checked, the AAII site (www.aaii.com) was running 39 value, growth, combined growth and value, small-cap, and specialty screens based on the stock picking strategies of the likes of Benjamin

Graham, John Neff, David Dreman, Geraldine Weiss, Warren Buffett, and many more. One relatively new addition is a screen based on Joseph Piotroski's value-stock selection criteria that inspired my detailed fiscal fitness exam described in Chapter 10,

AAII runs the screens monthly, so you can see the top stocks picked by each screen as of the end of the past month. AAII also updates each screen's performance figures at the same time and once a year compares the performance of all of the screens.

Summary

Consider the results of all screens, whether based on your ideas or the ideas of a guru, as a list of research candidates, not as a buy list.

PART TWO

ANALYSIS TOOLS

4

ANALYSIS TOOL #1:
ANALYZING
ANALYSTS' DATA

Disregarding day-to-day fluctuations, stock prices typically reflect the market's expectations for the underlying company's future earnings growth. Other things being equal, shareholders make money when expectations rise, and lose when they decline.

Stock market analysts came under fire in recent years, first for advising us to buy ridiculously overpriced tech stocks at the market peak in 2000, then in 2001 for urging us to buy Enron shortly before the energy-trader collapsed, and again in 2002 when government investigations revealed that some analysts were advising investors to buy stocks that they themselves believed were losers.

Despite their low repute, analysts' buy/sell ratings and earnings forecasts are the best measure of the market's expectations for a specific stock. Although their buy/sell ratings per se won't help you make money, you can find important information embodied in analysts' ratings and estimates and in their research reports.

The Sentiment Index described later in this chapter will help you determine if market expectations best qualify a stock as a value or as a growth candidate. Analysis of analysts' earnings growth forecasts and of the firm's surprise history will help you to further define the stock as a viable growth or value candidate. Revenue forecasts are a powerful new tool that you can use to validate the reasonableness of earnings growth forecasts.

Who Are the Analysts?

Stock analysts come in two varieties: buy-side and sell-side. Investment bankers, including most full-service brokerages, hire sell-side analysts to research stocks of interest. Originally, brokerages derived most of their income from commissions on stock sales, hence the term, sell-side analysts. These days, investment banking accounts for the lion's share of full-service brokerage income, but the sell-side label is still applied.

Brokerages employ scores of analysts. Each typically covers a specific industry such as semiconductor equipment or restaurants. Analysts write research reports on their industry as a whole, and on specific companies within the industry. The analysts devise sales and earnings forecasts, buy, hold, or sell recommendations, and target prices for companies they follow. They update their forecasts and recommendations after each company's quarterly report is released and at other times as events warrant. Sell-side analysts ratings and reports are widely distributed, and third parties such as Thomson Financial, Zacks Research, and Reuters tabulate their ratings and estimates and publish them in the form of analysts' consensus ratings and forecasts.

Mutual funds, pension plans, and other institutional players read the sell-side analysts' reports, but many also employ their own analysts. These buy-side analysts do their own research and arrive at their own opinions about a company's future prospects. The buy-side analysts' reports are rarely publicized.

All of the ratings and forecasts that we hear about or see compiled, come from sell-side analysts. Analysts publish an in-depth report describing the business model, industry, and competitive situation when they begin coverage of a new company. After that, most analysts' reports are short updates, typically responding to an earnings report or other news affecting the company's outlook. Each report or update includes the analysts' current buy/sell recommendation (rating), as well as earnings forecasts for upcoming quarters and for the current and next fiscal years. The report also provides background information justifying changes in the ratings or forecasts.

Analysts' Ratings

The point of an analyst's report is to advise clients whether to buy or sell the company's stock. However, it's not that simple. For instance, an investor planning on holding for five years might be buying a stock that an investor with a shorter horizon is selling. So analysts developed a variety of rating variations, and, to further confuse the issue, each brokerage has its own terminology.

For instance, Goldman Sachs will put a stock on its Recommended List if it thinks it's going up in short order, while Merrill Lynch might label it a short-term buy, and Prudential Securities would say strong buy. The only way you can be sure of a specific ratings definition is to consult the brokerage's rating explanation, sometimes included with the report and sometimes not.

It's not as complicated as it sounds, because in my experience, all analysts' ratings other than strong buy equate to sell. Regardless of the spin, anything short of strong buy means that the analyst is not excited about the stock's prospects and probably wouldn't add it to his own portfolio.

"Sell" Is a Four-Letter Word

Sell-side analysts are real people like you and me who happen to have very well-paying jobs. You can't blame them for wanting to hold onto those jobs. Their employers, mostly brokerages, derive much of their profits from investment banking, that is, working with companies when they issue more stock, make acquisitions, borrow money, and so forth. How much money is involved? Say an investment banker brings a new company public by underwriting its IPO. The underwriting fee is negotiable of course, but think 7 percent. So a deal is worth 7 percent of $150 million, or $10.5 million, if the new company issues 10 million shares at an initial offering price of $15. When one company acquires another, both firms hire investment bankers to advise them on the transaction, involving fees running into tens of millions of dollars.

With that much money involved, the competition among investment banks to land these juicy contracts is intense. Naturally, the client, say a new company going public, picks the bank it believes will do the best job, meaning the one that will get the most shares sold at the highest price, and equally important, keep the share price up after the IPO. The latter is important because company insiders personally own tons of shares they will eventually want to sell. That's where the analyst comes into the picture. A highly regarded analyst's strong buy recommendation can make a big difference in a stock's trading price. According to a January 29, 2001, *Wall Street Journal* story, analysts receive "bonuses of several hundred thousand dollars for helping their firms win big underwriting deals." You can connect the remaining dots on your own.

Most public corporations represent potential investment banking business of some sort. Executives at these companies usually have incentives to keep their firm's share price up. They may be on bonus plans tied to the share price, have stock options, or own shares outright. It's understandable that most take it personally when an analysts' sell recommendation tanks their company's stock price. Since they're in a position to get even by diverting investment banking business to another firm, analysts get the picture, and most don't see anything to gain by advising selling a stock.

Consequently, most analysts don't issue sell ratings. Instead they say, hold, neutral, or market perform, and the pros know that means sell.

On occasion, analysts do want to advise selling, but some brokerages don't allow sell ratings. So, the policy of the analyst's brokerage house determines whether a stock will be rated hold or sell, not the analyst's view of the stock's prospects. As a rule of thumb, interpret hold, sell, and strong sell ratings as sell.

Analysts use terms such as buy, accumulate, long-term buy, outperform, and the like, to specify ratings between strong buy and sell. These ratings mean that the analyst isn't sure which way the stock is headed, at least in the near future. *Note*: Standard & Poor's analysts are the exception to the hold means sell rule. S&P does issue sell ratings, and a hold recommendation means exactly that; don't sell if you own it, but don't buy it either.

Consensus Ratings

Firms such as Thomson Financial, Zacks, and Reuters compile the analysts' individual buy/sell ratings into a consensus figure. They do that by first assigning each brokerage's individual ratings into one of five categories: strong buy, buy, hold, sell, and strong sell. They assign each category a numerical weight as shown in Table 4-1.

The compiler tabulates and averages the individual analyst's ratings. For instance, if three analysts all rate a stock strong buy, the total equates to 3, and the average (total divided by number or ratings) is 1. The consensus rating for a stock with one strong buy (1) and one hold (3) would be 2 (4/2), equating to a buy, even though neither of the analysts actually rated the stock a buy. The consensus is 2.7 (16/6) if three analysts say hold (9), two say strong buy (2), and one rates the stock a strong sell (5). Table 4-2 illustrates how the ratings are shown on Yahoo's Analyst Estimates page.

Compiling consensus ratings this way enables you to get a sense of the ratings trend by comparing older ratings to the current value. For instance, you'd see that analysts are getting more excited about a stock if last month's rating was 2.2 (weak buy) and this month it's 1.8.

TABLE 4-1 Numeric values for analysts' buy/sell ratings.

Category	Numeric Value
Strong Buy	1
Buy	2
Hold	3
Sell	4
Strong Sell	5

TABLE 4-2   Analysts consensus rating of 2.0, equating to buy for Clayton Homes, even thought none of the six analysts following the stock had rated it buy.

Broker Recommendations	
	This Month
Strong Buy	3
Buy	0
Hold	3
Sell	0
Strong Sell	0
Mean	**2.0**

Some may differ on the meaning attached to particular consensus values, but here's my rule of thumb:

- 1.0 to 1.5: Strong Buy
- 1.6 to 2.4: Buy
- 2.5 to 3.5: Hold
- 3.6 to 5.0: Sell

Do Strong Buys Outperform Sells?

You'd logically assume that you'd make money buying strong buys and lose money investing in hold or sell rated stocks. However there's little evidence to support that assumption.

Research on the subject is inconclusive. Some studies show that holds outperform strong buys and others draw the opposite conclusion. One reason strong buys don't outperform sells is simply that analysts issue many more buys than sells and analysts can make some really dumb calls.

Consider ADC Telecommunications, a maker of broadband equipment for telephone, cable TV, and wireless communications systems. I'll track the advice given by one analyst who initiated coverage of ADC in February 2000, just before the collapse of the then still soaring telecommunications equipment market. The analyst calls related here are real, but I gave him a made-up name, Andy Analyst, because this analyst was just one of 20 or so making similar calls. Each entry lists ADC's share price as of the report date.

February 7, 2000 @ $17.25 (All prices adjusted for stock splits.)

Telecom equipment was a hot sector when Andy initiated coverage with an outperform rating calling ADC a "reasonably valued vehicle to gain exposure to the increased levels of investment by communications service providers." Shortly thereafter, Andy upgraded ADC to buy.

May 19, 2000 @ $29.16

Andy, noting ADC's strong second quarter results, increased his price target to $38, commenting that the shares, "currently trading at 50 times our calendar 2000 EPS estimate," were trading "at a discount to the current and expected growth rate." Can you imagine that? A stock changing hands at a 50 P/E based on current fiscal year forecasted earnings is trading at a discount.

August 18, 2000 @ $42.38

On the day its share price peaked, Andy raised ADC's price target to $55 after the firm reported results "crushing our top line estimate … and surpassing our $0.15 EPS estimate." "ADC continues to grow at rates well in excess of its historical guidance of 25 percent to 30 percent increases," gushed Andy.

October 6, 2000 @ $25.19

With ADC's share price down 40 percent, and word spreading that some of its customers could fail, Andy publishes a report headlined: "ADCT: Recent Concerns Overdone," and noted that he had recently raised capital spending forecasts for the telecom sector. Much of the telecom sector capital spending came from upstart telephone companies funded by recent IPOs that by that time were running out of money and couldn't raise more.

November 29, 2000 @ $19.06

With the stock down 55 percent, Andy stubbornly maintained his buy based on "another solid quarterly financial performance … slightly ahead of expectations." Andy wasn't concerned that many of ADC's telecom customers were facing bankruptcy, because, as he put it: "ADC endorsed consensus estimates for fiscal 2001."

January 22, 2001 @ $14.25

With news of the plunge in telecom equipment spending now widespread, Andy maintained his buy even after reporting that ADC said it now "expects its current quarter earnings to come in about 50 percent below previous forecasts."

February 16, 2001 @ $12.06

With the stock down more than 70 percent from its August 2000 peak, and down 30 percent from when he started coverage, Andy finally threw in the towel, changing his recommendation to neutral, which we were supposed to know meant sell. What caused the change of heart? On the day before, Andy noted that rival equipment maker Nortel said that it expected its current quarter results to come in "substantially below current estimates."

The moral of the story: You're on your own; you can't rely on analysts to make your buy and sell decisions for you. But don't go away, there is important information to be found in analysts' ratings.

Number of Analysts

Each analyst following a stock works for a different brokerage or investment banker. One brokerage may employ thousands of stockbrokers, and each of those brokers may have dozens, if not hundreds, of individual clients. So each analyst's report potentially reaches tens of thousands of investors. Equally significant, analysts' research reports circulate to mutual funds and other big buyers.

How many analysts is enough? Most well known larger companies have between 20 and 35 analysts. For instance, in early 2002, Cisco Systems had 33 analysts, Merck had 26, AOL Time Warner had 30, and Microsoft had 28 analysts. Smaller firms that have already attracted interest will have somewhere between 7 or 8 to 15 or so analysts.

For instance, Chico's FAS, a fast-growing women's clothing store operator, had 11 analysts when I checked. Firms that hadn't yet garnered much attention may only have coverage from one, two, or three analysts.

The number of analysts following a stock is significant, but its interpretation depends on your perspective. For instance, value investors seek out stocks given up for dead by the growth crowd, who make up the bulk of the market. All other things being equal, analysts go where the action is and usually drop coverage when a company's stock goes into the tank. So the lack of analyst coverage signals a potential value candidate.

However, often all other things aren't equal. Sometimes analysts continue covering a down-and-out stock but not because of investor interest. Investment bankers figure that the distressed company may have to raise cash by selling off operating divisions, selling bonds, bank borrowings, and the like. They know that the resulting fat consulting fees will go to investment banks that stuck with the firm and continued to provide analyst coverage during their dark days.

That's why, in January 2002, down and outers such as Xerox and Lucent Technologies still had coverage by 11 and 29 analysts, respectively. But you can still spot out-of-favor stocks if you take a closer look at the ratings. For instance, here's the ratings distribution for the 29 analysts that were following Lucent:

- Strong buy: 3
- Buy: 7
- Hold: 17
- Sell: 2
- Strong sell: 0

Most of the analysts covering Lucent were advising selling the stock (holds and sells), and only three issued strong buys. So there wasn't much enthusiasm for Lucent, even though 29 analysts covered the company.

Sentiment Index

The analysts' ratings tell you a lot about the market's expectations for the company. For instance, you'd interpret the information differently if 20 out of the 29 analysts covering Lucent said strong buy, instead of only 3 advising buying Lucent's shares.

I devised a rule of thumb for using the analysts' ratings to gauge the market's enthusiasm, or excitement for a stock, at least from the analysts' perspective. I call it the Sentiment Index. You calculate the Sentiment Index by adding points for strong buy ratings and subtracting points for holds and sells. Regular buys are ignored.

Sentiment Index

■ **Strong buy:** Add the number of "strong buy" ratings.

■ **Buy:** Ignore.

■ **Hold, sell, and strong sell:** subtract a point for each of these ratings.

For example, a stock with three strong buys and no other ratings would score 3. A stock with three strong buys and three buys would still score 3 because the buys aren't counted. A stock with three holds would score –3. A stock with three holds and one strong sell would score –4.

Interpret negative scores as meaning analysts want nothing to do with the stock. Scores of 9 and above reflect strong enthusiasm.

I'll give you an example of how the index works in practice. Back in March 1999, Nortel was trading at $15 (all prices split adjusted). With 26 analysts, Nortel had plenty of coverage, but only seven rated Nortel strong buy, four rated it hold, and the rest were at buy. So Nortel's sentiment score stood at 3.

By October 1999, Nortel's share price had almost doubled to $29. Out of 28 analysts covering Nortel, 11 rated it strong buy, two were at hold, and the balance rated it buy. Nortel's sentiment score had moved up to 9, a relatively high number.

By April 2000, Nortel's share price had soared to $59, and its sentiment index hit 14.

In June, with its stock trading at $63, Nortel's sentiment score hit 16, which turned out to be its peak level.

In July 2000, Nortel's share price hit $71, but its sentiment score had slumped to 13.

Nortel's share price peaked at $82 in August, before beginning its unrelenting slide to $5 in August 2001. By January 2002, Nortel's sentiment score registered –21, a notably unenthusiastic reading.

Consider ADC Telecom, another high-flyer that I mentioned in an earlier example. I started following ADC in June 1999, when its stock was trading at $12, pretty much where it had been for the previous three years. With 10 of 22 analysts rating ADC a strong buy, and 5 at hold, ADC's sentiment score totaled 5.

By December 1999, ADC's share price had moved up about 25 percent, and its sentiment score had moved up to 7.

ADC's sentiment score peaked at 17 in August 2000, the same month that its stock topped out at $41.

By July 2001, ADC, with a score of –6, was trading at $6, on the way to its $3.50 September 2001 low.

Not all high-flying stocks that I tracked hit teen sentiment levels in their heydays. Market maker Knight Trimark, for instance, doubled in price between March and July 1999. Its sentiment score peaked out at 9, and that was in August 1999 when the stock was already well off its July high.

Here's how I suggest applying the index—

Value Candidates

Stocks with negative scores are clearly in the doghouse, and your best bets. Value priced stocks with scores between 0 and 2 reflect weak sentiment and may also be value candidates.

Growth Candidates

Scores significantly below 0 (e.g., –4) reflect strong negative sentiment, and that doesn't bode well for growth stocks. Sentiment scores of 9 or higher reflect high risk, but that doesn't mean that they won't trade higher, as the Nortel example proves.

Scores between –2 and 8 are acceptable, but preliminary evidence indicates that growth stocks with lower scores, in the 0 to 2 range, have more upside potential than stocks with higher scores.

Inspiration for the Sentiment Index

My inspiration for the sentiment index came from CNET.com's (investor.cnet.com) momentum rating. CNET calculates its momentum rating by awarding four points for each strong buy and buy, and subtracting two points for each hold and six points for each sell or strong sell. The main difference between CNET's approach and mine is that I don't count buy signals, and I give the same weight to holds and sells. CNET interprets high scoring stocks as buy candidates, where I interpret high scores as signaling risk.

Analysts' Estimates

Analysts consensus earnings forecasts are the single most important factor influencing stock prices. Changes in consensus forecasts often precipitate major stock price moves. You can find analysts' forecasts on most major financial sites, but at this writing, Yahoo shows you more data than other sites, and displays all of the information on a single page, making it easier and faster to access. Consequently, I'll use Yahoo's format to explain how to use consensus forecasts.

Earnings Growth Forecasts

You would think that the consensus forecasts reflect sophisticated statistical processing of the analysts' raw forecasts. But in fact, consensus forecasts—the numbers that determine whether a company's stock moves up or down on report day—are simple averages of the individual forecasts.

For example, say four analysts publish forecasts for a company, and three expect $1 per share, while the fourth predicts a break-even quarter, that is, no earnings. The average of the four estimates is $0.75, even though no one expects the company to earn $0.75.

Yahoo displays consensus earnings per share (EPS) forecasts for the company's current quarter, next quarter, current fiscal year, and next fiscal year (see Table 4-3, which is based on Yahoo information). Yahoo shows you the number of analysts making estimates, the high and low estimates, and the year-ago reported EPS for each period. For example, 12 analysts had made forecasts ranging from $0.28 to $0.31 per share for Accredo Health's March 2002 quarter, averaging to $0.30, the consensus forecast. Accredo had reported $0.18 per share earnings in the year-ago, March 2001 quarter. Accredo's June quarter marks the end of its fiscal year.

Note: Often the year-ago earnings shown on earnings estimate reports don't match the income statement earnings because analysts typically go along with the reporting company's preference to use pro forma earnings rather than those calculated through generally accepted accounting principles.

TABLE 4-3 Analysts consensus earnings and revenue forecasts for Accredo Health. Get a quote like this on finance.yahoo.com and then select Analyst Estimates.

	This Qtr. (3/02)	Next Qtr. (6/02)	This Year (6/02)	Next Year (6/03)
Earnings Estimates				
Avg. Estimate	0.30	0.30	1.09	1.59
# of Analysts	12	12	12	11
Low Estimate	0.28	0.27	1.05	1.42
High Estimate	0.31	0.38	1.15	1.90
Year-Ago EPS	0.18	0.18	0.66	1.09
Revenue Estimates				
Avg. Estimate	$176 mil.	$158 mil.	$651 mil.	$859 mil.
# of Analysts	2	2	11	7
Low Estimate	$176 mil.	$154 mil.	$594 mil.	$735 mil.
High Estimate	$177 mil.	$162 mil.	$774 mil.	$1.4 bil.
Year-Ago Sales	$124 mil.	$124 mil.	$462 mil.	$651 mil.
Sales Growth	41.9%	26.8%	40.9%	31.9%

There's considerable information that can be gleaned from the earnings estimates data.

Forecast Spread

The difference between the high and low analysts' estimates, 31 cents versus 28 cents, is typical for a current quarter. Accredo's June 2002 quarter and both fiscal years' estimates show wider spreads, signaling that those forecasts will likely move closer over time. A wide spread (e.g., 5 cents or more) close to announcement date indicates the likelihood of a significant earnings surprise.

EPS Growth

Analysts expected Accredo's earnings to grow 65 percent year-over-year in its June 2002 fiscal year (1.09 vs. 0.66), and another 46 percent the following year (1.59 vs. 1.09).

Growth investors should focus on stocks with at least 15 percent forecast year-over-year earnings growth. Accredo's strong year-over-year earnings growth forecasts qualified the stock as an attractive growth candidate.

Value stock candidates will likely have low or nonexistent forecast earnings growth. Consensus growth forecasts exceeding 5 percent signal relatively high expectations. Accredo's strong earnings growth forecasts would disqualify it as a value candidate.

Forecast EPS Trend

Consensus earnings forecast trends are even more significant than the forecasts themselves.

The forecast trend is the current forecast for a period, say the current fiscal year, compared to forecasts for the same period one, two, or three months ago. A positive trend in forecasts tells you that analysts are becoming increasingly optimistic about the company's prospects, and a positive earnings surprise is likely. Conversely, a negative trend raises the specter of further forecast reductions and a negative surprise at report time.

Value Candidates

The best value candidates will show flat or negative forecast trends. Positive forecast trends signal increasing enthusiasm, which means that it's probably too late for value investors.

Growth Candidates

Stocks with flat (no trend) or positive forecast trends are valid growth candidates. But growth investors should avoid stocks with negative forecast trends.

Yahoo's EPS Trend report (see Table 4-4) shows consensus estimates going back 90 days for each of the two quarters and fiscal years covered. Pay most attention to the fiscal numbers because the quarterly results often fluctuate for a variety of short-term reasons. Ignore $0.01 changes.

TABLE 4-4 Earnings forecast trend report for Accredo Health.

	This Qtr. (3/02)	Next Qtr. (6/02)	This Year (6/02)	Next Year (6/03)
	EPS Trend			
Current	0.30	0.30	1.09	1.59
7 Days Ago	0.30	0.28	1.07	1.44
30 Days Ago	0.30	0.28	1.07	1.44
60 Days Ago	0.26	0.27	0.99	1.28
90 Days Ago	0.25	0.24	0.93	1.16

Analysts had been consistently increasing their estimates for Accredo. The magnitude and consistency of Accredo's positive earnings forecast momentum was stronger than most you'll find, and reinforced Accredo's standing as a strong growth candidate.

99 CENTS Only Stores' consensus forecast trend (Table 4-5) is more typical.

99 CENTS Only Stores' current fiscal year's forecasts had barely moved during the preceding three months, and its next fiscal year's forecast had moved up only 2 cents. 99 CENTS Only Stores' flat EPS trend signals less enthusiasm than Accredo's positive trend, but it wouldn't disqualify it as a growth candidate, and would also qualify it as a value prospect.

TABLE 4-5 99 CENTS Only Stores' consensus earnings forecast trend.

	This Qtr. (3/02)	Next Qtr. (6/02)	This Year (12/02)	Next Year (12/03)
	EPS Trend			
Current	0.23	0.25	1.11	1.34
7 Days Ago	0.23	0.25	1.11	1.34
30 Days Ago	0.22	0.25	1.10	1.30
60 Days Ago	0.22	0.25	1.10	1.30
90 Days Ago	0.23	0.25	1.11	1.32

TABLE 4-6   InFocus' consensus earnings forecast trend.

	This Qtr. (3/02)	Next Qtr. (6/02)	This Year (6/02)	Next Year (6/03)
EPS Trend				
Current	0.15	0.19	0.90	1.25
7 Days Ago	0.15	0.19	0.91	1.25
30 Days Ago	0.11	0.19	0.91	1.25
60 Days Ago	0.24	0.27	1.17	1.37
90 Days Ago	0.25	0.27	1.18	1.42

InFocus' earnings forecast trend (Table 4-6) tells a gloomier story. InFocus' earnings forecasts had been steadily trending down, and its fiscal year forecasts were both down substantially from 90 days before. InFocus' negative forecast trend was a red flag warning of further cuts and/or a negative earnings surprise.

Long-term Earnings Growth

Many analysts, as a matter of course, estimate a company's long-term (usually 5 years) average annual earnings growth. Those forecasts are averaged and listed on many sites. The company's consensus long-term growth forecast is the *G* in PEG, the valuation method favored by many growth investors (see Chapter 5). Although widely followed, the long-term growth forecasts are not tracked for accuracy. (PEG is the acronym for the ratio of the stock's P/E divided by the expected earnings growth.) Think about it! Have you ever heard of anyone looking up a particular analyst's long-term earnings growth forecast for say, Microsoft, from 5 years past, and then comparing it to what actually happened? Me neither!

Even so, long-term consensus forecasts work as an expectations gauge. High average annual growth forecasts reflect high expectations, and vice versa. The earnings growth rate for stocks making up the S&P 500 Index has averaged around 15 percent annually over the past few years. Using 15 percent as a base, forecast annual growth rates below 10 percent can be said to imply below average, or low expectations, while those above 20 percent reflect high expectations.

Long-term growth forecasts of 10 percent or less signal value candidates. Growth investors, however, should stick with stocks reflecting at least 15 percent long-term growth expectations.

Earnings Surprise

An earnings surprise is the difference between analysts consensus forecasts and the company's reported earnings. If the reported earnings come in below forecasts, it's a negative surprise, and a positive surprise if earnings come in above forecasts.

Surprises are usually quantified in cents, as in, "a two-cent positive surprise." Absent other overriding factors, a negative surprise of any amount drives the share price down, often sharply. Most companies routinely report a one or two-cent positive surprise, so that amount is not really a surprise and doesn't move prices much.

Positive surprises of four or five cents—or more—usually do move the share price up, although not nearly as much as a negative surprise forces it down. A big positive surprise, say 10 cents, can have a more pronounced effect. Surprisingly, the surprise percentage isn't as important as the number of cents. A 4-cent shortfall, say a company reported $4.04 instead of the expected $4.08, is about as significant as if the company reported $0.08 instead of $0.12.

Although the stock price reacts immediately, a significant surprise can have a longer lasting effect because the event forces analysts to reevaluate their earnings forecasts for coming quarters. For instance, analysts almost always increase their estimates following a large positive surprise.

Although a stock reacts to the magnitude of the surprise in cents rather than percentage, some investors believe that in the event of a positive surprise, the surprise percentage does foretell future price action. That is, stocks with higher percentage surprises gain more in the ensuing months than stocks with lower percentage surprises.

History Lessons

You can see a company's recent surprise history on most financial sites. Yahoo displays the estimated earnings, actual reported earnings and the cents and percentage surprise for each of the last four reported quarters.

Here were Mylan Laboratories' last four quarters' surprises listed in chronological order (oldest first) as of February 2002: +0.02, +0.09, +0.09, +0.06

From the data, it appeared that Mylan, at least in the past year, had been a habitual positive surpriser. Further research might give you a different slant, but based only on its surprise history, it looked likely that Mylan would surprise again on the upside when it reported its March 2002 results.

On the other hand, a history of negative surprises signals risk. Nothing is for sure in the stock market, but a habitual negative surpriser is more likely than the average firm to announce another negative surprise.

Value vs. Growth

Some research shows that growth stocks drop more, percentage-wise, than value-priced stocks in the event of a negative surprise. That's logical since growth stocks' valuations imply high expectations, and value stocks, by definition, are low expectation stocks. So for a value stock, a negative surprise is really no surprise since most players already view the company as a loser. Conversely, growth investors expect their picks to surprise on the upside, so a negative surprise is a real surprise.

Research results are mixed on positive surprises. Some studies show that growth stocks outperform value stocks in the event of a positive surprise, while other research shows the opposite result.

Sales Forecasts

Although sometimes it may seem so, analysts just don't pull their earnings forecasts out of thin air. Rather, they set up detailed earnings models, starting with estimated sales, and then deduct their estimated costs to arrive at their earnings forecast.

Earnings forecasts have been available for years, but the sales (revenue) forecasts used to derive the forecasted earnings have been hard to come by. That changed in 2001 when Yahoo added consensus revenue estimates to its Analyst Estimate report. The availability of sales forecasts is an important breakthrough that, so far, has gone unnoticed by many investors.

Consensus sales forecasts are most important when analyzing growth companies. Growth investors often don't realize that a company's recent earnings growth was driven by a large acquisition or another one-time event and won't be repeated. Reviewing sales forecasts would alert you to that instance. Other times, slowing sales growth estimates are your first clue that once hot earnings growth is about to slow.

You can see that reflected in Mentor Corporation's sales forecasts for its March and June 2002 quarters (Table 4-7). Mentor's year-over-year sales growth had totaled 20 percent, 22 percent, and 28 percent, respectively, in the three quarters prior to March 2002. But analysts were only forecasting around 11 percent year-over-year growth in its March and June 2002 quarters.

Analyzing revenue growth is covered in detail in Chapters 11 and 12.

TABLE 4-7 Mentor Corporation's revenue (sales) forecasts.

	This Qtr. (3/02)	Next Qtr. (6/02)	This Year (3/02)	Next Year (3/03)
Earnings Estimates				
Avg. Estimate	0.47	0.47	1.63	1.86
# of Analysts	4	4	4	4
Low Estimate	0.44	0.45	1.57	1.80
High Estimate	0.48	0.49	1.65	1.90
Year-Ago EPS	0.43	0.42	1.40	1.63
Revenue Estimates				
Avg. Estimate	$87 mil.	$90 mil.	$323 mil.	$364 mil.
# of Analysts	2	1	1	1
Low Estimate	$87 mil.	$90 mil.	$323 mil.	$364 mil.
High Estimate	$88 mil.	$90 mil.	$323 mil.	$364 mil.
Year-Ago Sales	$79 mil.	$81 mil.	$269 mil.	$323 mil.
Sales Growth	11.0%	11.5%	20.2%	12.6%

Regulation FD

In October 2000, a new SEC rule, Regulation FD (Fair Disclosure) outlawed selective disclosure of all material financial information. Prior to Reg. FD, corporations would routinely disclose important information, such as whether they would likely meet, beat, or come in below existing earnings forecasts to favored analysts. Other analysts might hear the same news later, if at all. Individual investors were shut out.

Reg. FD shut down that game and now most firms announce such changes in guidance via a press release, in a conference call open to the public, or both. Consensus forecasts change immediately since all analysts get the same news at the same time. Consequently, changes in guidance have the same effect on a stock price as an earnings surprise. However, so far as I know, nobody is tracking management guidance changes in the same way that surprises are tabulated.

Research Reports

I may not follow analysts' buy/sell advice because of their positive bias, but I still avidly read their research reports. Some don't say much, but many are filled with essential information about the company's business plan, the problems it's encountering, and the analysts' take on the competition and industry trends. That's valuable information that would require days of research if you did it on your own.

Further, you can often deduce that a buy rating really means sell by reading the report. For instance, in late June 2001, investment banker Credit Lyonnais reiterated its add recommendation for Global Crossing, then trading at around $9, but at the same time cut its price target from $25 to $12. Or consider ABN Amro's mid-August 2001 report reducing its 2002 and 2003 revenue and earnings estimates for Microsoft, while reiterating its add advice. Whether by reducing the target price, or cutting earnings estimates, an analyst is signaling reduced expectations, and reduced expectations translate to sell.

Reuters Investor offers research reports from dozens of brokerages. Most reports are for sale at prices ranging from $10 to $90 each. At those prices you can run up a big bill if you research many companies. However, many Web brokers offer free research reports to their customers. I suggest starting with your broker's offerings, and even consider opening a second account with a different broker to access additional free reports.

Summary

You won't fare well following analysts' buy/sell advice, but their recommendations and forecasts gives you information about the market's enthusiasm for any stock and can help you qualify stocks as viable value or growth candidates. Further, analysts' research reports can help you to understand a company's business and competitive standing, and often yield clues revealing the analysts' real view of the company's business prospects.

5

ANALYSIS TOOL #2: VALUATION

How much is a stock worth? If we knew, making money in the stock market would be easy. All we would have to do is buy stocks currently trading below their value, and then simply sit back and wait for them to move up to their "correct value." Of course it's not that easy. Unless it pays a meaningful dividend, a stock has no value, other than what another investor is willing to pay.

That said, there are a plethora of stock valuation schemes in use. Many originated when stocks did pay significant dividends. These measures originally valued stocks by calculating the present value of their expected future dividends. That made sense, but over time dividends faded in importance, and now most investors buy stocks for capital appreciation and don't consider dividends in their evaluations. You'd think that given that shift, analysts would have found new ways of valuing stocks. Many have, but many others simply replaced dividends with expected earnings or cash flow and continue using the same formulas. That makes sense from an academic perspective, but I doubt that you will find anyone willing to buy your shares at a price calculated by those methods.

In fact, stocks trade at whatever price investors are willing to pay today. The greed, excitement, fears, expectations, and enthusiasm that determine today's value are impossible to quantify. What you can do is evaluate the reasonableness of the expectations reflected in today's stock price. This section describes two ways to do that.

- Implied growth
- Growth at a reasonable price

The first, determining the earnings growth rate implied by a stock's current trading price, although employed by many professionals, is unknown to most individual investors. The second, growth at a reasonable price (GARP), applies only to growth stocks and is arguably the valuation formula most widely followed by individual investors and pros alike. That truth undoubtedly goes a long way toward explaining why so many got it so wrong in the 2000/2001 tech debacle.

After reading this chapter, all sane investors will no doubt glue the implied growth formula onto their foreheads. However, implied growth only conveys what is true today. You'll have to calculate target prices (see Chapter 6) to find out what happens next.

Implied Growth

Benjamin Graham, sometimes called the father of value investing, proposed a practical and easily calculated formula for estimating the intrinsic value of a growth stock in his pioneering treatise on fundamental analysis, "Security Analysis," co-written with David Dodd and first published in 1934. Don't be put off by the algebraic formulas that follow. They're included to justify the result. In the end, all you'll have to do is look up implied growth on Table 5-1. Graham and Dodd defined intrinsic value as:

Intrinsic Value = *Eps x [8.5 + (2 x forecast annual earnings growth %)]*

(where *Eps* is the TTM earnings per share)

Put into words, Graham said that a company's intrinsic value is its latest annual earnings multiplied by a factor equal to 8.5 plus twice the projected earnings growth rate.

Later, Graham modified the formula to account for the notion that stock valuations vary inversely with prevailing interest rates. That is, stocks tend to trade at higher valuations when interest rates are low, and vice versa (see Chapter 2). Graham used AAA (highest quality) corporate bond rates as a proxy for prevailing interest rates. The AAA corporate bond rates were around 4.4 percent when he first devised the formula, so the revised version looks like:

Intrinsic Value = *Eps x (4.4/AAA) x [8.5 + (2 x forecast annual earnings growth %)]*

(where *AAA* is the current yield of AAA-rated corporate bonds)

For example, if a company's latest earnings were $1 per share, the bond yield was 7.2 percent, and analysts forecast 20 percent average annual earnings growth over the next five years, the intrinsic value would be:

Intrinsic Value = *$1.00 x (4.4/7.2) x [8.5 + (2 x 20)] = $29.64*

The intrinsic value is $29.64, based on November 2001's 7.2 percent corporate bond yield.

Graham's intrinsic value calculation, per se, is interesting, but it isn't of much practical value since it hinges on analysts' long-term earnings growth forecasts. While analysts strive to accurately predict a company's current quarter's earnings, they'll undoubtedly revise their forecasts for the next quarter based on the current quarter's results. Consequently, their long-term growth forecasts are likely to be considerably off the mark.

However, Graham's formula can be very insightful used another way. If you substitute the current stock price for intrinsic value, and implied earnings growth for forecast growth, and then do some algebraic manipulation, you get:

Implied growth rate = *P/E (AAA/8.8) –4.25*

Implied growth, as I've defined it, is the long-term average annual earnings growth that the company would have to achieve to justify its current P/E.

To gain further insight, assume for the moment that the AAA corporate bond rate is 8.8 percent. Then the formula simplifies down to:

Implied growth rate = *P/E –4.25*

For example, using the simplified formula, a P/E of 50 implies a growth 46 percent average annual earnings growth rate.

According to Graham's formula, the implied growth rate corresponding to a particular P/E moves in tandem with the corporate bond rate. For example, the market will support higher P/Es if interest rates drop. Table 5-1 shows how it works out. You can use the table to look up the long-term average annual growth rate corresponding to your stock's P/E.

The current AAA corporate bond rate is available at www.neati-deas.com/aaabonds.htm.

Most tech stocks sported P/E ratios well in excess of 50 during the 1998/1999-tech boom. For instance, Cisco Systems, using its July 2000 fiscal year earnings and its July 30, 2000, closing share price, sported an off-the-chart 175 P/E. As you can see in Table 5-1, a 100 P/E implies that the market is expecting earnings growth in the 53 to 96 percent range.

TABLE 5-1   Implied annual EPS growth rates for various AAA corporate bond rates.

P/E	5%	6%	7%	8.8%
10	1%	2%	4%	6%
15	2%	6%	8%	11%
20	7%	9%	12%	16%
25	10%	13%	16%	21%
30	13%	16%	19%	26%
35	16%	19%	23%	31%
40	18%	23%	27%	36%
50	24%	30%	35%	46%
60	30%	37%	43%	56%
80	41%	50%	59%	76%
100	53%	68%	75%	96%

What's a reasonable annual earnings growth rate expectation? Here's a look at some well-known tech stocks. I'll start with sales growth, since in the end, that is what determines earnings growth. Table 5-2 shows each company's average annual sales growth for the most recent five years and for the five years before that. Table 5-3 illustrates how those sales growth rates translated to earnings growth.

TABLE 5-2   Average annual sales growth. (Growth rates are as of the last reported fiscal year data available on 12/01/01.)

Company	Last 5 years	Prior 5 years
Microsoft	23%	38%
Cisco	19%	86%
Qualcomm	27%	55%
Sun Micro	21%	16%
IBM	4%	1%
Dell	43%	57%
Intel	16%	33%

TABLE 5-3   Average annual earnings growth. (Growth rates are as of the last reported fiscal year data available on 12/01/01.)

Company	Last 5 years	Prior 5 years
Microsoft	25%	38%
Cisco	24%*	72%
Qualcomm	119%*	losses
Sun Micro	12%	21%
IBM	20%	-8%
Dell	57%	43%
Intel	25%	38%

* 2001 fiscal year excluded because the company had negative EPS.
In these instances, growth data covers the four years ending in fiscal 2000.

Most of these companies saw their growth slow in the most recent five years compared to the earlier period. You can draw your own
conclusions. My take is that 20 percent to 30 percent annual earnings
growth is a realistic expectation for mature tech companies, and 30 percent to 40 percent is reasonable for younger firms.

You can look up the current AAA corporate bond rate on the Financial Forecast Center (www.neatideas.com/aaabonds.htm). What corporate bond rates should you assume for the future? Use history as your
guide. Table 5-4 show historical ranges dating to the 1920s. You can
draw your own conclusions, but my take is that barring a period of run-
way inflation, rates are likely to hover in the 6 percent to 9 percent
range.

Table 5-1 gives you the earnings growth rate implied by your
stock's P/E. It's up to you to determine the reasonableness of the implied
rate. However, a little common sense goes a long way.

For instance, say that you're a value investor looking at a candidate with a 5 percent implied annual earnings growth rate. Assume that
you think the firm will see earnings growth in the 10 percent to 20 percent range when it recovers from its current plight. For now, you don't

TABLE 5-4   Historical AAA corporate bond rates.

Years	Low	High
1920-29	4.6%	6.4%
1930-39	2.9%	5.2%
1940-49	2.5%	3.0%
1950-59	2.6%	4.6%
1960-69	4.2%	7.7%
1970-79	7.1%	10.8%
1980-89	8.4%	15.5%
1990-94	6.7%	9.6%
1995-99	6.2%	8.5%
2000-04	5.0%	8.0%

* Source: Moody's via Financial Forecast Center (www.neatideas.com).

care whether the market ends up pricing the company as a 10 percent or 20 percent grower because either is well above its current valuation.

On the other hand, say that you're a growth investor looking at a hot stock priced to grow earnings 50 percent annually. With a 50 percent growth rate priced in, what happens to its stock price if it only achieves 40 percent growth?

Growth at a Reasonable Price

Many growth investors don't spend much time worrying about the subtleties of stock valuation. Instead, they adhere to a "keep it simple" philosophy. In their view, valuation boils down to earnings and earnings growth.

These investors look for a balance between price and expected earnings growth. Specifically, they want to buy growth at a reasonable price (GARP). The reasonable price is determined by comparing a stock's P/E to the company's expected annual earnings growth rate.

PEG and Fair Value

A stock is said to be fairly valued when its P/E equals its growth rate, undervalued when trading at a P/E below its expected growth, and overvalued when trading above. For example, if a company is expected to grow earnings 25 percent annually, its stock is fairly valued when its P/E is 25. It's undervalued when trading at P/Es below 25, and overvalued when trading at P/Es higher than 25.

PEG is the acronym for the ratio of the stock's P/E divided by the expected earnings growth.

$$\text{PEG} \ = \ \frac{\text{P/E}}{\text{Forecast Annual EPS Growth}}$$

A PEG of 1 translates to fair value. PEGs below 1 signify undervalued and above 1, overvalued.

Presumably, defining fair value as the condition when P/E equals the growth rate is based on a mathematically elegant principle, but I've never been able to find any basis for the relationship. Possibly, just that the concept is widely followed gives it validity.

Most players adjust the fair value definition to market conditions. Few growth stocks traded at PEGs below 2 during the 1998/1999 momentum market, so growth investors changed their PEG definition of fair value to 2 (PE equal to twice the earnings growth rate) instead of 1. Doing that isn't as silly as it sounds. In the end, P/E measures the market's enthusiasm for a stock, and most stocks trade at higher valuations during a bull market.

While the definition sounds precise, calculating PEG isn't cut and dried. The only factor universally agreed is *P*, the latest closing stock price.

The "E" in P/E

Everyone agrees that the *E* in P/E is 12-months' earnings, but which 12 months, and which earnings? Some use the last four quarter's earnings, adhering to generally accepted accounting principles (GAAP), while others prefer the pro forma earnings favored by many reporting companies and by their analysts because it omits a variety of charges and thus is higher than the GAAP earnings. Most analysts and many money managers prefer, however, to use analysts consensus forecast earnings for the current year. Since we're talking about growth stocks, forecast earnings are higher than historical earnings, thus reducing the P/E. Besides, using forecast earnings avoids the GAAP versus pro forma debate, since analysts always forecast pro forma earnings.

Pro Forma Earnings

Some companies highlight pro forma earnings instead of GAAP earnings in their quarterly reports. The pro forma earnings calculation omits certain costs that the reporting company deems not representative of its operating performance. There are no standards defining which expenses should or should not be included in pro forma earnings. It's up to the discretion of the reporting company.

Growth Rate

The earnings growth rate, the *G* in PEG, could be historical long-term earnings growth, but most participants use analysts consensus forecast growth. Here again, there's room for discussion. Some practitioners use analysts' five-year average annual earnings growth forecasts, while others prefer the current, or the next fiscal year's, year-over-year forecast earnings growth.

The growth money managers and analysts that I interviewed use PEG, despite the inaccuracies, because it's close enough. They say that they're not calculating PEG down to decimals. If the P/E is 20, and forecast earnings growth is 40 percent, the stock is undervalued. The logic still works, even if the company ends up growing earnings at 30 percent annually instead of 40 percent.

Realistic Earnings Growth Estimates

Successful emerging growth companies often chalk up supercharged earnings growth in their early years. Sales are growing rapidly, but more important, many are near the breakeven point, and gross profits are just beginning to exceed fixed costs. As revenues grow, higher percentages of gross profits fall to the bottom line, driving earnings up faster than sales.

Eventually, sales growth slows to levels similar to its market sector. The timing depends on the particulars, but in my experience that happens sooner than most market analysts expect.

Once a company is past that initial growth spurt, earnings growth, although volatile quarter to quarter, trends down toward the level of sales growth. That happens because a company can only grow earnings faster than sales by increasing its profit margins, and margin expansion opportunities diminish over time. That said, for the best companies you could probably expect annual earnings growth to exceed sales growth by 10 to 20 percent on an ongoing basis. That means that a well-run company may be able to grow earnings from 22 percent to 24 percent annually on only 20 percent sales growth.

Table 5-5 shows historical long-term sales growth rates for a few representative industries. The best companies exceed these industry averages by taking market share from weaker competitors.

Estimating Maximum Growth Using ROE

Many analysts say that return on equity (ROE) defines a firm's maximum earnings growth rate. That concept has mathematical validity, and is fully explored in Chapter 11. However, it assumes that the company will not increase its profit margins or raise additional funds through borrowing or by selling more stock.

While high ROE is desirable, many firms do manage to increase profit margins and raise additional funds, and it's not clear that in practice ROE works well to define a company's maximum annual earnings growth.

TABLE 5-5   Historical Average Annual Sales Growth.

Industry	Average Annual Longterm Sales Growth
Advertising	9%
Apparel	7%
Banks	0%
Biotechnology	17%
Drugs	11%
Educational Services	16%
Food Processing	7%
Grocery	5%
Healthcare Info Systems	18%
Homebuilding	11%
Hotel/Gaming	13%
Household Products	12%
Life Insurance	0%
Medical Services	14%
Office Equipment	9%
Restaurants	12%
Retail Stores	10%
Securities Brokerage	16%
Semiconductor Equipment	13%
Semiconductors	8%
Software	14%
Telecom Equipment	10%
Wireless Networking	15%

Dividends

The valuation formulas described here do not take dividends into account. That's okay for the most part because relatively few stocks pay significant dividends. Some do, however, and in these instances, the dividend payout should be considered when valuing the stock. One way to estimate the value added by dividends is to divide the annual dividend payout by the AAA corporate bond rate. For instance, if a company is paying $1.00 per share annually, and the corporate bond rate is 7 percent, the value added by the dividend is $14.28 ($1.00/0.07). That equation assumes that the dividend payout will continue indefinitely at the same level. Dividends growing over time would warrant a higher valuation.

Summary

Market analysts all too often ignore the earnings growth expectations built into the current price when they tell us to buy their favorite stocks. But you can check the reasonableness of their recommendations yourself. Simply look up the current AAA corporate bond rate on the Web and then find the growth rate implied by a stock's P/E in Table 5-1.

6

ANALYSIS TOOL #3:
ESTABLISHING
TARGET PRICES

Many professional money managers compute a target price, the price they expect to sell it at if all goes well, before they buy a stock. The target price defines the potential profit on the investment, and if it isn't high enough to justify the risk, they don't buy the stock.

Computing target prices is not the same as determining the reasonableness of a stock's current price (described in Chapter 5). Instead, the target price calculation forecasts a stock's trading range at some future time. How far depends on your goals and investing style. Value investors usually find themselves analyzing distressed companies, and they don't know when a candidate will regain its footing. So it's necessary for them to look three to five years ahead. Growth investors usually have shorter timeframes and may only look 12 months to 18 months ahead, typically to the end of the next fiscal year.

The beauty of the target price method is that it doesn't matter. The accuracy of your target prices depends on the accuracy of your assumptions, not the time span. Once you understand the process, you can vary the number of look-ahead years to suit your needs.

Why is setting target prices important? Consider an example. Say that you're analyzing two stocks, both in similar businesses and both are currently trading for $30 per share.

Now assume that after analyzing relevant factors, you determine that if all goes as you predict, two years from now Stock A will be trading between $35 and $40, while Stock B will be trading in the $60 to $70 range. Your analysis could be wrong, of course, or events may not go as expected, but given that information, most would agree that Stock B presents the better opportunity.

The target price approach, unlike other valuation methods, doesn't use analysts' earnings forecasts in the computation. On the other hand, consensus sales (revenue) forecasts, if available, can be very helpful.

The Process

Because it relies on historical performance, the target price approach is most effective analyzing companies that have been in business long enough to amass a significant track record, say seven or eight years minimum.

Developing target prices involves seven steps. Don't be put off by that. You can do the whole calculation in less than 10 minutes.

1. Forecast sales in the target year.
2. Estimate profit margin in the target year.
3. Compute the target year net income by multiplying your sales forecast (Step 1) by your estimated profit margin (Step 2).
4. Estimate the number of shares outstanding at the end of the target year.
5. Estimate the target year EPS by dividing your net income forecast (Step 3) by your estimated number of shares outstanding (Step 4).
6. Estimate the likely high and low P/E when the target year's results are announced.

7. Compute high and low target prices by multiplying your estimated EPS (Step 5) by your forecast high and low P/Es (Step 6).

I'll demonstrate the process by estimating pharmaceutical maker Alpharma's target prices for early 2005, after its 2004 fiscal year results would have been announced. I wrote this chapter in April 2002, so I was estimating Alpharma's target prices a little less than three years into the future. Alpharma had been a steady grower, but it made several missteps in 2001, dumping its share price and making it a potential value candidate.

	Avg P/E	Price / Sales	Price / Book	Net Profit Margin (%)
12/01	NA	1.20	1.32	-3.7
12/00	31.60	1.43	1.52	6.6
12/99	25.30	1.57	3.29	5.3
12/98	30.40	1.58	3.56	4.0
12/97	23.20	1.10	2.31	3.5
12/96	NA	0.65	1.71	-2.4
12/95	24.90	1.09	2.76	3.6
12/94	NA	0.93	2.41	-0.4
12/93	44.80	0.89	1.63	2.5
12/92	36.30	1.88	3.02	3.9

	Book Value / Share	Debt / Equity	Return on Equity (%)	Return on Assets (%)	Interest Coverage
12/01	20.11	1.16	NA	-1.5	0.2
12/00	28.84	0.59	7.1	3.8	2.9
12/99	9.36	1.67	11.2	3.4	2.6
12/98	9.91	1.60	9.1	2.7	2.5
12/97	9.41	0.94	7.3	2.8	2.5
12/96	8.55	1.26	NA	-1.9	0.2
12/95	9.47	1.07	9.2	3.0	2.4
12/94	8.40	1.21	NA	-0.3	1.1
12/93	8.58	0.44	4.7	2.0	3.2
12/92	8.57	0.40	8.8	4.4	2.7

FIGURE 6-1 MSN Money's Key Ratio 10-Year Summary report for Alpharma. From MSN Money's main page, get a stock quote, then choose Financial Results under Research, and click on Key Ratios. You'll also need the 10-Year Financial Summary report. Click on Statements and then select 10-Year Summary from the Financial Statements dropdown menu.

The analysis is best-done using fiscal year data. MSN Money is the best resource because its Financial Statement and Key Ratio 10-Year Summary reports list sales, profit margins, shares outstanding, and P/E data going back 10 years. Figure 6-1 shows MSN Money's Key Ratio 10-Year Summary report for Alpharma.

(1) Forecast Target Year Sales

You have two resources at your disposal to help you forecast your target year sales: (1) MSN Money's 10-Year Summary lists annual sales going back 10 years, and (2) Yahoo's Analyst Estimates report shows analysts consensus sales (revenues) forecasts for the current and next fiscal year.

You can use the 10-year sales history by itself to forecast future sales growth, you can use the consensus sales forecasts, or you can use both resources.

The most appropriate approach depends on the circumstances. Yahoo's consensus forecast is often your best resource if you're looking only a year or so ahead, and a combination of the two is usually best if you're looking further ahead. Circumstances often call for exceptions to these guidelines, as the Cisco Systems example later in this chapter illustrates, so use common sense.

To demonstrate the process, I'll estimate Alpharma's 2004 sales using its 10-year sales history alone, and then in combination with the consensus sales forecasts.

USING HISTORICAL SALES HISTORY

MSN Money listed Alpharma's sales going back to 1992, as shown in Table 6-1.

Alpharma's sales grew in every year except 1996. Sales increased by about $137 million in 1999, and by another $177 million in 2000, before the firm stumbled in 2001. The most recent years before the stumble are probably the best predictors of future growth, so I averaged the 1999 and 2000 sales growth figures to come up with $157 million. I rounded that number down to $150 million to be conservative, and I settled on $150 million as representative of Alpharma's typical (normalized) annual sales growth.

I figured that Alpharma was likely to spend 2002 retrenching and reorganizing and it wouldn't see significant growth until 2003. So I estimated 2002 sales at $975 million, and then estimated $150 million

TABLE 6-1 Alpharma's historical sales as shown on MSN Money's 10-Year Financial Summary Report.

Fiscal Year	Sales
12/01	975.1
12/00	919.5
12/99	742.2
12/98	604.6
12/97	500.3
12/96	486.2
12/95	520.9
12/94	469.3
12/93	338.2
12/92	295.1

annual sales growth in 2003 and 2004, bringing estimated sales in 2004 to $1,275 million.

ADDING REVENUE FORECASTS TO THE MIX

Looking up Alpharma's consensus revenue forecasts on Yahoo's Analyst Estimates report (finance.yahoo.com, get quote, then select Analyst Estimates) showed that analysts were projecting sales in 2002 of $1,100 million, considerably above my $975 million estimate. Consensus forecasts for 2003 were $1,370 million, which was $195 million above my estimate. Yahoo's forecasts cover only the current and next fiscal years, so I added my normalized $150 million annual growth estimate to the analysts' 2003 figure, and that brought the estimated 2004 sales forecast up to $1,520 million.

Researching recent news stories about Alpharma, I found that the analysts 2002 consensus sales estimates were based on Alpharma's own forecasts. I assumed that Alpharma's management was probably too optimistic and that I was probably too pessimistic. I averaged my $1,275 million original forecast with the analysts' $1,520 million figure to come up with $1,400 million (rounded) estimated sales for fiscal 2004.

(2) Estimate Net Profit Margin

The best way to estimate a company's future net profit margins (net income divided by sales) is by reviewing its historical performance. Table 6-2 summarizes Alpharma's historical profit margins. The margins were erratic until 1997, and then they climbed steadily from 3.5 percent in 1997 to 6.6 percent in 2000, before turning into a loss in 2001.

Alpharma's 2001 setback represents the "problem" that value investors typically look beyond to forecast target prices after the firm recovers.

Given the 2001 setback, I estimated that Alpharma's profit margins would also be depressed in 2002 but would recover in 2003 and return to historical levels by 2004. I forecast that Alpharma's 2004 margin would at least reach its 1999 figure of 5.3 percent, and I used that number for my 2004 estimated profit margin.

TABLE 6-2   Alpharma's net profit margin history.

Fiscal Year	Net Profit Margin (%)
12/01	-3.7
12/00	6.6
12/99	5.3
12/98	4.0
12/97	3.5
12/96	-2.4
12/95	3.6
12/94	-0.4
12/93	2.5
12/92	3.9

(3) Compute Net Income

Net income is sales multiplied by profit margin. I've forecasted Alpharma's 2004 sales and profit margin, so multiplying the two figures gives Alpharma's estimated net income for 2004.

Net Income = Sales x Profit Margin

2004 Net Income—$1,400 million x 5.3 percent = $74.2 million

Alpharma's estimate 2004 net income is $74.2 million.

(4) Estimate Shares Outstanding

Most firm's number of outstanding shares increases annually because they issue stock to raise money, make acquisitions, or provide employee stock options. You can use the 10-year history of shares outstanding shown on MSN Money's 10-year Financial Summary report to gauge the historical annual share inflation and estimate the number of shares outstanding at the end of your target year, in this case, 2004 (Table 6-3).

TABLE 6-3   MSN Money lists Alpharma's number of shares outstanding at the end of each fiscal year.

Fiscal Year	Shares Outstanding (Millions)
12/01	44.3
12/00	29.9
12/99	37.9
12/98	27.0
12/97	25.3
12/96	21.8
12/95	21.7
12/94	21.6
12/93	21.5
12/92	21.5

MSN Money showed that Alpharma had 37.9 million shares out at the end of 2000, and 44.3 million shares out by the end 2001, but only 29.9 shares out in 2000. I figured that the 2000 figure was probably an error and I ignored it. Alpharma appeared to be a habitual share inflator in recent years. I estimated that it would add around two million shares annually, bringing the 2004 year-end total to 50 million shares.

(5) Convert to EPS

Once you have the estimated net income and the number of outstanding shares, you can compute the EPS by dividing the estimated income found by the number of shares:

$$EPS = Net\ Income/Shares\ Outstanding = \$74.2/50 = \$1.48$$

Dividing the $74.2 million estimated earnings by 50 million shares yielded $1.48 estimated EPS in 2004.

(6) Estimate P/E Range

This step, estimating the probable P/E range in early 2005, is the hardest. Some analysts use a firm's industry P/E or the overall market P/E as a basis for the estimate. However, most of the managers that I interviewed look to a company's own historical valuation ratios for guidance.

That makes sense because valuation ratios reflect the markets' enthusiasm about a company, and each company has its own sizzle factor. You'll find that similar companies in the same industry often trade at different valuation ratios for extended periods. For instance, pharmaceutical maker Merck typically trades with P/Es between 20 and 30, while rival Pfizer garners much higher P/Es, usually ranging from the mid-20s to the mid-60s. Although both firms are dominant forces in the same industry, it's unlikely that they will ever trade at the same P/E at the same time.

MSN Money Key Ratios report lists average P/E ratios going back 10 years. Table 6-4 shows MSN Money's P/E data for Alpharma.

Alpharma recorded losses in 3 of the last 10 years and thus had no P/E in those years. Its P/E mostly ranged between 25 and 35 during the 7 profitable years listed. I estimated that Alpharma's P/E in early 2005 would end up in that same range, between 25 and 35.

TABLE 6-4 Average of Alpharma's high and low P/E ratios going back 10 years.

Year Ending	Average P/E
12/01	n/a
12/00	32
12/99	25
12/98	30
12/97	23
12/96	n/a
12/95	25
12/94	n/a
12/93	45
12/92	36

(7) Compute Target Price Range

The final step is to use the forecast EPS and high and low P/Es to calculate a target price range. If you do the algebra you'll find that a stock price is equal to its P/E multiplied by its EPS:

price = P/E x EPS

Or for our purposes, the target price is the estimated earnings per share from Step 5 multiplied by the estimated P/E.

Target Price = P/E x EPS

I had forecast that Alpharma would trade at a P/E ranging between 25 and 35 in early 2005, so the estimated target prices are:

Low Target = 25 x $1.48 = $37

High Target = 35 x $1.48 = $52

The analysis says that Alpharma will likely be trading somewhere between $37 and $52 in early 2005.

You can also use the high and low target prices to determine a target buy price. As a rule of thumb, the target buy price should be no more than 50 percent to 55 percent of the average of the low and high target sell prices.

Average Target: $44.50

Low Buy Target = Average Target x 50% = $22.25

High Buy Target = Average Target x 55% = $24.50

Alpharma was trading in the $16 range when I did the analysis, so it was well within the buy range from a target price perspective. Don't buy a stock only because it is trading below its buy target price range. The target price calculation is only one step in the analysis procedure.

Cisco Systems

Here's another example, this time determining target prices for tech favorite, Cisco Systems. Cisco's fiscal year ends in July, and when I did this analysis I had fiscal year data through July 2001. I analyzed Cisco's target price for a shorter timeframe, as of its fiscal year ending July 2003.

(1) Forecast Target Year Sales

The tech industry was in a tailspin when I did the analysis, and projecting sales growth in a recovery was a guessing game. Given the circumstances, I decided that Cisco's sales history was a better prognosticator of its future sales growth than analysts' forecasts. So I ignored consensus sales forecasts when I computed Cisco's 2003 fiscal year's sales. Table 6-5 shows MSN Money's 10-year sales data for Cisco.

Cisco's sales rose around $2 billion a year in fiscal 1997 and 1998. Then annual sales growth shot up to $3.7 billion in 1999 and to $6.7 billion in 2000. In fiscal 2001, Cisco's growth slowed to $3.4 billion.

Cisco's 2000 sales growth bulge was related to the explosive buildup of the Internet, which I assumed was a one-time event. However, I guessed that in a recovery Cisco's sales would likely grow faster than the $2 billion rate it saw before the dot-com buildup took off in its fiscal 1998. I estimated Cisco's annual sales growth at $3 billion when that happened.

TABLE 6-5 Cisco Systems
10-year sales history.

Fiscal Year	Sales (Millions)
7/01	22,293
7/00	18,928
7/99	12,154
7/98	8459
7/97	6440
7/96	4096
7/95	1979
7/94	1243
7/93	649
7/92	340

Further, I assumed that Cisco's sales would remain flat through fiscal 2002, and its recovery would take place starting in Cisco's fiscal 2003 year that started in August 2002. Based on those assumptions, I came up with sales remaining at $22.3 billion in 2002 and increasing to $25 billion (rounded down) in its July 2003 fiscal year.

(2) Estimate Profit Margin

Table 6-6 lists Cisco's historical profit margins that I used to forecast its target year margin.

Cisco's net profit margins bounced around over the years, but mostly ranged between 16 percent and 18 percent. I figured that 17 percent was a reasonable average.

TABLE 6-6   Cisco Systems' net
profit margin history from fiscal
July 1992 to July 2001.

Fiscal Year	Net Profit Margin (%)
7/01	-4.5
7/00	14.1
7/99	17.2
7/98	16.0
7/97	16.3
7/96	22.3
7/95	21.3
7/94	25.3
7/93	26.5
7/92	24.9

(3) Compute Target Year Net Income

Once you have the estimated sales and profit margin, you can
compute the forecasted net income.

Net Income = Sales x Profit Margin

I estimated Cisco's net income at $4.3 billion ($25 billion x
17%) for its July 2003 fiscal year.

(4) Estimate Shares Outstanding

You need to estimate the number of shares outstanding at the end
of your target year to convert the net income to earnings per share. MSN
Money's Financial Statements 10-year Summary lists number of shares
outstanding for each of the last 10 fiscal years. Table 6-7 lists MSN
Money's share data for Cisco Systems.

TABLE 6-7 Cisco Systems number of shares out-standing at the end of each fiscal year.

Fiscal Year	Shares Outstanding (Billions)
7/01	7.3
7/00	7.1
7/99	6.6
7/98	6.3
7/97	6.0
7/96	5.8
7/95	4.9
7/94	4.6
7/93	4.4
7/92	4.3

Cisco had been adding about 0.3 billion shares annually. Assuming share inflation continued at the same rate, Cisco would have 7.9 billion shares out by July 2003.

(5) Convert to EPS

Convert your forecast net income to EPS by dividing the net income by your estimated number of shares outstanding.

EPS = Net Income/Shares Outstanding

Dividing Cisco's $4.3 billion estimated total earnings by 7.9 billion shares yields $0.54 per share earnings estimated for Cisco in its July 2003 fiscal year.

(6) Estimate P/E Range

Next, use the average P/E history shown on MSN Money's 10-year Key Ratio report (Table 6-8) to estimate the likely high and low P/Es after Cisco reports its target year results.

TABLE 6-8   Cisco Systems average P/E ratios from MSN Money's 10-Year Key Ratio Summary report.

Fiscal Year	Average P/E
7/01	n/a
7/00	153
7/99	72
7/98	60
7/97	41
7/96	31
7/95	28
7/94	28
7/93	28
7/92	25

Cisco's average P/E prior to 1997 was fairly stable at around 28. My guess was that the market's love affair with Cisco wasn't going to end, and its P/E probably wouldn't head back to the pre-1997 levels in a recovery, but I didn't think it would hit its 1999 and 2000 levels again either. So I estimated that Cisco's P/E would probably end up between 30 and 50 after it reported its July 2003 fiscal year results in September or October of that year.

(7) Compute Target Price Range

Once you have the P/E range and the EPS, you can compute the target prices.

Target Price = P/E x EPS

Based on those assumptions, I came up with:

Low Target = 30 x $0.54 = $16

High Target = 50 x $0.54 = $27

Average Target = $22

Multiplying Cisco's average $22 target price by 50 percent and 55 percent yields a buy price range of $11 to $12. Cisco's shares were changing hands at around $20 when I did the analysis.

Based on target prices alone, Alpharma appeared to have considerable more upside potential than Cisco Systems.

Summary

Your target prices will only be as good as your estimates. Even a company's key executives can't accurately forecast sales and profit margins two or three years down the road, so errors are inevitable. It's important to review your targets whenever new data becomes available.

Even with the inherent errors, calculating target prices will give you insight into a stock's upside potential that you wouldn't otherwise have.

7

ANALYSIS TOOL #4: INDUSTRY ANALYSIS

The first three analysis tools dealt with abstract numbers such as earnings forecasts and P/E ratios and the like without regard to the company's business. Given the same numbers, your conclusions would have been identical whether you were analyzing a maker of chewing gum, buggy whips, guided missiles, or computer chips.

Now it's time to learn about your candidate's business, its industry, and its competition.

The Business

Your first step is to determine what the company does, that is, the products and services that it sells. That's a no-brainer if you're talking about Wal-Mart, but how many investors know what Lucent Technology or Network Appliance do for a living?

Surprisingly, few investing sites do a good job of providing that information. One that does, however, is Reuters Investor. Its Overview offers a concise but readable paragraph describing a company's products and services.

Reuters Company Profile page goes into more depth than the overview, describing each of the company's major products and services, probably in more detail than you'll want to know at this stage of your research, but you'll need it later.

Morningstar also offers a concise company overview on its Snapshot page, which is different, although not necessarily better than Reuters. I suggest reading both to gain a better understanding of the company's business.

Morningstar also offers a longer review, written by a Morningstar analyst, for many, but not all stocks. The review gives you the analysts' take on the company's business plan, and on its competitive position. Morningstar's analyst review is concise, doesn't go into much depth, and you must be a paid subscriber to see it. Still, it's a worthwhile read, usually giving you a better perspective on the company's operations than you'd otherwise have. It's worth paying the $12 or so monthly fee.

Industry Growth Outlook

Once you understand a company's line of business, your next step is to research its industry, starting with growth prospects.

Why? If you're a growth investor, you want growing companies, and you'll find them mostly in growing industries. Otherwise, your picks will have to grow earnings by cutting costs, by taking market share from competitors, or by acquiring other industry players. Although many firms have successfully practiced these strategies, they are inherently riskier than participating in a growth industry.

The competition is less intense in a fast-growing market because there is plenty of business for all contenders. As an industry matures, and growth slows, companies change their focus to increasing market share. That usually translates to price-cutting, which leads to eroding margins and reduced earnings.

Value investors, although satisfied with a slower pace than growth investors, should still be concerned about their candidate's industry growth prospects. It's tough, even for value investors, to make money holding companies that are battling to survive in a declining industry.

Industry growth means sales growth, but industry sales growth forecasts are hard to find. However, analysts consensus earnings growth forecasts are readily available for most industries. So we'll start with industry earnings growth forecasts, and then convert the earnings growth numbers to sales growth.

Analysts' Forecasts Are Good Enough

Why would you want to rely on analysts' forecasts when few trust their buy/sell ratings?

For starters, although analysts may have conflicted interests, most try to come up with accurate earnings growth forecasts. The industry growth forecasts are compiled from consensus long-term earnings growth forecasts for all the companies making up each industry. Since the industry forecasts are the average of many individual forecasts, they are probably more accurate than the individual company forecasts.

Secondly, predicting long-term growth is easier said than done, and despite their failings, analysts' forecasts are probably as good as anyone's. Besides, you need ballpark figures, not precise estimates. Despite their other shortcomings, analysts' growth forecasts are good enough for this purpose.

MSN Money's Earnings Estimates page (Figure 7-1) is a good place to find the industry earnings growth forecasts. I'll use network storage device maker Network Appliance to demonstrate the process.

MSN Money reported analysts consensus 5-year average annual growth forecasts of 24 percent for Network Appliance and 21 percent for its industry, computer storage devices.

Earnings Growth Rates	Last 5 yrs.	FY 2002	FY 2003	Next 5 yrs.	02 P/E
Company	NA	-65.60%	108.70%	24.30%	179.00
Industry	-13.90%	-14.60%	34.70%	21.30%	-112.00
S&P 500	8.40%	-21.70%	12.90%	7.50%	27.10

FIGURE 7-1 MSN Money's analysts' consensus long-term earnings growth forecasts for Network Appliance, its industry, and the S&P 500.
Get there by requesting a quote, selecting Earnings Estimates, and then Earnings Growth Rates.

Convert Earnings Growth to Sales Growth

Once you have the industry forecast, you can convert the earnings growth forecast to sales growth. By analyzing historical data, I've found that on average, long-term industry earnings growth typically outruns sales growth by 15 percent or so. Also, analysts' long-term forecasts usually run high, probably by 10 percent to 15 percent.

Taking those two factors, together, I figure that discounting long-term earnings forecasts by 30 percent is a reasonable rule of thumb for estimating industry sales growth. Sure, this method is based on all kinds of assumptions, but so are everybody's forecasts. In reality, it's all guesswork, and this technique is probably as close as anyone's.

Applying the 30 percent discount factor, I estimated 15 percent annual sales growth for computer storage, Network Appliance's industry. Is 15 percent good or bad? It depends. Table 7-1 lists suggested guidelines for evaluating industry growth rate forecasts.

The moderate 10 percent to 15 percent growth range is a favorite for many value investors, because to them, 15 percent is high, and they think it's unrealistic to expect more. Moderate growth industries are suitable for growth investors, but only if they can pinpoint firms growing faster than their peers.

Growth investors generally need faster growth than value investors and find their best prospects in industries growing between 15 percent and 25 percent annually. The best performing companies in these industries could score 30 percent to 50 percent, or even higher annual sales gains. Value investors, although unbelievers, may still find beaten up value candidates left for dead by the growth crowd after the company tripped up.

TABLE 7-1   Industry growth guidelines for value and growth investors.

Expected Industry Annual Sales Growth	Value	Growth
Declining Industry (less than 3%)	n/g	n/g
Slow Growth (3-10%)	good	n/g
Moderate Growth (10-15%)	best	fair
Fast Growth (15-25%)	good	best
Super Growth (25% +)	fair	good

Look at high industry growth forecasts skeptically, since analysts sometimes get carried away. That's especially true when an industry is experiencing super-heated growth, such as the telecommunications industry saw in the late-1990s.

> ### Industry & Sector Terminology
>
> *While we're on the subject of industries, here's a rundown on the terminology.*
>
> *A sector is a major business category such as technology, and an industry is a subset of the sector such as computers or semiconductors. Some sites confuse the terminology. For instance Hoover's describes Network Appliance as being in the Data Storage Industry of the Computer Hardware sector. The terminology doesn't matter as long as in the end you figure out that Network Appliance sells data storage equipment.*

Here are five industries considered by many analysts as having the best long-term growth prospects.

- Financial Services
- Health Care
- Entertainment Products
- Consumer products for a healthy lifestyle
- Technology

Industry Concentration

Concentration refers to the number of major competitors in a given industry. The best industries, from an investing perspective, are near monopolies, that is, highly concentrated industries.

Leading firms in concentrated industries, those with only two or three major competitors, typically report higher profit margins than companies in fragmented markets. These firms give a higher priority to increasing profit margins than to gaining market share through price-cutting. Oil refiners and automobile makers are examples of concentrated industries.

TABLE 7-2   Guidelines for best industry fragmented vs. concentrated characteristics.

Expected Industry Annual Sales Growth	Fragmented	Concentrated
Declining Industry (less than 3%)	n/g	n/g
Slow Growth (3-10%)	n/g	okay
Moderate Growth (10-15%)	fair	good
Fast Growth (15-25%)	good	best
Super Growth (25% +)	best	best

Conversely, fragmented markets with many participants vying for position are usually price competitive, resulting in lower profit margins. For instance, the apparel industry with dozens of companies battling for market share generates net profit margins around 6 percent, compared to the 11 percent average margin for all companies making up the S&P 500 Index.

New, high-growth industries start out fragmented, and then concentrate over time as the winners emerge. Therefore, whether a fragmented market is a good thing or a bad thing depends on the industry's maturity and growth rate. Table 7-2 lists some guidelines.

Growth investors usually do well picking the strongest player in a concentrated, high growth industry. Microsoft and Intel during the early- to mid-1990s are prime examples. However, picking the eventual winner in a still-fragmented emerging industry can be even more profitable because the biggest stock market profits typically accrue to the winners. Here are some examples:

- Intel's $232 billion market capitalization not only dwarfs number two Texas Instruments' $58 billion, but exceeds the combined value of all general-purpose chip makers.

- Wal-Mart's $252 billion market-cap similarly overwhelms second banana Target's $36 billion, and Costco places a distant third at $20 billion. Wal-Mart's market capitalization exceeds the combined value of all other discount variety stores.

- In the software industry, Microsoft's $367 billion towers over number two Oracle's $85 billion.
- Citigroup's $252 billion similarly overwhelms number two banker Bank of America's $98 billion market-cap.

Picking Winners in an Emerging Fragmented Industry

Picking the eventual winner starts with identifying the players.

The SEC requires companies to include competitive information in their annual reports (but not in the quarterly reports). Most companies do a reasonably complete job of describing both their major and lesser competitors in the report, but they often don't say which is which. The company's competitive discussion is always included in a section titled "Competition." The annual reports are lengthy, so use your browser's find function (Ctrl-F on a PC, Cmd-F on a Mac) to search for "competition" rather than scrolling through the entire report.

Reuters frequently copies the annual report's competitive discussion almost verbatim into the last paragraph of its Company Profile, so check there first because it's a quicker access.

Hoover's is an alternative source for a short list of the competitors if for some reason you can't access either Reuters or the annual report on the SEC Edgar database. Hoover's lists its take on a company's top three competitors on its Fact Sheet (Figure 7-2). Hoover's accuracy in nailing the top three is usually good, but Hoover's doesn't give you any detail.

It's no longer a complete rout. Cisco Systems controls almost two-thirds of the global market for routers and switches that link networks and power the Internet. It also makes network access servers and management software. Not content to dominate the computer networking market, Cisco competes with giants such as Nortel and Lucent in the telecommunications sector with products designed to accommodate data, voice, and video traffic. Market conditions have caused the company to decelerate its typically frenzied acquisition pace (more than 70 acquisitions since 1993), and while it still dominates the networking sector, Cisco faces increasing competition from relative upstarts such as Juniper Networks.

Top Competitors
Juniper Networks | Lucent | Nortel Networks

FIGURE 7-2 Hoover's profile for Cisco Systems zeroed in on Cisco's major competition.

For instance, in 2001, Cisco Systems and Juniper Networks were the strongest players in the Internet router arena, although Cisco had, by far, the largest market share.

In its SEC report, Juniper Networks clearly tabbed Cisco Systems as its major competitor, and Reuters effectively relayed that information in its company description. Hoover's, however, listed Avici Systems, Cisco, and Nortel Networks as Juniper's top competition, but it didn't discriminate among the three.

To its credit, in its Cisco Systems profile, Hoover's listed Juniper Networks as one of Cisco's top competitors. That showed that someone at Hoover's gave some thought to the listing, since Cisco mentioned a dozen competitors in alphabetical order in its SEC filing without identifying Juniper as the strongest, and Reuters simply repeated Cisco's list.

Identifying the Strongest Competitors

How do you pick the eventual winner in an up and coming industry? Let's see what we can learn from history.

DATABASE SOFTWARE INDUSTRY

Here's a snapshot of the database software industry during the mid-1990s when Oracle, though the market leader, was still battling contenders Sybase and Informix for control of the still young industry. I've listed four performance items for each contender:

- **Revenue:** Total sales for the year.
- **Percent Revenue Growth:** The sales for the listed year compared to the previous year.
- **Operating Margin:** A measure of a company's profits resulting from its operations without considering interest, income taxes, and income from investments.
- **SG&A Percent of Sales:** SG&A (sales, general, and administrative expenses) includes all expenses but research and development (R&D) and the direct costs of producing the company's goods or services. SG&A is often referred to as overhead. Computing the SG&A percent of sales measures the company's operating efficiency. The lower the percentage, the more efficient the company.

As you'll see, tracking just these four items will help you recognize a winner emerging from the pack.

We'll pick up the story in 1993, when Oracle, although the market leader, was still in a dogfight with Sybase and Informix. Table 7-3 summarizes the four performance items from 1993 to 1997.

By the end of 1993, Sybase had just ridden an 83 percent year-over-year sales gain to grab the number two spot away from Informix. At that time, Informix was the slowest grower of the three but had recorded the highest operating margin, indicating that it wasn't giving the store away to gain sales. Oracle, however, was the most efficient operator of the bunch, with SG&A sapping only 44 percent of sales compared to Informix's 48 percent, and 51 percent for Sybase. From the data, it appears that Sybase sacrificed profits to gain market share in 1993.

Sybase increased market share again in 1994, racking up a 70 percent sales gain. But again, Sybase, with the lowest operating margin, was sacrificing earnings for market share. The numbers show that Informix, with increasing costs and diminishing operating margin, was struggling to stay in the game.

Oracle took over the market in 1995, gaining share while Sybase and Informix apparently slashed profits in a vain attempt to remain competitive.

Finally, in 1997, Sybase faltered, recording a drop in revenues, while Informix crashed and burned when its executives were caught cooking the books. From that point on, Sybase and Informix fell by the wayside.

TABLE 7-3   Direct to consumer PC industry key performance measures.

	Revenue (millions)	% Revenue Growth	OM%	SG&A % of Sales
1993				
Oracle	2001	33	21	44
Sybase	484	83	16	51
Informix	353	24	24	48
1994				
Oracle	2967	48	22	43
Sybase	825	70	16	49
Informix	470	33	20	51
1995				
Oracle	4223	42	21	42
Sybase	957	16	2	57
Informix	633	35	10	56
1996				
Oracle	5684	35	22	40
Sybase	1011	6	-7	59
Informix	735	16	-8	66
1997				
Oracle	7144	26	17	38
Sybase	904	-11	5	59
Informix	664	-10	-54	76

PC WARS: DELL VS. GATEWAY

Here's another example illustrating how tracking the same four items would have helped you discern that Dell was emerging victorious in its mid-1990s battle with Gateway for dominance in the direct-to-consumer segment of the PC industry.

IBM originally dominated the personal computer market, but steadily lost share, and by the early-1990s the market was free for all. Many contenders came and went in the 1990s, but I've focused on the battle between just two players, Dell and Gateway. They are the only survivors following direct-to-customer distribution models, and PCs account for an overwhelming majority of each company's sales. Table 7-4 lists the same four performance measures we tracked for the database software industry.

Gateway was coming on strong in 1993. Dell was hitting higher sales numbers, but it was unprofitable and struggling while Gateway was gaining market share.

Gateway looked even better in 1994, more than doubling Dell's sales growth rate, narrowing the market share gap. Dell, however, returned to profitability, while Gateway's operating margin dropped precipitously. It looks as though Gateway was sacrificing profits for market share.

In 1995, Dell's sales growth rocketed, while Gateway faltered. Gateway's operating margin partially recovered, equaling Dell's. Gateway's reduced sales growth rate, combined with its higher margins, suggests the company may have ditched its former market share at any cost strategy. But notice the jump in Gateway's SG&A percentage of sales. Where was that extra money going? Probably for increased advertising and other marketing expenses.

The turning point came in 1996. Dell was still increasing market share, but even more significant, the Texas-based upstart was making 29 percent more (9 percent operating margin versus 7 percent for Gateway) money on each computer sold.

Gateway cut margins to the bone in 1997 in a futile attempt to hold onto market share. Meanwhile Dell further increased its operating efficiency and profitability. Gateway, no longer able to produce and sell computers as cheaply as Dell, became a minor player.

By the way, notice how both contenders' profitability wilted when industry growth slowed in the 1998-2000 timeframe.

Tracking just four performance measures made Dell's market dominance crystal clear as 1996 drew to a close. Was it too late to profit from analysis? Not hardly. Dell's share price gained 719 percent from January 1, 1997, through December 31, 2001. Gateway's shareholders lost 40 percent during the same period.

TABLE 7-4 Direct to consumer PC industry key performance
measures.

	Revenue (millions)	% Revenue Growth	OM%	SG&A % of Sales
1992				
Dell	2014	126	7	13
Gateway	1107	77	9	8
1993				
Dell	2873	43	-1	15
Gateway	1732	56	9	7
1994				
Dell	3475	21	7	12
Gateway	2701	56	5	8
1995				
Dell	5296	52	7	11
Gateway	3676	36	7	10
1996				
Dell	7759	47	9	11
Gateway	5035	37	7	12
1997				
Dell	12,327	59	11	10
Gateway	6294	25	3	13
1998				
Dell	18,243	48	11	10
Gateway	7703	22	6	12

TABLE 7-4 Direct to consumer PC industry key performance measures. *(continued)*

	Revenue (millions)	% Revenue Growth	OM%	SG&A % of Sales
1999				
Dell	25,265	38	9	9
Gateway	8965	16	7	14
2000				
Dell	31,888	26	8	10
Gateway	9601	7	5	16

Industry Scuttlebutt

The final step is to get up to speed on the current trends and issues facing the industry. You can do that by reading the news and in-depth reports usually found on industry trade magazine Websites. You'd be hard pressed to find an industry that isn't covered by at least two or three trade magazines. The easiest way to find them is to search for the industry name and "trade magazine" on Google (www.google.com).

Summary

Growth investors will do best picking candidates in fast-growing industries. You can score the biggest profits by pinpointing the eventual winner in a still-fragmented emerging industry. Focusing on just four factors—sales (revenue), sales growth, operating margin, and SG&A compared to sales—will help you pick the winners.

Keeping tabs on industry happenings by reading industry trade magazines will keep you up to speed on industry developments and ensure that you haven't overlooked an important industry player or a significant event that might change the outlook for particular competitors or for the industry as a whole.

8

ANALYSIS TOOL #5: BUSINESS PLAN ANALYSIS

If you were considering buying a local business, say a bicycle shop, would you base your purchase decision entirely on how much money the seller said he or she made last year or on the seller's profit forecast for this year?

I'll bet not. Instead, you'd probably want to know where the shop gets its bicycles, how much it pays, and whether the competition is paying the same prices.

You would check for alternative sources in the event that an important supplier goes out of business or decides to open its own outlet and stop selling to you. You'd also want to know something about your customers. Are they mostly individual consumers, or did one or two bicycle courier services account for a big hunk of last year's purchases?

Most people would evaluate such topics if they were, in fact, thinking of buying a bicycle store. Yet all too often, investors skip this vital step when analyzing a stock.

For evidence, consider the dot-com startups that each raised hundreds of millions of dollars from millions of investors, both amateur and professional. Many of them had nonsensical business plans with zero chance of success. For instance, there was at least one Web retailer that planned to, and actually did, sell every product at its cost or less.

In this chapter, you'll learn to analyze the pluses and minuses of your candidate's business model. Many of the concepts presented were inspired by the ideas of Harvard Business School Professor Michael Porter, considered by many to be the guru of competitive analysis.

Introduction

Nothing attracts competition more than high profit margins. But no matter how strong the market looks in the beginning, the unimpeded entry of new players leads to supply exceeding demand and tumbling profit margins as players fight for market share. That's why you need to consider a company's competitive advantages, or barriers to entry, in your analysis.

Barriers to entry discourage new players from entering the market. Without sufficient barriers to entry, a company's long-term success is problematical, because it will be easy for new competitors to enter the market.

Barriers to entry can take many forms. The following paragraphs describe some of the more common barriers. You will uncover others when you analyze prospective candidates. A barrier to entry enjoyed by one company translates to a risk factor for its competition. Besides barriers to entry, every company's business model embodies a variety of additional risk factors.

To streamline the analysis, I've combined similar barriers to entry and risk factors into single rating factors. Most of the factors considered can evaluate as an advantage or a disadvantage, depending on the circumstances.

Use the Business Plan Score card provided on page 121 to assess each candidate's business model. Score each business plan factor as a one, minus one, or zero depending on whether you evaluate it to be an advantage, disadvantage, or not applicable, respectively.

Brand Identity

Many consumers will pay more for Coca Cola, Scotch Tape, Duracell batteries or Gillette razors than they would for lesser brands or for generics. These products have achieved a combination of brand awareness and perceived superior quality in consumers' minds. A strong brand identity often translates to higher selling prices and higher profit margins.

Hewlett Packard's name is synonymous with computer printers and HP enjoys a strong reputation for quality products. Those factors taken together equate to strong brand identity, explaining why HP printers outsell Lexmark by more than five to one, even though Lexmark's products may be as good or better than HP's.

For another example, consider the experiences of Oakley and Sunglass Hut. Oakley makes designer sunglasses, and Sunglass Hut, a retail chain, is the largest seller of designer sunglasses in the U.S. Going into 2001, Sunglass Hut was Oakley's largest customer, accounting for 19 percent of its sales. Then, in mid-2001, Luxottica Group, an Italian firm, acquired Sunglass Hut. That created a problem for Oakley because Luxottica already owned Ray-Ban, a competing sunglass brand. Sure enough, Luxottica dropped Oakley's products shortly after taking over Sunglass Hut.

But Sunglass Hut's shoppers wanted Oakley, not Ray-Ban. By mid-December, the chain was once again stocking Oakley's glasses, a testament to the power of the Oakley brand.

A strong brand identity gives its owner a competitive advantage, and acts as a barrier to entry to new players. Give one point to companies with strong brand identities, and subtract one point for companies facing a competitor with strong brand identity.

Other Barriers to Entry

You will uncover candidates with other barriers to entry in your analysis. Add one point for additional significant barriers to entry, and subtract one point from companies facing additional barriers. Add or subtract one point maximum for this category.

Distribution Model

In the early days, home PC and business computer makers addressed different markets. Firms such as Dell and Gateway prospered in the home PC sector, while IBM and Compaq dominated the corporate market. Those lines blurred when personal computer power increased and prices plunged. In the early 1990s, Compaq, losing market share to Dell, abandoned its high-cost proprietary designs and instead followed Dell's lead of assembling computers using readily available generic parts. From then on there were no significant product differences. Personal computers had become commodities, and buyers, whether multimillion dollar corporations, or home hobbyists, were drawn to the lowest price solution.

Although Dell and Compaq's production costs were similar, the companies had developed different distribution strategies.

Compaq adhered to the traditional model, selling to distributors who in turn sold to retail stores and systems builders. Compaq designed standard models, built them in bulk quantities, and warehoused the completed systems until it received orders. Each step of the process— building systems ahead of orders, warehousing and selling through distributors and retailers—added costs.

Dell had a different idea. Dell had no dealers, distributors, or warehouses full of prebuilt computers. Instead of standard models, Dell built each computer to buyer's specifications. Dell undoubtedly incurred higher costs because it was dealing with thousands of individual customers instead of a few distributors. But on balance, it was the lowest cost producer because it didn't have to pay for warehousing, and there were no middlemen taking a cut. Dell's unique distribution system enabled it to overtake Compaq's once commanding market share lead.

You may never find another example exactly like Dell versus Compaq, but be on the lookout for companies with similar operational advantages in areas such as order processing, production techniques, marketing, and the like. Score one for companies enjoying such operational advantages and minus one for firms facing competitors with distribution model advantages.

Access to Distribution

If you were to start a new book publishing business, getting your products into bookstores wouldn't be a difficult problem. Bookstores buy mainly from distributors, and book distributors readily buy from new publishers.

Contrast that scenario to starting up a new line of laundry detergents, which are mostly sold in supermarkets where shelf space is at a premium. There's no room for a new detergent without eliminating an existing brand, and Proctor and Gamble and its ilk deploy legions of salespeople to ensure that that doesn't happen.

In the late 1990s, upstart broadband Internet service providers Covad and Rhythm Connections tried to enter a business where the distribution channels were controlled by their competition, the established telephone companies. Neither Covad nor Rhythm ever made money, and they both eventually went bankrupt.

Locked-up distribution channels represent a strong barrier to entry. Award one business model point to companies enjoying distribution channel advantages, and subtract one point from scores of companies facing competitors with those advantages.

Product Useful Life/Product Price

Long product-life items such as automobiles, home entertainment systems, computers, and copy machines are discretionary purchases that can usually be put off. However food, healthcare products, cigarettes, and office supplies are quickly used up and inventories must be frequently replenished. For example, it's unlikely that WorldCom stopped buying staples when it slashed its capital spending budget in 2001. Companies selling short-lived products have a business plan advantage.

This principle isn't limited to consumer products. Cabot Microelectronics makes slurries, used in the semiconductor production process. Something like toothpaste, the slurries are used up in the process and must continuously be replenished. Consequently, Cabot's sales increased 25 percent in its September 2001 fiscal year, a period when semiconductor sales plunged.

Similarly, companies with inexpensive products have an advantage over companies with expensive products, especially in a weak economy. For instance, when times are tough, consumers will put off buying a new home, but they'll still buy breakfast cereals.

Award one point to companies with short lived and/or low-priced products, and subtract one point from companies selling discretionary purchase products.

Access to Supply/Number of Suppliers

Most firms enjoy a choice of multiple vendors eager to supply needed services and materials. But sometimes you'll encounter a company where that is not the case.

Syncor International markets Cardolite, the product you drink before going in for cardiac imaging diagnostic tests. Syncor markets other products, but in 2000, Cardolite accounted for 45 percent of its revenues. Unfortunately, Syncor doesn't make Cardolite. It buys it from a unit of Bristol-Meyers under an agreement that, as of late 2001, was set to expire at the end of 2003.

Regardless of how Syncor fares in its efforts to come up with a new agreement with Bristol Meyers, its dependency on a single supplier adds risk to Syncor's business model.

In other instances, companies may have multiple suppliers but face an industrywide shortage of critical components. That happened in the late 1990s when computer makers couldn't get sufficient quantities of flat panel screens used in their laptop models.

Subtract one point from companies that face tight supply, allocated markets, or are dependent on only one or two suppliers.

Revenue Stream Predictability

It's much easier to forecast a company's future earnings if you have a good handle on its likely sales. Companies with long-term contracts or stable client bases have predictable revenue streams. Examples include insurance companies, health plans, pharmaceutical companies, credit card processors, and telephone and cable TV companies. Firms with predictable revenue streams suffer less year-to-year volatility in revenues and earnings than those that don't.

Conversely, media companies, makers of designer clothing, sporting goods, durable goods (e.g., washing machines), fad items (e.g., cigars, scooters, George Forman grills), semiconductors, computers, computer software, cameras, and so on all have unpredictable revenue streams. Hence, their earnings are equally unpredictable.

Award one point to companies with predictable revenues and subtract one point from companies with unpredictable revenue streams.

Number of Customers

Companies with just a few customers accounting for a majority of sales are vulnerable to shifts in the growth rates of their customers, and/or changes in their customers' strategies. Loss of a single customer to a competitor can severely impact a company's performance.

Further, an important customer can squeeze a supplier's profit margins by insisting on lower prices. This is a common occurrence in the automobile industry where automakers such as Ford and General Motors routinely ask their vendors to "share their pain" by reducing prices.

Add one point to companies with thousands of customers, zero points to companies with a few hundred customers, and subtract one point if fewer than 10 customers account for 50 percent or more of the firm's sales.

Product Cycle

The product cycle is the length of time that a product is on the market before it's replaced by a newer version. Companies with short product cycles, including most technology manufacturers, are riskier investments than those with long product cycles, such as candy makers. The short product cycle companies must continuously develop new products and run the risk of seeing their creations made obsolete by a hotshot new competitor.

Add one point to companies with long product cycle products such as calculators and linens, and subtract one point from makers of high-tech and other short-cycle products.

Product/Market Diversification

Firms offering just a single product line are riskier than companies with a variety of products because something unforeseen can happen to unexpectedly kill the sales of almost any product.

Similarly, companies serving a single business segment, such as telecommunications, the automobile industry, or the airline industry, will suffer when that industry goes into a downturn. Consider the semiconductor industry's recent experience.

Sales growth, especially for chips used in telecommunications equipment, soared during the 1998/1999 tech boom. At the time, it appeared as if the growth cycle was unstoppable. But as it turned out, telecom equipment makers such as Nortel Networks, Lucent Technologies, and Cisco Systems, or their suppliers, accounted for much of the growth.

Then in 2000 the telecom equipment makers' customers—mostly AT&T, WorldCom, Sprint, new telephone companies, and dot-coms—all, virtually simultaneously, ran out of cash and quit buying routers and servers, compelling the equipment makers to cancel their chip orders.

Firms producing multiple products serving a variety of markets are less susceptible to those sorts of mishaps and to economic downturns than less diversified companies.

Award one point to companies with multiple products serving diversified markets, and subtract one point from single product, or single market firms.

Growth by Acquisition

In the beginning, most firms grow organically, that is, their growth comes from selling more products, or by opening new stores. Eventually growth slows as supply catches up with demand or new competition appears. Then management must find new ways to sustain the growth rate; otherwise the slowing growth will sink the firm's stock price.

At that point, most firms develop new products or enter additional markets, but others turn to an acquisition strategy to maintain growth.

Growth by acquisition is an appealing strategy. Purchasing an established company already serving a market saves the acquirer the time and expense of learning the business and developing products from scratch. The process is relatively inexpensive because the acquirer often uses its own newly issued shares to pay for the acquisition.

The strategy is often successful early on and the acquiring firm is able to maintain a strong growth rate, keeping the market happy and its share price up. The latter is an important factor since the firm's stock is the currency enabling the acquisitions.

Many firms pull it off for years, but acquisition-fueled growth is somewhat like a pyramid scheme. Consider the math. A company with $100 million in annual sales can achieve a 25 percent sales increase by acquiring a company selling $25 million annually. However once it achieves the $200 million level, it must acquire a company with $50 million in annual sales to maintain the same growth rate. Compounding the problem, the bigger it gets, the fewer the number of acquisition candidates.

Eventually something goes wrong. Perhaps the acquirer overpays. Maybe the acquired company doesn't perform to expectations or expected cost cutting synergies fail to materialize. Perhaps a clash between corporate cultures disenchants key employees in the acquired company, and they leave.

Whatever the cause, the serial acquirer fails to meet earnings growth forecasts, torpedoing its stock price. The lower stock price takes away its acquisition currency, further slowing growth and thereby putting more pressure on its share price. In essence, it's game over!

When one company acquires another, it usually pays more than the accounting book value for the acquired firm. The difference between what it pays and the acquired firm's book value is supposed to be added to the goodwill total on its balance sheet, although in some instances it appears on the intangibles' line. A company that never acquired another firm for more than its book value would show no goodwill and very little intangibles on its balance sheet.

Thus, you can gauge a firm's acquisition history by comparing its goodwill and other intangibles to its total assets. For brevity, call the result of dividing goodwill plus intangibles by total assets the GI/A ratio. The higher the ratio, the more acquisitive the firm.

Drugstore chains Walgreen and CVS afford a good example. Both are relatively fast-growing firms. Walgreen relies entirely on internal growth, while CVS uses a combination of internal growth and acquisitions to increase its sales. According to the most recent annual balance sheets available in April 2002, Walgreen's GI/A ratio was a flat zero, compared to 10 percent for CVS.

Table 8-1 shows GI/A ratios for firms that have employed acquisitions for much of their recent growth. For comparison, Table 8-2 shows the GI/A ratios for firms that have grown mostly organically.

TABLE 8-1   Goodwill plus intangibles / total assets for serial acquirers.

Company	Company + Intanglibles % of Total Assets
Allied Waste Industries	60
Black Box	57
Cisco Systems	12
Clear Channel Communications	85
Tyco International	34
VeriSign	75
Waste Management	26
WD-40 Company	52

TABLE 8-2   Goodwill plus intangibles divided by total assets for organic growers.

Company	Company + Intanglibles % of Total Assets
Bed, Bath, & Beyond	0
Chico's FAS	0
Columbia Sportswear	3
Dell Computer	0
Harley-Davidson	2
Home Depot	1
Microsoft	3
Outback Steakhouse	0

As you can see, there is a wide divide between the ratios of serial acquirers and organic growers. As a rule of thumb, organic growers usually show ratios below 5 percent, and ratios of 10 percent or more identify firms growing at least partly by acquisition.

Award one point to companies with GI/A ratios less than 5 percent, and subtract one point from companies with ratios greater than 10 percent.

Overblown Competitive Advantages

Factors That Should Make a Difference But Often Don't

Some supposed competitive advantages sound good but somehow never amount to much in practice. Here are two competitive advantages that you'd be better off ignoring unless you're an expert in the field.

Patents

The pharmaceuticals industry effectively employs patents as a barrier to entry. However, pharmaceuticals are more the exception than the rule. For instance, tech companies file hundreds, if not thousands, of patents annually. Yet new competitors constantly pop up, and it's hard to think of a tech name that has turned its patents into an effective barrier to entry.

VISX, for example, made laser systems that enable quick and painless eye surgery to correct vision problems. In 1999, its share price soared from $20 to $100 after its system was approved for use in the U.S. The company and most analysts following VISX thought that it had lock-tight patents on the process. Nevertheless, competitors brought their own systems to market in short order. To stay competitive, VISX was forced to slash prices, killing profits. VISX was eventually acquired for around $25 per share.

Few investors have the expertise to judge a patent's value as a barrier to entry. Even in the pharmaceuticals industry, it's difficult to assess the value of a particular patent. A new drug may sound miraculous, but there could be an even better treatment on the way from a competitor.

Qualcomm, with its proprietary wireless phone technology, and Rambus, owner of a proprietary high-speed memory chip technology, are more examples of patented technologies that somehow failed to produce the expected profits.

Ignore patents as a significant barrier to entry unless you are an expert in the field *and* a patent attorney.

Proprietary Technology/Production Processes

In theory, a company's superior production processes or equipment could be an effective barrier to entry. In practice, these advantages often fail to produce the expected results.

For example, again comparing Lexmark to Hewlett Packard, Lexmark enjoys laser printer production cost advantages compared to HP because Lexmark makes its own printer engines (the guts of the printer), while Hewlett Packard buys it engines from Canon. Somehow, that advantage has never meant much. Hewlett Packard still dominates the industry, and Lexmark has failed to gain significant market share.

Every CEO, given the opportunity, will tell you why his or her company's products are technologically superior. That's their job. Many market analysts repeat that same mantra as truth. As with patents, unless you're an expert, you'd be well advised to remain skeptical about touted technological advantages.

Business Plan Score Scorecard

Award one point for each category where a company has a significant advantage, and subtract one point for categories where it is at a disadvantage. Score zero where the category is not relevant. Consult Chapters 15 and 16 for further details on the relevance of the categories to each strategy.

Summary

Professional money managers routinely evaluate a firm's business plan before investing, and you should too. Technology candidates will usually score lower than firms in other industries because many do not enjoy strong brand identity that separates them from the field, most offer expensive products with short life cycles, and many depend on acquisitions for growth.

BUSINESS PLAN SCORECARD

Brand Identity   ___

Other Barrier to Entry   ___

Distribution Model   ___

Access to Distribution   ___

Product Useful Life/Product Price   ___

Access to Supply/Number of Suppliers   ___

Revenue Stream Predictability   ___

Number of Customers   ___

Product Cycle   ___

Product/Market Diversification   ___

Growth by Acquisition   ___

Total Score   ___

9

ANALYSIS TOOL # 6: MANAGEMENT QUALITY

Many professional money managers consider evaluation of management quality to be an important consideration in their analysis. They often visit the company and spend a day or two talking with management to determine if its key officers are in tune with stockholders' best interests. It's not practical for individual investors to visit companies and meet with management. However, we have clues at our disposal to accomplish the job.

Key Executive and Board Quality

Start by reviewing key officer's résumés. Reuters Officers and Directors report offers biographies of key executives and board members.

Look for officers with relevant experience. At least some should be crusty veterans with years of experience in the same industry.

Imagine that you're doing the hiring. Would you hire these people based on their experience? Notice how long the key executives have been on the job. Numerous recent management changes signal problems.

Fast food chain Boston Chicken was one of the hottest IPOs ever when it went public in November 1993, and its stock remained a hot item until the company failed, filing bankruptcy in 1998. Somehow in all the excitement, nobody seemed to notice that the company's executives had no experience in the restaurant business. Both its CEO and its president came from Blockbuster Entertainment.

Look at the makeup of the board of directors. The best boards are filled mostly with CEOs of successful firms in the same field, not consultants and venture capitalists.

For an example of what you don't want to see in a candidate, consider Webvan, the online grocery business offering home delivery that went public in November 1999, and filed bankruptcy less than two years later.

Selling groceries is a tough business, so you'd expect Webvan to fill its top management and board with grocery industry veterans. Here's a sampling of the top officers at the time of the IPO—

CEO: Before taking the helm of Webvan, just two months prior to its IPO, George Shaheen spent the prior 32 years with Andersen Consulting.

Senior Vice President, Corporate Operations and Finance: Kevin Czinger, a lawyer, worked at Merrill Lynch for one year before joining Webvan. He was in the media industry before that.

V.P., Merchandising: Gregory Butler, the man responsible for ordering the groceries, came from General Electric's GE Lighting division.

What about the board of directors?

Louis Borders, chairman, founded Webvan in December 1996. Borders also founded Borders Books in 1971, but although remaining on the board until 1992, he ran the company on a day-to-day basis only until 1983. After leaving Borders, he dabbled in investing and in a software startup.

The remaining board members that were not also company officers included two venture capitalists and the CEOs of E*Trade and Yahoo.

Not one key executive or board member had any experience with the nuts and bolts of operating a grocery store.

Not all executives need be from the same industry as long as you have experienced people in key operational positions, such as food buyers and merchandisers in the Webvan example. Troubled companies often successfully bring in turnaround specialists that are not necessarily from the same industry.

Clean Accounting

Many professional money managers point to clean and straightforward accounting as a hallmark of good management. They consider repeated one-time, nonrecurring, and extraordinary charges as an indicator of questionable accounting practices.

The beauty of nonrecurring expenses in the eyes of some corporate managers is that they don't have to count them when they tabulate pro forma earnings. Since the pro forma calculation doesn't deduct nonrecurring costs to come up with earnings, the more expenses that can be defined as nonrecurring, the higher the reported earnings.

Pro forma originally meant "as if" and was mainly employed to present the results of recently merged companies "as if" they had always been a single company. In recent years, though, some corporate managers figured out that they could make their earnings look better by emphasizing pro forma results in their quarterly reports.

It's easy to spot nonrecurring charges because both Reuters and MSN Money list nonrecurring items on a separate line of each company's income statement. The entries are labeled Unusual Expense/Income on Reuters and Special Income/Charges on MSN Money.

The raw numbers don't mean much by themselves, so it's best to compare nonrecurring expenses to total sales, also shown on the income statement. You can do that by dividing the nonrecurring expenses by the sales and computing the result as a percentage. For instance, the ratio would be 10 percent if a company recorded sales of $1,000 and listed $100 in nonrecurring charges (100/1000). Some firms can get creative when it comes to labeling charges that they don't want to count in their pro forma results, so to be on the safe side, consider all charges labeled unusual, restructuring, purchased R&D, extraordinary, accounting changes, and discontinued operations in the calculation.

Table 9-1 lists the nonrecurring to sales percentages for a variety of companies.

TABLE 9-1 One-Time, Nonrecurring, and Extraordinary Charges as
Percentage of Annual Sales (in %). *

Company	2001	2000	1999	1998	1997	1996	1995
Bed, Bath, & Beyond	0	0	0	0	0	0	0
Dell Computer	2	1	1	0	0	0	0
Computer Associates		-4	13	23	0	15	37
Cisco Systems	9	7	4	7	8	0	4
Intel	1	0	1	1	0	0	0
Lucent Technologies	57	3	-8	4	5	0	0
Microsoft	0	1	0	0	2	0	0
Tyco International	4	1	7	1	12	12	2

* Figures shown are from fiscal year data closest to the calendar year columns, compiled from Reuters income statements. Charges considered include unusual expenses, restructuring, purchased R&D, extraordinary items, accounting changes, and discontinued operations.

Judging management quality is a subjective exercise. Most firms will from time to time incur costs that are truly nonrecurring, such as charges associated with losing a lawsuit, closing factories, writing off worthless patents, and so on. The trick is to differentiate the companies that persistently come up with nonrecurring expenses to boost pro forma earnings.

The pattern of the past few years is more significant than any single year's nonrecurring charges. You can see that by eyeballing the results or, since both MSN Money and Reuters list five year's worth of data, by computing the ratios for each of the five years and then averaging them. If you do it that way, consider any company with a five-year average ratio of 3 percent or higher as a suspected nonrecurring expense abuser.

Earnings Growth Stability

Looking at a firm's historical earnings pattern can also help you evaluate management quality. Every company has its bad years, but overall, solid managers manage to turn out relatively consistent earnings growth. Conversely, some firms' roller coaster earnings history cast doubt as to whether management is really in control.

Reuters Financial Highlights report shows you up to four years reported earnings in a format ideally suited to visually evaluate earnings growth stability. It shows each fiscal year's quarterly earnings in a column so that you can compare the same quarter of each year (e.g., March quarter), and thus eliminate seasonal variations. Figure 9-1 shows the recent quarterly earnings history for Caremark Rx, a company with relative stable earnings growth, while Figure 9-2 shows an example of inconsistent earnings.

Stock Ownership

It's reassuring to know that key management, particularly the CEO and CFO, hold large positions in a firm. What constitutes a large position varies with the size of the firm, but think millions for the CEO and hundreds of thousands of shares for the CFO. It's disconcerting if key officers hold only a few thousand shares and sell immediately after exercising stock options.

EARNINGS PER SHARE				
Quarters	1998	1999	2000	2001
MAR	0.030	0.060	0.090	0.150
JUN	0.009	0.060	0.090	0.160
SEP	0.060	0.070	0.110	0.190
DEC	0.060	0.100	0.140	0.230
Totals	0.159	0.290	0.430	0.730

FIGURE 9-1 Caremark Rx' consistent earnings history reflects quality management. Always compare earnings to the year-ago period, not the previous quarter, to eliminate seasonal distortions. (Courtesy of Reuters.com.)

EARNINGS PER SHARE				
Quarters	1999	2000	2001	2002
JUL	0.860	0.720	-0.610	-0.340
OCT	0.840	0.840	-0.100	-0.380
JAN	0.590	0.480	-6.260	0.310*
APR	0.660	0.370	-1.360	
Totals	**2.950**	**2.410**	**-8.330**	**-0.410***

FIGURE 9-2   Fleetwood Enterprises inconsistent earnings casts doubt on management quality. (Courtesy of Reuters.com.)

Yahoo is the best place to see how many shares insiders own. Low shareholdings by key officers isn't a deal breaker, per se, but it should be considered along with the other management quality factors.

Summary

Management quality is probably the single most important determinate of a company's success. Reviewing key officers' résumés is a good check on management's qualifications for the job. Analyzing the firm's accounting cleanliness tells you whether its officers are a conservative lot looking out for the firm and its shareholder's long-term interests, or are bending the rules to achieve short-term gains. Analyzing earnings growth stability and key officer's shareholdings gives you further perspective on management quality.

10

ANALYSIS TOOL #7: FINANCIAL FITNESS EVALUATOR

Financial Fitness Counts

Stocks move up or down on a daily basis for any number of reasons. But in the long-term, only two factors account for most stock losses:

1. Something happens to reduce earnings growth expectations.

2. The market believes that the company is in danger of running out of cash, and may file bankruptcy.

Most analysts and individual investors concentrate on number one and don't worry much about number two.

For proof, look no further than energy trader Enron Corporation's spectacular implosion in late 2001. Despite numerous warning signals, and a plunging stock price, most analysts continued advising buying until a month or so before bond-rating agencies downgraded

Enron's bonds to junk status, crippling the debt-laden company and forcing it into bankruptcy.

That said, a company doesn't have to file bankruptcy to ruin your day; just coming close is enough to drive its stock price into the ground. Xerox and Amazon.com are two examples of companies whose stocks got hammered when the market started worrying about their financial solvency.

Given the consequences, you'd think that financial strength would be an important consideration when market analysts decide on their buy/sell ratings. But it isn't, so you're on your own in this department.

Fortunately, the information you need to do the analysis is readily available. Since your goal is simply to determine if a company is a potential bankruptcy, not whether its bonds should be rated AAA or AA, the process is straightforward and easily implemented. This chapter describes different methods for evaluating a firm's financial fitness depending on whether it's a low- or high-debt firm.

Low-debt firms are the easiest to analyze and that may be sufficient incentive to convince you to restrict your research to firms in that category. High debtors are best analyzed employing the fiscal fitness exam, which requires retrieving information from a firm's financial statements. If you're not so inclined, we describe two alternative checks later in this chapter: looking up the firm's current bond ratings, and/or checking to see if bond traders are pricing a risk premium into the firm's bond prices, indicating perceived default risk.

Pinpointing Financially Challenged Companies

Bankruptcy candidates typically fall into one of three categories:

1. **Busted Cash Burners:** Newer firms that spend more than they take in are running short of cash, and can't raise more. These companies have little or no long-term debt because they were originally funded via IPOs and by follow-on stock offerings.

2. **Overburdened Debtors:** Typically, large, mature companies with a history of using debt to enhance productivity. Then, something happens, and they can no longer generate sufficient cash to service their debt.

3. Solvent and/or profitable companies: Established firms that file bankruptcy to avoid crippling lawsuits, such as asbestos-related claims.

Here, we'll focus on tools to detect the first two categories. But these tools won't protect you from firms that massively misrepresent their financial condition. For instance, software maker Lernout & Hauspie showed $1 billion or so of nonexistent cash on its books prior to its early-2001 bankruptcy filing.

Simplify the Problem

Since most firms don't file bankruptcy, it's a waste of time doing a detailed examination of every stock. Consequently, priority number one is to separate the strong from the potential basket cases. Start by determining if your candidate falls into the low- or high-debt category.

Low Debt

Comparing total liabilities to shareholder's equity is the best gauge of high debt versus low debt. Both are balance sheet items. The result is the total liabilities to equity ratio (TL/E).

TL/E = total liabilities/shareholders equity

Don't confuse the TL/E ratio with D/E and the *total debt* to equity ratios listed on many financial sites. The D/E ratio compares long-term debt to shareholders equity, and the total debt to equity ratio compares the total of short- and long-term debt to equity. Total liabilities, by contrast, include *all* of the company's liabilities, whether they're labeled debt or something else.

The difference between using TL/E compared to the traditional D/E ratios is substantial. Consider Lucent Technologies.

By the end of 2001, after reporting losses totaling $13 billion in its last four quarters, Lucent could hardly be considered a pillar of financial strength. Here are the three ratios for Lucent using its December 31, 2001, financial statements. Typically, firms with D/E ratios below 0.5 are considered low-debt, and those with ratios of 1.0 or more are classified high-debt.

- Debt/Equity: 0.3

- Total Debt/Equity: 0.3

- Total Liabilities/Equity: 1.8

Judging by traditional measures Lucent qualified as a low-debt firm, but the TL/E ratio tells a different story. Why the difference?

Comparing total liabilities to equity always results in higher ratios than D/E because it includes accounts payables and payroll liabilities that aren't normally counted as debt. But usually the difference isn't enough to move a company from the low- to high-debt category.

However Lucent's balance sheet listed $5.1 billion as other current liabilities, twice the $2.5 billion combined total of its accounts payable and payroll entries. Lucent also listed $8.6 billion as other long-term liabilities. Both the $5.1 billion and the $8.6 billion would not be counted in its D/E ratios.

For another example, consider Bethlehem Steel, which filed bankruptcy in 2001. Bethlehem reported $853 million of long-term debt on its December 2000 fiscal year-end balance sheet. However that figure was dwarfed by $2.6 billion retirement benefit obligations listed as other liabilities that would not been have been counted using the traditional measures. Using total debt, Bethlehem's 0.8 D/E ranked it in the gray area between low and high debt, but its 3.9 TL/E ratio clearly labeled the steelmaker as a potentially overburdened debtor.

Lucent and Bethlehem probably followed all of the rules. But that doesn't matter. Few of us have the time to interpret the nuances of every financial statement entry. Both Lucent and Bethlehem owed big money that wouldn't have been detected using the conventional D/E ratios.

You won't find the TL/E ratio listed on any Web site, but all balance sheets list total liabilities and total equity in close proximity to each other near the bottom. It's easy to divide the two to come up with the TL/E.

The TL/E ratio is the best measure of debt and thus determines the required financial fitness analysis. My suggested guidelines are illustrated in Table 10-1.

The busted cash burner analysis is described next and the detailed fiscal health exam description can be found later in the chapter.

TABLE 10-1   TL/E ratio determines required fiscal fitness analysis.

Ratio Value	Analysis
TL/E less than 0.5	Busted Cash Burners
TL/E 0.5 or higher	Detailed Fiscal Health Exam

Detecting Potential Busted Cash Burners

Detecting potential busted cash burners entails comparing a company's cash flow to its working capital. Let's define those terms first.

Cash Flow

A company could be burning cash, meaning that it is spending more cash than it takes in (negative cash flow), even though it reports positive earnings quarter after quarter.

To illustrate, assume that Company A reports a $1,000 sale to Customer B. Further, assume that Company A logs the $1,000 order as shipped, but Customer B hadn't paid for the goods by the end of the quarter (the $1,000 unpaid bill is added to accounts receivables).

Following the rules, Company A records the $1,000 as a completed sale, deducts the product cost and other expenses, and logs the difference, say $200, as net income.

Company A showed the $200 profit on its income statement, but since it received no cash from the customer, it actually spent $800 in real cash. Consequently its cash flow, more specifically, its operating cash flow, was a negative $800.

Let's modify that scenario and assume that Customer B did pay before the books were closed. But to get the best prices, Company A ordered enough materials to build two of the products, say $600 worth. So Company A has an extra $300 worth of materials in its inventory. Assuming that Company A paid cash for the materials, it ended up with $100 less in the bank ($200 net income on the product sold less $300 for extra inventory). So it recorded $200 income on the sale, but its operating cash flow resulting from the sale was a minus $100.

Finally, assume a third scenario where Customer B paid before the end of the quarter, but Company A had to buy a new machine costing

$2,000 to produce the product. So Company A's operating cash flow was $200, but after shelling out $2,000 in capital expenses, it was, in fact, $1,800 poorer for the transaction. Free cash flow is accounting terminology for operating cash flow minus capital expenses (plants and equipment). In this example, Company A's free cash flow was a negative $1,800.

Financially distressed companies will probably cut capital expenses to the bone, so we'll use operating cash flow to analyze potential busted cash burners.

Working Capital

Examining a company's cash flow tells only half the story. You must also measure its financial resources, termed working capital, to determine if it's a potential busted cash burner. Working capital is the company's current assets minus its current liabilities. In accounting terminology, current refers to assets and liabilities that are short-term in nature.

CURRENT ASSETS

Current assets include cash and other assets such as inventories and accounts receivables. It doesn't include nonliquid assets such as buildings, capital equipment, patents, and the like.

Cash includes the cash in the bank plus short-term investments. Inventory includes finished products ready to be shipped to customers, raw materials, and partially built products (work in process). Accounts receivables are the monies owed by customers for goods that have been shipped, but not paid for.

CURRENT LIABILITIES

Current liabilities include unpaid taxes, accounts payables, short-term debts, and anything else the company will have to pay out during the next 12 months.

COMPARING CURRENT ASSETS TO CURRENT LIABILITIES

Working capital is simply current assets minus current liabilities, the cash available to run the business. Current ratio is another term that describes the same information. Instead of subtracting, simply divide the current assets by the current liabilities to determine the current ratio.

Cash Burner Analysis

You can do the analysis using balance sheet and cash flow data offered by a variety of financial sites. However, Morningstar compiles the data into the needed format. Especially important, Morningstar displays the trailing twelve-month's (TTM) operating cash flow, a figure vital to the analysis.

It shouldn't take you longer than a minute or two to complete the entire busted cash burner analysis using Morningstar's prosaically named "5-yr Restated" financial report (Figure 10-1). Morningstar's balance sheet breakdown lists cash and other current assets on separate lines. Start by adding those two items together to compute the company's current assets. Then calculate the working capital by subtracting the current liabilities from the current assets. Using Morningstar's terminology:

Working capital = cash plus other current assets minus current liabilities

Cash Flow $Mil

Fiscal year-end: March

	1999	2000	2001	TTM = Trailing 12 Months TTM
Operating Cash Flow	124	224	325	415
- Capital Spending	25	28	61	122
= Free Cash Flow	98	196	263	294

Balance-Sheet Breakdown

Assets	$Mil	%
⬤ Cash	1,187.4	49.2
⬤ Other Current Assets	274.4	11.4
⬤ Long-Term Assets	953.0	39.5
Total	**2,414.8**	**100.0**

Liabilities and Equity	$Mil	%
⬤ Current Liabilities	557.6	23.1
⬤ Long-Term Liabilities	602.4	24.9
⬤ Shareholders' Equity	1,254.9	52.0
Total	**2,414.8**	**100.0**

FIGURE 10-1 Morningstar's cash flow and balance sheet breakdown for Symantec. Find it by selecting Financials Statements and then 5-yr Restated.

Next, estimate the likely operating cash flow for the current year. Morningstar lists the operating cash flow for the last three fiscal years in addition to the TTM amount. Usually, the TTM number is a good estimate. However, you may need to modify it if the historical cash flows are inconsistent from year to year. For instance, say that the last three fiscal years' cash flows are –50, 50, and –20, respectively and that the TTM cash flow is 30. That much inconsistency makes the TTM number suspect. You have to exercise judgment in those instances, and I'd probably assume a zero cash flow value in that example.

Based on the working capital and cash flow values that you come up with, each company that you analyze will fall into one of four categories:

1. Cash flow positive and working capital positive
2. Cash flow positive and working capital negative
3. Cash flow negative and working capital positive
4. Cash flow negative and working capital negative

Cash Flow Positive and Working Capital Positive

This is the best result, and in fact, you wouldn't go wrong requiring that every stock you buy meet this requirement. The company is generating positive cash flow from its operations, and it has positive working capital. These companies already have enough working capital to pay their bills, and they are consistently adding more cash to the pile.

Security software maker Symantec's December 2001 financials (Figure 10-1) illustrate the point. The company had $1,187 million in cash and another $274 million in other current assets on its balance sheet. Subtracting the $558 million current liabilities left Symantec with working capital of $903 million. Further, Symantec generated $415 million in TTM operating cash flow. Comparing the TTM cash flow to the last three fiscal years shows the TTM number to be reasonable.

There may be other reasons why Symantec's shares might not have been a smart buy, but the company wasn't a busted cash burner candidate, either.

Cash Flow Positive and Working Capital Negative

These companies are typically former cash burners that have turned the corner and are now generating cash. However their liabilities outdistanced their assets when they were burning cash. You must determine if their now-positive cash flow is sufficient to overcome their working capital deficit.

Oil drilling instrument maker Global Technovations offers a good example. As of December 31, 2000, Global's balance sheet showed current assets of $14 million compared to $31 million in current liabilities, so in terms of working capital, it was $17 million in the hole.

The company posted positive TTM operating cash flow, but it only amounted to $2 million, not much compared to the $17 million deficit. The company would have still been $13 million in the hole, even if you had assumed that its cash flow would double to $4 million in 2001. Global filed bankruptcy in December 2001.

As a rule of thumb, the estimated annual operating cash flow should at least equal the working capital deficit.

Cash Flow Negative and Working Capital Positive

Most cash burners that you encounter will have positive working capital. In these instances, you'll need to estimate how long the company can continue operating at its present burn rate before it runs out of cash.

The best way to get a handle on that is to convert the TTM operating cash flow to a monthly burn rate (divide by 12) and then compare the burn rate to the working capital. For example, the company has a 10 months' supply of cash if it's burning $10 million monthly and has $100 million in working capital.

How much is enough? There's no hard and fast rule, but a company probably has a good shot at surviving if it has enough cash to last at least two years. If the company's business plan makes sense, it's likely to attract more capital, or better yet, become cash flow positive in that timeframe.

Conversely, firms with less than 12 month's working capital are in dangerous waters unless they can raise additional funds in short order. To illustrate, consider two examples—Calico Commerce and DoubleClick:

• *CALICO COMMERCE*

E-commerce software maker Calico Commerce had burned $50 million in the four quarters ending in June 2001, around $4 million per month. With current assets of only $14 million, Calico had only enough working capital to last around three or four months.

Calico was very much a busted cash burner candidate, and in December 2001, Calico made a deal to file bankruptcy and then be acquired by Peoplesoft for a grand total of $5 million. Calico's shareholders netted around $0.14 per share in the deal, a long way from the $60 that Calico shares had fetched 18 months earlier.

• *DOUBLECLICK*

Internet advertising company DoubleClick burned $8 million in the four quarters ending September 30, 2001. However the dot-com survivor had $186 million in the bank, plus another $501 million in other current assets. Since its current liabilities amounted to only $142 million, DoubleClick's working capital totaled $545 million, enough to last 68 years, at DoubleClick's then current burn rate.

With that much working capital, DoubleClick was bound to figure out how to make money before it ran out of cash.

Cash Flow Negative and Working Capital Negative

Companies in this condition are as good as gone, and normally you wouldn't find many firms in such dire straights. However they were plentiful in 2000 and 2001.

E-learning infrastructure supplier Caliber Learning Network is one such example. According to its March 2001 report, the company had burned $22 million in the previous four quarters, leaving it with a $20 million working capital deficit. The firm filed its March report on May 22, 2001, and filed bankruptcy three weeks later.

Simple Analysis Is Good Enough

This simple analysis assumes that the TTM cash flow burn rate will continue into the future, and that each company's working capital will be completely converted to cash in time to pay its operating expenses. In practice, a firm running close to the edge will figure out how to reduce its cash burn rate, but conversely, not all of its working capital will convert to cash. Not all of its inventory will be sold, and not all of its accounts receivables will be collected. All in all, the assumption errors tend to be self-canceling, and the estimate is close enough for our purposes.

Some Will Survive

Not all busted cash burner candidates will file bankruptcy. Some will find additional financing, and others will be acquired.

You can do more research to identify likely survivors. Start by checking the news for each company. Firms that have found additional funding will say so in a press release.

For instance, wireless telecommunications product distributor Airgate PCS was a persistent cash burner. The company burned $41 million in the 12 months ending September 30, 2001. Worse, the company's working capital was in the hole by $6 million. However, Airgate had a commitment from Lehman Brothers for loans up to $98 million, which Airgate's management considered sufficient to fund the company through 2002, when the company expected to achieve breakeven operating cash flow.

If you don't find out anything by checking the news, you could continue your research by reviewing each company's SEC reports, but you should first decide whether the time wouldn't be better spent locating a more promising candidate.

Detailed Fiscal Fitness Exam

A landmark study done in the early 1990s showed that value-priced stocks outperform growth stocks. More recently, Joseph Piotroski, an accounting professor at the University of Chicago business school, took another look at the study.

He found that although the value portfolio outperformed the growth portfolio, a few outperformers skewed the portfolio returns. In fact, more value stocks underperformed the market than outperformed.

Piotroski, an unusually practical sort for an academic, wondered about the relevance of a strategy that "relies on the strong performance of a few firms, while tolerating the poor performance of many deteriorating companies." Say five stocks out of a hundred accounts for the outperformance. What are the chances you'll pick one of those outperformers if you're only buying 10 or 15 stocks?

Piotroski reasoned that since value stocks became value priced because something went wrong, many were financially distressed and would be hard pressed to survive. Piotroski figured that you could boost the performance of the value portfolio by getting rid of the weakest players. To do that, he devised a simple nine-step test, using financial statement factors to evaluate financial strength.

Each step posed a question, and awarded one point if the company passed. For instance, did the company earn money last year? Give it one point for a yes and zero for a no. Same thing for operating cash flow; one point if it was positive last year, and zero if not. The remaining seven questions looked at performance measures such as return on assets, gross margins, asset turnover ratio, working capital, and so forth. Each question was worth one point, so total scores ranged between zero and nine.

Piotroski classified companies scoring below five as financially weak, and five and above as financially strong. He compared the performance of a portfolio limited to financially strong firms to a portfolio of all value-priced stocks. He found that the strong firms outperformed the all value portfolio by 7.5 percent annually. Most significant, he found that weak (low scoring) firms were five times more likely to delist for performance-related reasons than strong firms.

You could use Piotroski's formula to find value candidates, and the American Association of Individual Investors (AAII) maintains a stock screen based on the formula in the Screens section of its site (www.aaii.com). See Chapter 3 for more on that. However, with some modifications, Piotroski's scoring system can be used to evaluate the financial strength of all high-debt firms, not just value-priced distressed firms.

I tested Piotroski's scoring formula on a variety of stocks, both value and growth, and further researched the factors common to financially stressed firms. Based on that research, I devised a modified version that is applicable to a wide range of medium to high-debt companies. However, it breaks down when applied to very low-debt firms, sometimes giving failing scores to very strong companies that recently reported negative cash flow and earnings.

Consequently, the detailed fiscal health exam should be applied only to high-debt firms (TL/E ratios of 0.5 or higher).

I'll explain the modifications that I made to Piotroski's original scoring formula as I describe the new version.

Measuring Fiscal Fitness

Piotroski's scoring formula consisted of nine tests each worth either zero or one point. I modified some of his original tests and added two new tests. One of my additions can have a score of minus one, zero, or plus one. So the range of possible scores is from minus one to eleven.

Piotroski grouped his nine tests into three categories: profitability, leverage and liquidity, and operating efficiency. All tests measure the company's performance over a 12-month period, either the last four reported quarters or the last fiscal year. You'll find it easier to compute the scores using fiscal year data, but the last four reported quarters' data is timelier.

Many of Piotroski's tests involved comparing ratios at the beginning of the test period to the same ratio at the end. For instance, did the return on assets (net income divided by total assets) increase during the period. I take some shortcuts rather than computing the beginning and ending ratios. For instance, to find out if the ROA did increase, I compare the percentage increase in net income to the percentage increase in total assets. It's mathematically identical to comparing ratios, but easier to compute.

Revenues, income, cash flow, and so on, are always measured over 12 months. For balance sheet items such as assets and debts, always compare values at the beginning and end of the 12-month period.

The following paragraphs provide detailed descriptions of Piotroski's original nine tests plus the two that I added.

PROFITABILITY

Profits are, of course, the key to financial strength, for without profits, most companies will eventually fail. Here are four profitability tests, essentially the same as those defined by Piotroski. Tests 1 and 2 determine if the company is profitable based on both net income and a cash flow basis. Tests 3 and 4 gauge the quality of the reported profits.

1. Net Income: Net income, the firm's bottom line after-tax profits, is an important factor in determining a firm's financial health. Award one point if the after-tax income is a positive number.

2. Operating Cash Flow: Net income results from a variety of accounting decisions, while operating cash flow measures whether the company made money on a cash basis. Award one point if the operating cash flow is positive.

3. ROA: ROA, the net income divided by total assets, measures management's effectiveness in converting available resources into profits. Piotroski wanted to see a year-over-year increase in ROA. I measure that by requiring that the net income growth exceed the growth in total assets. Award one point if that condition is met.

4. Quality of Earnings: Operating cash flow typically exceeds net income since depreciation and other noncash items reduce the income, but not the cash flow. Low cash flow compared to net income signals that noncash accounting entries could be inflating income. Award one point if the operating cash flow exceeds the net income.

DEBT AND CAPITAL

Is the company sinking deeper in debt or is it digging its way out? Tests 5 and 6 award points for declining debt levels. If the debt situation is improving, is it due to profitable operations, or is the company raising cash by selling more stock? Test 7 penalizes companies that raise cash by selling shares rather than from their operations. The test also penalizes firms issuing shares to grow by acquisition, rather than organically.

5. Total Liabilities to Total Assets: TL/A ratio, the company's total liabilities compared to its assets, measures the company's debt load. Increasing debt levels isn't necessarily a bad thing for strong companies, but Piotroski, dealing mostly with financially distressed firms, looked for shrinking debt. I substituted total liabilities where Piotroski called for long-term debt, because TL is a better debt measure. Award one point if the percentage increase in total assets exceeds the percentage increase in total liabilities.

6. Working Capital: The difference between current assets and current liabilities, the funds available to run the business. Piotroski wanted to see an increase in working

capital to signal that the company's financial condition is improving. However, there's no advantage for healthy companies to continually increase their working capital beyond needed levels, so I modified Piotroski's requirement, and only penalize companies with shrinking working capital.

The current ratio (current assets divided by current liabilities) is an alternative way to express working capital. The current ratio increases when working capital increases. Award one point if the latest current ratio is equal to, or greater than, the year-ago ratio.

7. **Shares Outstanding:** Piotroski penalized companies that increased the number of shares outstanding during the year, figuring that they sold stock to raise cash or to make an acquisition. However, employee stock options inflate the shares outstanding total, even if the firm isn't using stock for acquisitions or to raise cash. I researched the annual share inflation rate of several companies that don't make many acquisitions or pay cash when they do. Share inflation for these firms averaged slightly under 2 percent annually. I modified Piotroski's test to award one point if the number of shares outstanding increased less than 2 percent during the prior 12-months.

OPERATING EFFICIENCY

These two tests, in effect, take the company's operational pulse. Rising gross margins along with improving asset turnover signals that both the company's competitive position and its productivity are notably improving.

8. **Gross Margin:** Declining gross margins (gross income divided by sales) often warn of a deteriorating competitive position and signal problems regardless of the company's financial condition. Piotroski rewarded firms with increasing gross margins, and I kept that requirement. Award one point if the gross margin for the trailing 12 months is higher than the year-ago figure.

9. Asset Turnover: Asset turnover, which is revenues divided by total assets, is a standard productivity measure. Piotroski rewarded companies with improving asset turnover ratios. That makes sense since assets rising faster than sales could signal inflating inventories and receivables, indicating earnings quality issues.

I implement the test by comparing the sales growth to the asset growth, and award one point if the percentage sales increase exceeds the percentage increase in assets.

ADDED TESTS

I added two new tests to better differentiate between companies that are on the ropes and the financially strongest companies.

10. Total Liabilities/EBITDA: A gauge favored by lenders, EBITDA measures a company's income before deducting for interest, taxes, depreciation, and amortization. Credit analysts believe that EBITDA best measures a company's ability to service its debt. Lenders believe so strongly in this gauge that they often require debtor companies to maintain a specified total debt/EBITDA ratio. Failure to maintain the required ratio allows the lenders to call their loans, meaning that they want their money immediately, an action that can drive a company into bankruptcy. Of course, lenders would do that only as a last resort, since bankruptcy means that they'll end up collecting only a fraction of the money owed. Ratios of seven to eight, or higher, typically give lenders the option of calling the loans.

Credit analysts also consider the ratio a measure of a company's credit quality. Companies with ratios below 5 are considered investment quality, and these companies can borrow funds at lower rates than firms with higher ratios.

Analysts and lenders' reliance on the total debt/ EBITDA ratio makes it more important than any other single factor, so I've given it more weight. Companies with investment quality ratios of 5 or lower get one point. Ratios above 5 and below 8 get zero. Ratios of 8 or above signal extreme danger, and I deduct a point.
I substituted total liabilities for total debt to ensure that the test considers all debt. Making that change does not significantly change the ratio values for most firms.

11. **Total Liabilities to Operating Cash Flow:** I added this test to differentiate firms that generate significant cash flows compared to their liabilities (cash flow at least 25 percent of total liabilities) and are in little danger of insolvency as long as that condition persists. Add one point if the TL/OCF ratio is less than 4.

Add the individual test results to determine the test score.

Passing Grade

In Piotroski's original 9-point system, 5 points constituted a passing grade. My changes didn't affect Piotroski's passing criteria much. I've found that companies that ended up going bankrupt almost always scored between 1 and 4 points, based on analyzing their most recent fiscal year's financial statements prior to filing bankruptcy.

The scoring system is designed to highlight companies with high risk of financial solvency problems. Obviously, not all companies with low scores will end up in financial trouble, but all of the troubled companies that I analyzed had low scores.

No red flag is raised if a company scores 5 or higher. Piotroski's tests showed that higher is better; that is, firms scoring 7 showed better future performance than those scoring 6, and so on. However, Piotroski's value-priced distressed stock universe is not representative of all stocks, and I haven't found any indication that 10-point stocks perform better than 6-point stocks.

Tables 10-2 through 10-6 list sample scores for a variety of companies. The date column in each table refers to the financial statement analyzed. For instance, 12/00 means that I analyzed the 12 months performance ending 12/31/00.

Enron's positive cash flow and net income contributed to its relatively high December 2000 score. It lost a point in June 2001 due to deteriorating asset turnover. Even with its famous off-balance sheet accounting, checking Enron's score would have gotten you out long before most of the experts.

Exodus, with positive cash flow, strong revenue growth, and improving gross margins, scored relatively high, but it was overwhelmed by its $3.4 billion debt.

Lernout & Hauspie showed hundreds of millions of nonexistent funds on its balance sheet, accounting for its high score.

Webvan only owed $162 million when it went under, the lowest debt of any of the bankrupt companies. The only problem was Webvan didn't have any earnings, cash flow, or EBITDA, the stuff necessary to meet a payroll.

XO Communications had much the same problems as Webvan, except it also owed more than $5 billion.

In April 2001, *The New York Times* said Computer Associates (Table 10-3) had been "using accounting tricks to overstate its profits and revenues for years." The company denied the allegations, and by December 2001, nothing had come of the charges.

Lucent scored a respectable 7 as of the end of its 1999 fiscal year, but its foundering revenue growth and increasing debt sunk its score only three months later to bankruptcy candidate level.

In March 2000, MicroStrategy got caught recording sales that hadn't yet happened, knocking its share price down to $87 from $294 a couple of weeks earlier.

Skyrocketing debt and faltering fundamentals accounted for Xerox's plunge to prime bankruptcy candidate in its fiscal 2000 year. Many thought Xerox wouldn't avoid bankruptcy in 2001, but by year's end, it looked as though it would survive.

All of 2001's big movers (Table 10-4) racked up passing scores early in the year except Genesis Micro. Genesis makes integrated circuits for controlling flat panel displays. Negative cash flow, negative EBITDA, and a variety of other items hurt its score.

TABLE 10-2 Companies that filed bankruptcy in 2001 or early 2002.

Company	Date	Score
Act Manufacturing	12/00	2
Act Manufacturing	6/01	3
At Home	12/00	1
Bethlehem Steel	12/00	3
Burlington Industries	9/01	3
Enron	12/00	4
Enron	6/01	3
Exodus	12/00	4
Global Crossing	12/00	2
HA-LO Inudstries	12/00	2
KMart	1/01	4
KMart	10/01	2
Lernout & Hauspie	12/99	8
McLeod USA	12/00	1
Polaroid	12/00	2
Webvan	12/00	1
XO Communications	12/00	3

TABLE 10-3 Bankruptcy near misses, firms accused of accounting shenanigans, etc.

Company	Date	Score
Computer Associates	3/01	3
Lucent	9/99	7
Lucent	12/99	4
MicroStrategy	12/99	3
Xerox	12/99	7
Xerox	12/00	1

TABLE 10-4 Strong stocks in 2001.

Company	Date	Score
American Woodmark	4/01	9
CACI	6/01	6
Chico's	1/01	9
Christopher & Banks	2/01	9
D & K Wholesale	6/01	5
DRS Technologies	3/01	9
Escalade	12/00	8
Foodarama Supermarkets	10/00	5
Genesis Micro	3/01	2
Nash Finch	12/00	6
Nvidia	1/01	6
Nvidia	7/01	8
Penn National Gaming	7/01	8

TABLE 10-5 Miscellaneous well-known stocks.

Company	Date	Score
Cisco Systems	7/01	5
Dell Computer	1/01	8
Gap	10/01	8
Gateway Computer	9/01	4
General Electric	12/00	9
Home Depot	1/01	8
Intel	12/00	10
Lowes Co.	1/01	7
Microsoft	6/01	9
Staples	1/01	6
Wal-Mart	1/01	7

Intel (Table 10-5) missed a perfect score only because its current ratio dipped slightly at the close of 2000 compared to the year-ago level. Microsoft's slumping sales growth combined with negative earnings growth cost it a perfect score. Cisco's score suffered from the ramifications of its $1 billion loss in its July 2001 fiscal year.

Table 10-6 lists a sampling of firms, chosen randomly, with high D/E levels. Strong profitability kept all except for Georgia Pacific out of the danger area. Georgia Pacific's combination of high and growing debt combined with negative income accounted for its low score.

TABLE 10-6 Large companies with high debt.

Company	Date	Score
American Express	12/00	7
Caterpillar	12/00	7
Cendent	12/00	5
Coca Cola Enterprises	7/01	5
Georgia Pacific	9/01	2
Textron	12/00	6

Computing Fiscal Fitness Scores

MSN Money is a good source for the financial strength data because it displays EBITDA as a line item, saving you the work of computing it.

A fiscal fitness worksheet is shown on page 167. Make copies and use the worksheet to tally the scores when you analyze a company. The process looks formidable, but you should be able to score a company in less than 10 minutes once you've done it a couple of times.

The worksheet is divided into two sections. The top section is used to gather the data and make necessary calculations, and the lower section is used to tabulate the scores.

FIGURING PERCENTAGES

The worksheet requires two types of percentage calculations: (1) simple percentages and (2) year-over-year comparisons.

To calculate simple percentages, divide one number by the other. For instance, gross margin is gross profit divided by sales. If the gross profit is 10, and the sales are 25, the gross margin is

10/25 = 0.40 or 40 %

Calculate year-over-year percentage growth by dividing the latest figure by the year-ago value, and subtract 1 from the result. For instance, if the recent value is 10, and the year-ago number is 7:

Percentage Growth = (10/7) -1 = 1.43 –1 = 0.43 or 43%

Do this calculation when A versus B is indicated.

Do all calculations in millions, and compute numbers to only one decimal place.

Following is an example calculation using Microsoft's June 2001 fiscal year results as displayed on MSN Money's Annual Income Statement (Figure 10-2).

Gathering and Calculating

The form is organized so that you can gather the needed data from the income statement, balance sheet, and cash flow statement in sequence. Figure 10-3 illustrates the income statement portion.

Annual Income Statement (Values in Millions)	6/2001	6/2000
Sales	25,296.0	22,956.0
Cost of Sales	1,919.0	2,254.0
Gross Operating Profit	23,377.0	20,702.0
Selling, General & Admin. Expense	10,121.0	8,925.0
Other Taxes	0.0	0.0
EBITDA	13,256.0	11,777.0
Depreciation & Amortization	1,536.0	748.0
EBIT	11,720.0	11,029.0
Other Income, Net	-195.0	3,090.0
Total Income Avail for Interest Exp.	11,525.0	14,275.0
Interest Expense	0.0	0.0
Minority Interest	0.0	0.0
Pre-tax Income	11,525.0	14,275.0
Income Taxes	3,804.0	4,854.0
Special Income/Charges	0.0	156.0
Net Income from Cont. Operations	7,721.0	9,421.0

FIGURE 10-2 Portion of MSN Money's display of Microsoft's annual income statement. MSN Money shows EBITDA as a separate line item, avoiding the need to calculate the figure.

INCOME STATEMENT

a) Record the most recent year's and the previous year's sales (revenues) and compute the percentage increase. For Microsoft, the sales figures are 25,296 million (latest) and 22,956 million (year-ago) for a year-over-year increase of 10.2 percent [(25296/22956) −1].

Sales Growth: TTM Sales vs. Year ago TTM Sales : 25,296 vs. 22,956 = 10.2%

b) Record the latest period's Gross Profit and the Sales. For Microsoft, the gross profit is 23,777 and the sales are 25,296.

TTM Gross Margin is Gross Profit/Sales (%): 23,777 / 25,296 = 94.0%

c) Repeat step b) using year-ago figures.

Year-ago Gross Margin: year-ago Gross Profit/Sales (%): 20,702 / 22,956 = 90.2%

FISCAL FITNESS EXAM WORKSHEET

COMPANY _____ as of (financial statement date): _____

Income Statement

a) Sales Growth: TTM Sales _____ vs. Year-Ago TTM Sales _____ = ____%

b) TTM Gross Margin: Gross Profit _____ / Sales _____ = ____%

c) Year-ago Gross Margin: Year-Ago Gross Profit _____ / Year-Ago Sales _____ = ____%

d) TTM EBITDA: _____

e) Net Income Growth: TTM Net Income _____ vs. Year-Ago NI _____ = ____%

Balance Sheet

f) Asset Growth: Total Assets _____ vs. Year-Ago Total Assets _____ = ____%

g) Total Liabilities Growth: Latest T.L. _____ vs. Year-Ago T.L. _____ = ____%

h) Current Ratio (Latest): Current Assets _____ / Current Liabilities _____ = ____

FIGURE 10-3   Income statement portion of Fiscal Fitness Exam Worksheet.

d) Record the EBITDA figure from the Income Statement

*TTM EBITDA: 13,256_*

e) Record the most recent year's and the previous year's Total Net Income and compute the percentage increase. For Microsoft, the income figures are 7,346 (latest) and 9,421 (year-ago) for a year-over-year change of minus 22.0 percent.

Net Income Growth is TTM Net Income vs. Year ago NI: 7,346 vs. 9,421 = -22.0%

Next, fill in the balance sheet data (Figure 10-4).

BALANCE SHEET

f) Record the latest and the year-ago Total Assets figures, and compute the percentage change. For Microsoft, the numbers were 59,257 (latest) and 52,150 (year-ago).

a) Sales Growth: TTM Sales _____ vs. Year-Ago TTM Sales _____ = ____%

b) TTM Gross Margin: Gross Profit _____ / Sales _____ = ___%

c) Year-ago Gross Margin: Year-Ago Gross Profit _____ / Year-Ago Sales _____ = ___%

d) TTM EBITDA: _____

e) Net Income Growth: TTM Net Income _____ vs. Year-Ago NI _____ = ___%

Balance Sheet

f) Asset Growth: Total Assets _____ vs. Year-Ago Total Assets _____ = ____%

g) Total Liabilities Growth: Latest T.L. _____ vs. Year-Ago T.L. _____ = ___%

h) Current Ratio (Latest): Current Assets _____ / Current Liabilities _____ = ___

i) Current Ratio (Year-Ago): Year-Ago Current Assets _____ / Y-Ago Current Liabilities _____ = ___

j) Shares Out: Latest _____ Year-Ago _____ Year-Ago x 1.02 _____

k) Total Liabilities to EBITDA Ratio: Total Liabilities (Latest) _____ / EBITDA _____ = _____

Cash Flows

l) TTM Operating Cash Flow (OCF): _____

Tabulate Score

Profitability

1) Net Income (NI) Positive: _____   _____

2) Operating Cash Flow Positive? _____

FIGURE 10-4   Balance sheet portion of Fiscal Fitness Exam Worksheet.

Asset Growth: Total Assets/Year ago Total Assets: 59,257 vs. 52,150 = 13.6%

g) Record the latest and the year-ago Total Liabilities, and compute the percentage change. For Microsoft, the numbers were 11,968 (latest) and 10,782 (year-ago).

Total Liabilities Growth: Latest TL/Year ago TL: 11,968 vs. 10,782 = 11.0%

h) The Current Ratio is the total current assets divided by the total current liabilities. By custom, the current ratio is not expressed as a percentage. This step computes the latest period current ratio. For Microsoft, the current assets are 39,637 and the current liabilities are 11,132.

Current Ratio (latest) is Current Assets/Current Liabilities: 39,637 /11,132 = 3.6

i) Compute the year-ago current ratio. For Microsoft, the year-ago current assets were 30,308, and the current liabilities were 9,755.

Current Ratio (year-ago) is year-ago Current Assets/year-ago Current Liabilities: 30,308 / 9,755 = 3.1

j) The number of (common) shares outstanding at the end of each period is shown near the bottom of the balance sheet. Record the number of shares outstanding for the current and year-ago periods. Multiply the year-ago figure by 1.02 (two percent increase).

Shares Out: Latest 5.4 bil   Year Ago 5.3 bil x 1.02 = 5.4 bil

k) Compute the total liabilities to EBITDA ratio by dividing the total liabilities (item g) by the EBITDA (item d).

Total Liabilities to EBITDA ratio: T.L./EBITDA: 11,968 / 13,256 = 0.9

There is only one entry required on the Cash Flows portion of the worksheet (Figure 10-5).

j) Shares Out: Latest _____   Year-Ago _____   Year-Ago x 1.02 _____

k) Total Liabilities to EBITDA Ratio: Total Liabilities (Latest) _____ / EBITI

Cash Flows

l) TTM Operating Cash Flow (OCF): _____

Tabulate Score

Profitability

1) Net Income (NI) Positive:

FIGURE 10-5   Cash flows portion of Fiscal Fitness Worksheet.

CASH FLOWS

l) The operating cash flow (net cash from operating activities) is listed about midway down the cash flow statement. Record the most recent four quarter's (TTM) operating cash flow.

TTM Operating Cash Flow (OCF): 13,422

That was the hard work. Now all that remains is filling in the blanks on the rating form.

Tabulating Scores

The Tabulate Score section of the worksheet is divided into four sections: Profitability, Debt & Capital, and Operating Efficiency, all categories of Piotroski's original formula, plus an added section that includes my two new tests. Figure 10-6 shows the Profitability section.

l) TTM Operating Cash Flow (OCF): _____

Tabulate Score

Profitability

1) Net Income (NI) Positive: _____

2) Operating Cash Flow Positive? _____

3) Net Income Growth > Total Asset Growth: NI Growth ____% Asset Growth ____%

4) Operating Cash Flow > Net Income: OCF _____ NI _____

Debt & Capital

5) Asset Growth > Total Liabilities Growth: Asset Growth ____% TL Growth ____%

FIGURE 10-6 Profitability score.

PROFITABILITY

1) Net Income: Use the TTM net income (item e). Score one point if the income is a positive number, no matter how small.

Net Income (NI) Positive: 7,346 = 1

2) Operating Cash Flow: Use the most recent year's operating cash flow (item m). Score one point if it is a positive number.

Operating Cash Flow Positive? 13,422 = 1

3) Return on Assets: Record the Net Income Growth (item e) and the Total Asset Growth (item f). Score one point if the income growth exceeds the asset growth. If both growth figures are negative, score one point if the NI Growth dropped less than the Asset Growth.

Net Income Growth > Total Asset Growth: NI Growth –18.0%
Asset Growth 13.6% = 0

4) Quality of Earnings: Score one point if the operating cash flow (Step 2) exceeds the net income (Step 1). This test measures quality of income, not whether the income or cash flow figures are positive. If the net income is negative, score one point if the cash flow is less negative than the net income (e.g., score one point if the net income is –100 and the operating cash flow is –10)

Operating Cash Flow > Net Income: OCF 13,442 NI 7,346 = 1

Next, fill in the Debt and Capital portion of the score (shown in Figure 10-7).

```
1) Net Income (NI) Positive: _____                                    ____

2) Operating Cash Flow Positive? _____                                ____

3) Net Income Growth > Total Asset Growth: NI Growth ____%  Asset Growth ____%     ____

4) Operating Cash Flow > Net Income: OCF _____ NI _____              ____

Debt & Capital

5) Asset Growth > Total Liabilities Growth: Asset Growth ____% TL Growth ____%     ____

6) Current Ratio >= Year-Ago CR: Latest CR ____  Year-ago CR ____       ____

7) Shares Out <= Year-ago Shares Out + 2%: Latest ____  Year-Ago + 2% ____    ____

Operating Efficiency

8) Gross Margins > Year-Ago GM: GM ____% Year-Ago GM ____%              ____

9) Sales Growth > Asset Growth: Sales Growth ____% Asset Growth ____%    ____

Added Tests

10) Total Liabilities/EBITDA: Ratio ____ (0 to 5 =1, & 8+ = -1)          ____

11) Total Liabilities vs. Operating C.F. Ratio < 4: T.L ____ / OCF ____  =
```

FIGURE 10-7   Debt and capital scores.

DEBT AND CAPITAL

5) Total Liabilities/Assets Ratio: Award one point if the assets growth (item f) exceeds the total liabilities growth (item g). If the total liabilities growth is negative, award one point if the asset growth is positive or less negative than the liabilities growth.

Asset Growth > Total Liabilities: Asset Growth 13.6% Total Liabilities Growth 11.0% = 1

6) Working Capital: Award one point if the latest current ratio (item h) equals or exceeds the year-ago ratio (item i).

Current Ratio >= Year-Ago CR: Latest CR 3.6 Year-ago CR 3.1 = 1

7) Shares Outstanding: Award one point if the latest number of shares outstanding (item j) is less than, or equal to, the year-ago figure plus two percent (item j).

Shares Out <= Year-ago Shares Out + 2%: Latest 5.4 Year-Ago + 2% 5.4 = 1

Next, record the operating efficiency scores (Figure 10-8).

5) Asset Growth > Total Liabilities Growth: Asset Growth _____ % TL Growth ___

6) Current Ratio >= Year-Ago CR: Latest CR _____ Year-ago CR _____

7) Shares Out <= Year-ago Shares Out + 2%: Latest _____ Year-Ago + 2% ___

Operating Efficiency

8) Gross Margins > Year-Ago GM: GM _____% Year-Ago GM _____%

9) Sales Growth > Asset Growth: Sales Growth _____% Asset Growth _____%

Added Tests

10) **Total Liabilities/EBITDA:** Ratio _____ (0 to 5 =1, & 8+ = -1)

11) Total Liabilities vs. Operating C.F. Ratio < 4: T.L _____ / OCF _____ = ___

FIGURE 10-8 Operating efficiency scores.

OPERATING EFFICIENCY

8) Gross Margin: Award one point if the latest GM (item b) exceeds the year-ago GM (item c).

GM > Year-ago GM: GM 94.0% Year-ago GM 90.2% = 1

9) Asset Turnover: Award one point if the sales (revenue) growth (item a) exceeds the total assets growth (item f). Both figures can be negative. In those cases, award one point if the sales shrinkage is less than the asset shrinkage.

Sales Growth > Asset Growth: Sales Growth 10.2% Asset Growth 13.6% = 0

Finally, enter the scores for the two added tests (Figure 10-9).

5) Asset Growth > Total Liabilities Growth: Asset Growth _____% TL Growth _____%

6) Current Ratio >= Year-Ago CR: Latest CR _____ Year-ago CR _____

7) Shares Out <= Year-ago Shares Out + 2%: Latest _____ Year-Ago + 2% _____

Operating Efficiency

8) Gross Margins > Year-Ago GM: GM _____% Year-Ago GM _____%

9) Sales Growth > Asset Growth: Sales Growth _____% Asset Growth _____%

Added Tests

10) Total Liabilities/EBITDA: Ratio _____ (0 to 5 =1, & 8+ = -1)

11) Total Liabilities vs. Operating C.F. Ratio < 4: T.L _____ / OCF _____ = _____

TOTAL

FIGURE 10-9   Added tests.

ADDED TESTS

10) Total Liabilities to EBITDA ratio: Record the Total Liabilities/EBITDA ratio (item k). Award one point if the ratio is equal to, or less than 5.0. Subtract one point if the ratio is equals 8.0 or higher.

Total Liabilities/EBITDA: Ratio 0.9 = 1

11) Total Liabilities Compared to Operating Cash Flow: Award one point if the ratio of total liabilities (item g) divided by operating cash flow (Step #2) is less than 4.0.

Total Liabilities/OCF < 4.0 : TL 11,968 / OCF 13,422 = 0.9 = 1

Total Score: 9

Microsoft's 9 score is higher than most companies that I've tested. Companies scoring 4 or less are risky from a financial health perspective and should be avoided. Firms scoring 5 or higher are not high bankruptcy risks, but that's all it means. There is no data showing that the stocks of high-scoring firms outperform the stocks of lower scorers.

Bond Ratings

The fiscal fitness exam performs a thorough analysis, but it takes some time and effort. Another way to get a reading on a firm's financial health is to piggyback on bond analysts' research.

Rating agencies such as Moody's Investors Service (www.moodys.com), Standard & Poors (www.standardandpoors.com), and Fitch (www.fitchratings.com), perform in-depth financial strength analyses of corporations that raise funds by issuing bonds or similar credit instruments. The company being rated pays for the analysis because it needs the rating to sell its bonds. So you won't find bond ratings for companies that raise funds strictly by selling stock.

Don't confuse bond ratings with the stock analysts' buy/sell ratings. Unlike stock analysts who are concerned mainly with earnings growth prospects, bond analysts concentrate on a company's ability to service its debt. They evaluate financial statements, management quality, the competitive environment, and overall economic conditions. Where stock analysts are optimists, bond analysts focus mostly on what can go wrong.

Bond ratings reflect the agencies' view of the risk that a company will default on its bond payments. That information is important to stock investors as well as bond investors because a bond default always destroys the issuing company's stock price. Also, the company's rating determines its access to, and its cost of, borrowing. A lowered bond rating can impact the company's earnings by increasing its interest expenses, and lack of access to new borrowings can stifle a company's growth or even drive it into bankruptcy.

The agencies use a combination of letters, numbers, and plus or minus signs such as AAA, BA1, B- and the like to rate corporate bonds.

■ The combination of symbols used by each rating service varies somewhat, but AAA always indicates the highest quality rating, and any rating starting with A signifies high quality debt. Three letter ratings starting with B such as BAA or BBB indicate lower quality debt than A ratings, but are still considered investment quality. Companies with A or three letter B ratings will probably be able to raise additional funds without problems.

- Two letter B ratings such as BB or Ba1 signify noninvestment grade, or junk bond securities. Corporations with bonds in the junk category may be able to raise additional funds, but it's problematic, and they will have to pay higher interest rates.

- Single letter B ratings such as B1, and all double or triple C rated bonds such as CC and CCC signify substantial risk. Companies with bonds carrying these ratings will probably not be able to raise funds from normal sources.

- Single letter C ratings indicate that the company has filed bankruptcy, and D ratings signify that the company has defaulted on its bond payments.

S&P often adds a + or a - symbol to the rating to indicate that it falls at the top or bottom of its rating group. For instance, a + indicates that the rating falls at the top end. Moody's adds the numbers 1, 2, or 3 to fine-tune their ratings, where 1 indicates rating at the top end of the range, 2 signifies midrange, and 3 indicates the lower end of the rating category. Rating agencies frequently place a rating on credit watch or under review if they are considering changing a rating.

Any A or triple letter B rating is good enough for our purposes because it signals that the rating agency sees little risk of default. There is no evidence that stocks issued by AAA rated companies outperform BBB rated companies' stocks.

Rating agencies also publish ratings that apply to the issuer's general credit worthiness instead of to a specific bond issue. Moody's uses the same rating codes for corporate credit as for specific bond issues, but S&P uses different codes for corporate credit:

- A-1, A-2, and A-3: Best or good quality
- B: Risky credit
- C: Riskier than B
- D: Already in default

You can see each of the three major ratings services ratings on their Web sites. You can look up S&P and Moody's bond ratings together on sites such as BuySellBonds (www.buysellbonds.com) and you can see S&P's credit ratings on the Business Week site (www.businessweek.com) under Estimates & Opinions.

The downside of relying on bond ratings is that they can be too slow to change in fast-moving situations, as the Enron example shows.

By March 2001, when Moody's upgraded Enron's bond ratings from Baa2 to Baa1, the energy trader's share price was changing hands in the mid $50 range, down from $85 in January. Moody's considers Baa bonds medium-grade obligations, meaning the "security to principal and interest are considered adequate, but elements may be present which suggest a susceptibility to impairment some time in the future"— in other words, the low-end of investment quality. The modifier 1 indicates that the obligation ranks toward the top of its rating category. Baa1 means that Moody's rated Enron's bonds at the upper end of the Baa category. Paraphrasing: In March 2001, Moody's moved Enron up from mediocre investment quality to better than mediocre investment quality. S&P's BBB+ rating jibed with Moody's call.

By mid-August, with Enron's shares trading at around $40, CEO Jeff Skilling, citing personal reasons, quit after only six months on the job.

Enron's shares were down to the mid-$30 range, when, on October 16, the company surprised analysts by reporting a $638 million September quarterly loss and by taking substantial asset-value write downs. Enron's report inspired Moody's to place Enron's bond rating on review for downgrade, while S&P reaffirmed its BBB+ ratings.

On October 22, 2001, Enron revealed that the SEC had opened an investigation into transactions between Enron and outside partnerships run by Enron's chief financial officer. That news drove Enron's share price down to $20.

Enron's shares changed hands at $16 on October 24, the day Enron's CFO took a leave of absence. The next day, S&P affirmed its BBB+ bond ratings, but it revised its long-term ratings outlook to negative.

On October 29, 2001, after the market closed, Moody's downgraded Enron's bond ratings back to the January Baa2 level, and kept them under review for further downgrade. The next day, Enron's stock closed at $14.

On November 1, 2001, with Enron's shares still trading in the low teens, the SEC opened a formal investigation of the company's dealings with related parties, and S&P reduced Enron's bond rating from BBB+ to BBB (still investment quality).

On November 8, Enron said it was restating earnings for 1997 though 2000 and for the first two quarters of 2001 to reflect losses incurred by its off-balance sheet partnerships. The news pushed the stock price down to $8.

November 9 was a busy day. Moody's downgraded Enron's bonds to Baa3, the lowest possible investment quality rating, and said it was keeping Enron's bonds under review for further downgrade. Then Enron said it had agreed to sell the company for $8 billion in stock to rival Dynegy (Dynegy later backed out of the deal). Finally, S&P cut its bond ratings from BBB to still investment-grade BBB- and put Enron on credit watch with negative implications. Enron's stock moved up to $9.

On November 19, 2001, with its shares still trading in the $9 range, Enron announced that the bond rating downgrades had triggered a payoff clause requiring the firm to repay some $690 million worth of bonds within one week. The next day the stock closed at $7.

Finally on November 28, with the share price down to $4, both Moody's and S&P downgraded Enron's bonds to noninvestment grade (junk), driving Enron's share price below $1. Unable to finance its debt, Enron filed bankruptcy on December 2, 2001.

The speed of Enron's demise, along with the complexity of its operations that made it difficult to analyze, may, at least partially, account for the bond rating agencies failure to keep up with events as they unfolded.

The Enron debacle was a huge embarrassment for the rating agencies, and the experience compelled them to rethink their rating revision timetables. It's likely that the revisions process will be faster paced by the time you read this book.

Use Bond Risk Premiums to Identify Risky Debtors

As Enron's stock price action illustrates, word of a company's troubles often leaks out to investors before analysts change their ratings. Just as stock prices sometimes move ahead of news, bond prices may also signal changes in a company's outlook before the news is reflected in the bond ratings. In those instances, bond investors will demand a higher bond yield, or a risk premium, to compensate for the added risk before they'll buy a company's bonds. Thus, checking a company's bond risk premiums could hint toward potential financial problems.

For instance, Kmart finally threw in the towel and filed bankruptcy in early 2002, but its bonds traded at close to a 3 percent risk premium during all of 2001. Web-hosting company Exodus' bonds traded at a 28 percent risk premium more than six weeks before its September 26, 2001, bankruptcy filing. Enron's risk premiums, mostly in the 5 percent to 7 percent range, signaled problems a month before the energy trader filed for bankruptcy on December 2, 2001.

Here's what you need to know to interpret risk premiums.

Bond Basics

Most corporate bonds are bought and sold by individual dealers. Some keep an inventory and buy and sell for their own account, while others act as agents for other dealers. Unlike stocks, there is no national quotation system for bonds, and you'd most likely pay different prices for the same bonds, purchased at the same time, from different dealers. Further, the dealer's price normally includes a markup reflecting the dealer's costs and profit.

Bonds are usually sold in $5,000 denominations but are quoted as if the bonds were traded in $100 increments. For instance, a bond price of $105 means that the bond traded at $105 per $100 of face value, or at a 5 percent premium.

You'll need the following definitions to analyze bond yields:

- **Maturity:** The date when the corporation must redeem the bond for its face value. Bonds with maturities of four years or less are termed short-term bonds, those with maturities of more than 12 years are deemed long-term, and those between are medium-term bonds.

- **Rate:** Most corporate bonds pay a specified fixed interest rate, called the coupon rate, based on the issue price.

- **Current Yield:** Your return rate on the bond, which is typically different than the bond rate. For instance, say that you buy a bond with a 6 percent interest rate (based on its original $100 issue price) for $95. You receive $6 in interest, annually, but your yield is 6.3 percent (6 divided by 95) since you only paid $95 for the bond.

■ Yield to Maturity: The total of principal and interest payments that you would receive if you held the bond to maturity. For instance, if you bought a 6 percent bond with a maturity date 12 months out for $95, your yield to maturity is $106 (the $100 principal you'll receive plus $6 interest) divided by the $95 that you paid, or 11.6 percent.

■ **Callable or non-callable (bonds can be either):** If callable, the corporation can redeem the bonds before the scheduled maturity date. Most bonds are noncallable, and for simplicity, we'll stick with that category.

Bond prices and bond yields are inversely related, meaning the yield rises when bond prices fall. Bond yields and bond prices can be influenced by external factors such as overall interest rates, and the current appeal of corporate bonds as investment vehicles. Its bond rating, years to maturity, and whether it's callable or noncallable also influence a specific corporate bond's price and yield.

Yahoo's Bond Screener (bonds.yahoo.com) makes analyzing risk premiums doable because you can use it to see bond yields to maturity based on recent trades for each of S&P's bond ratings for years to maturity ranging from 1 to 12 years, in one-year increments.

Here's how to determine a bond's risk premium.

Get Bond Yield

Start by getting the current bond quotes for the company that you're researching. Restrict your search to non-callable bonds. Figure 10-10 illustrates the bond quote format you'll find on BuySellBonds.com. When I looked up Wal-Mart in August 2005, I found 24 quotes involving 11 different bonds. Since quotes for the same bond often vary in price, you'll see different yields to maturity listed for the same bond. I've found that it's best to find a bond with three or more quotes.

You only need to look at three items: the S&P bond rating, the maturity date, and the yield. I found three quotes for a Wal-Mart AA rated bond maturing in August 2009, four years away. The yields to maturity on all three were around 4.2 percent.

Qty Min Incr/MBR	Ratings Industry	Issue Call Information	Coupon Maturity ▲	Price YTM LY
50 25	Aa2/AA Industrial	Wal Mart Stores Inc Non Callable, Spec Redemp	5.450 08-01-2006	102.309 2.922 Mat
100 25	Aa2/AA Industrial	Wal Mart Stores Inc Non Callable, Spec Redemp	5.450 08-01-2006	102.352 2.876 Mat
250 25	Aa2/AA Industrial	Wal Mart Stores Inc Non Callable, Spec Redemp	5.450 08-01-2006	102.308 2.923 Mat
50 25	Aa2/AA Industrial	Wal Mart Stores Inc Non Callable, Spec Redemp	4.375 07-12-2007	101.621 3.475 Mat
250 25	Aa2/AA Industrial	Wal Mart Stores Inc Non Callable, Spec Redemp	4.375 07-12-2007	101.408 3.592 Mat
100 25	Aa2/AA Industrial	Wal Mart Stores Inc Non Callable, Spec Redemp	4.375 07-12-2007	101.571 3.503 Mat
50 25	Aa2/AA Industrial	Wal Mart Stores Inc Non Callable, Spec Redemp	3.375 10-01-2008	98.510 3.889 Mat
250 50	Aa2/AA Industrial	Wal Mart Stores Inc Non Callable, Spec Redemp	3.375 10-01-2008	98.268 3.973 Mat
100 25	Aa2/AA Industrial	Wal Mart Stores Inc Non Callable, Spec Redemp	3.375 10-01-2008	98.466 3.904 Mat
50 25	Aa2/AA Industrial	Wal Mart Stores Inc Non Callable, Spec Redemp	6.875 08-10-2009	109.768 4.172 Mat
250 25	Aa2/AA Industrial	Wal Mart Stores Inc Non Callable, Spec Redemp	6.875 08-10-2009	109.746 4.177 Mat
250 25	Aa2/AA Industrial	Wal Mart Stores Inc Non Callable, Spec Redemp	6.875 08-10-2009	109.827 4.156 Mat

FIGURE 10-10 Corporate bond quotes are available on several sites including BuySellBonds.com. The figure shows a partial list of Wal-Mart's bonds offered for sales in August 2005.

Determine Average Yield

The next step is to compare Wal-Mart's yield to maturity to the average yield for similar bonds.

Use Yahoo's Bond Screener to find corporate, non-callable bonds with a four-year to five-year maturity range (see Figure 10-11). You can't specify four-years for both your minimum and maximum because the screener will only list bonds maturing four-years to the month from the date you run the screen, which probably won't be sufficient to do the analysis.

My screen turned up 25 bonds sorted by maturity date. The average yield of the 13 bonds maturing by December 2009 was 4.2 percent. There was no risk premium since Wal-Mart's bonds, at 4.2 percent, were trading right at the average.

Analyzing Ford Motor Company illustrates a case where a risk premium does exist.

Following the same procedure for Ford, I found quotes involving three BB+ rated bonds, all a little more than four years out, maturing in October 2009 with yields to maturity averaging 7.0 percent.

Finding the average yield to maturity for a BB+ rated bond requires another step because Yahoo lists BB and BBB ratings, but not BB+.

Since BB+ is between BB and BBB, I averaged those two ratings' for bonds maturing between August 2009 and March 2010, coming up with 5.4 percent versus Ford's 7.0 percent yield to maturity.

Ford's 1.6 percent risk premium meant that bond traders saw risk in owning its bonds, not necessarily that Ford will default. For instance, Xerox's bonds traded at 8 percent risk premiums in October 2001, but the company didn't default.

BOND SCREENER RESULTS

Type	Issue	Price	Coupon(%)	Maturity	YTM(%)	Current Yield(%)	Rating	Callable
Corp	BANK ONE CORP	104.90	6.000	1-Aug-2008	4.207	5.720	AA	No
Corp	BANK OF AMERICA CORPORATION	97.64	3.250	15-Aug-2008	4.100	3.328	AA	No
Corp	FIFTH THIRD BK CIN OHIO MTN BE	98.00	3.375	15-Aug-2008	4.095	3.444	AA	No
Corp	PROCTER & GAMBLE CO	101.01	4.300	15-Aug-2008	3.937	4.257	AA	No
Corp	WACHOVIA CORP 2ND NEW	98.31	3.500	15-Aug-2008	4.108	3.560	AA	No
Corp	WELLS FARGO & CO NEW	99.56	4.000	15-Aug-2008	4.160	4.018	AA	No
Corp	MERRILL LYNCH & CO INC MERRILL	98.56	3.700	18-Aug-2008	4.215	3.754	AA	No
Corp	FEDERAL NATL MTG ASSN	100.03	4.000	2-Sep-2008	3.991	3.999	AA	No
Corp	MERRILL LYNCH & CO INC MERRILL	99.36	3.750	2-Sep-2008	3.975	3.774	AA	No
Corp	ONTARIO PROV CDA	104.68	5.500	1-Oct-2008	3.881	5.254	AA	No
Corp	WAL MART STORES INC	98.47	3.375	1-Oct-2008	3.904	3.428	AA	No
Corp	MERRILL LYNCH & CO INC	106.66	6.375	15-Oct-2008	4.091	5.977	AA	No
Corp	ASSOCIATES CORP NORTH AMER	106.44	6.250	1-Nov-2008	4.070	5.872	AA	No
Corp	CITICORP MTN SUB BE	106.76	6.375	15-Nov-2008	4.112	5.971	AA	No
Corp	HANCOCK JOHN FINL SVCS INC	104.78	5.625	1-Dec-2008	4.044	5.368	AA	No

FIGURE 10-11   Yahoo's Bond Screener makes it possible to find the yields to maturity for all of Standard & Poor's major bond ratings, for a wide range of years to maturity. This feature makes analyzing risk premiums practical.

Summary

Few would argue that evaluating a firm's financial health should be done for every investment candidate. You'd think that market analysts would take that step before advising investors to buy a stock, but since they don't, you have to do it on your own.

You can simplify the task by sticking with low-debt firms showing positive cash flow and positive working capital. You can get a quick read on high-debt firm's financial health by checking their bond ratings and their bond risk premiums, but the Detailed Fiscal Fitness Exam is the best way to determine a potential financial basket case.

FISCAL FITNESS EXAM WORKSHEET

COMPANY _____ as of (financial statement date):_____

Income Statement

a) Sales Growth: TTM Sales _____ vs. Year-Ago TTM Sales _____ = ____%

b) TTM Gross Margin: Gross Profit _____ / Sales _____ = ____%

c) Year-ago Gross Margin: Year-Ago Gross Profit _____ / Year-Ago Sales _____ = ____%

d) TTM EBITDA: _____

e) Net Income Growth: TTM Net Income _____ vs. Year-Ago NI _____ = ____%

Balance Sheet

f) Asset Growth: Total Assets _____ vs. Year-Ago Total Assets _____ = ____%

g) Total Liabilities Growth: Latest T.L. _____ vs. Year-Ago T.L. _____ = ____%

h) Current Ratio (Latest): Current Assets _____ / Current Liabilities _____ = ____

i) Current Ratio (Year-Ago): Year-Ago Current Assets _____ / Y-Ago Current Liabilities _____ = ____

j) Shares Out: Latest _____ Year-Ago _____ Year-Ago x 1.02 _____

k) Total Liabilities to EBITDA Ratio: Total Liabilities (Latest) _____ / EBITDA _____ = _____

Cash Flows

l) TTM Operating Cash Flow (OCF): _____

Tabulate Score

Profitability

1) Net Income (NI) Positive: _____   _____

2) Operating Cash Flow Positive? _____   _____

3) Net Income Growth > Total Asset Growth: NI Growth ____% Asset Growth ____%   _____

4) Operating Cash Flow > Net Income: OCF _____ NI _____   _____

Debt & Capital

5) Asset Growth > Total Liabilities Growth: Asset Growth ____% TL Growth ____%   _____

6) Current Ratio >= Year-Ago CR: Latest CR _____ Year-ago CR _____   _____

7) Shares Out <= Year-ago Shares Out + 2%: Latest _____ Year-Ago + 2% _____   _____

Operating Efficiency

8) Gross Margins > Year-Ago GM: GM ____% Year-Ago GM ____%   _____

9) Sales Growth > Asset Growth: Sales Growth ____% Asset Growth ____%   _____

Added Tests

10) Total Liabilities/EBITDA: Ratio _____ (0 to 5 =1, & 8+ = -1)   _____

11) Total Liabilities vs. Operating C.F. Ratio < 4: T.L _____ / OCF _____ = ____   _____

TOTAL   _____

11

ANALYSIS TOOL #8:
PROFITABILITY ANALYSIS

You've probably heard the popular sports cliché about winning being the only thing. Similarly, in the stock market, earnings is the only thing that matters at report time. But, except in cases of fraud or very creative accounting, earnings don't come out of thin air. In this chapter, you'll learn how to analyze the underpinnings of a company's reported earnings and its future earnings prospects. The components of profitability analysis include:

- Sales and sales growth
- Profit margins
- Profitability ratios
- Cash flows

The first two, sales and profit margins, determine reported earnings. The latter two, profitability ratios and cash flow, tell you what's behind the raw numbers.

Where Do Earnings Come From?

Sales and profit margins combine to produce earnings. It takes both. Here's the formula:

earnings = sales x profit margin

I call it the E=SP formula. Memorize it, even if you hate math and flunked algebra.

The E=SP formula makes it clear that sales and margins both determine earnings. It's tough for companies to report consistent earnings growth if sales rise, but profit margins drop, or vice versa. Let's flesh out the concept with numbers.

Suppose that a company sold $1,000 worth of products during the last quarter at a 15 percent profit margin. According to E=SP, the company earned $150.

earnings = $1,000 x 0.15 = $150

If nothing changes in the next quarter, the company will again rack up sales of $1,000 and it will again earn $150.

That would create a problem for shareholders if it did happen because earnings growth, or the expectation of earnings growth, is usually what drives stock prices up.

E=SP tells us that the only way to boost earnings is to increase sales and/or profit margins. In the best case, good management can combine sales growth with growing profit margins, and then earnings grow faster than sales.

The bottom line number announced on earnings report day is earnings per share (EPS), which is net income divided by the number of outstanding shares.

earnings per share = net income/shares outstanding

A company with lackluster growth can boost its EPS by buying back its stock, thereby reducing the number of shares outstanding.

Table 11-1 shows the relationship between annual sales growth, net income, and earnings per share growth for a variety of companies.

Costco, Gap, Microsoft, Pfizer, and Walgreen results characterize most companies, with net income and earnings per share closely tracking sales.

Avon Products and IBM typify companies that, despite lackluster sales growth, still manage to grow earnings at a respectable rate by productivity improvements combined with share buybacks.

Intel embodies the ideal situation; fast-growing sales and even faster growing earnings. That's history, though. Notice that Intel's sales growth slowed markedly in the 1997 to 2000 timeframe, even though the tech sector was flying high.

Cisco Systems, the fastest grower of the group, hasn't done a good job of translating sales growth to profits. Worse, EPS growth didn't track net income, reflecting Cisco's inclination to use its stock to boost sales via acquisitions, consequently diluting shareholder value.

Bottom line, you won't go wrong starting with the assumption that, long-term, most companies' earnings growth will track sales growth. In the short-term it's a different story. Stock prices respond to all sorts of stimuli. It's up to you to filter out the fundamentally significant information from the day-to-day noise.

Analyzing Sales (Revenue) History

You'll be most productive starting your analysis with sales growth, since it's the crucial ingredient of long-term growth. First analyze long-term sales growth trends and then zero in on the most recent data.

MSN Money's 10-Year Summary report is a good resource for long-term sales data. Table 11-2 shows the data for a variety of companies.

Looking at the big picture gives you perspective. For instance, many gurus consider Gillette to be a growth company, but the shaver-maker's last meaningful growth year was 1996. You'd have to go back to 1995 to see real growth from Coca Cola, also considered by many to be a growth stalwart. A similar story for Intel, whose last big growth year was 1997. Of the biggies listed, Pfizer looks like the only consistent long-term growth story.

TABLE 11-1   Average annual net income and EPS growth vs. average annual sales growth.

	Sales Growth (%)	Net Income Growth (%)	EPS Growth (%)
Typical			
Costco			
9/91 to 9/96	10	3	4
9/96 to 9/01	12	19	16
9/91 to 9/01	11	11	10
The Gap			
1/91 to 1/96	18	20	19
1/96 to 1/01	26	20	22
1/91 to 1/01	22	20	21
Microsoft			
6/91 to 6/96	36	37	33
6/96 to 6/01	24	29	26
6/91 to 6/01	30	33	30
Pfizer			
12/90 to 12/95	9	14	13
12/95 to 12/00	12	9	9
12/90 to 12/00	10	11	11
Walgreen			
8/91 to 8/96	12	14	14
8/96 to 8/01	16	19	18
8/91 to 8/01	14	16	16

TABLE 11-1 Average annual net income and EPS growth vs. average annual sales growth. *(continued)*

	Sales Growth (%)	Net Income Growth (%)	EPS Growth (%)
Good EPS Growth Despite Lackluster Sales Growth			
Avon Products			
12/90 to 12/95	5	8	7
12/95 to 12/00	5	11	16
12/90 to 12/00	5	9	12
IBM			
12/96 to 12/01	3	5	12
12/94 to 12/01	4	11	20
Strong Sales Growth and Even Stronger EPS Growth			
Intel			
12/91 to 12/96	34	45	43
12/96 to 12/00	13	20	20
12/91 to 12/00	24	33	32
Fast Grower with Diminshing Productivity			
Cisco Systems			
7/91 to 7/96	86	84	72
7/96 to 7/00	47	31	25
7/91 to 7/00	67	58	49

TABLE 11-2   Examples of long-term sales histories (in millions).

Calendar Year	Intel	Adv. Micro.	Coca-Cola	Gillette	The Gap	Chico's	Pfizer
12/01	26,539	3891	20,092	8.961	13,848	378	32,259
12/00	33,726	4644	20,058	9295	13,673	259	29,574
12/99	29,389	2857	19,805	9897	11,635	155	16,204
12/98	26,273	2542	18,813	10,056	9055	107	13,544
12/97	25,070	2356	18,868	10,062	6508	75	12,504
12/96	20,847	1953	18,456	9698	5284	64	11,306
12/95	16,202	2430	18,018	6795	4395	60	10,021
12/94	11,521	2135	16,172	6070	3723	59	8281
12/93	8782	1648	13,597	5411	3296	47	7478
12/92	5844	1514	13,074	5163	2960	33	7230

Growth investors need strong sales growth and should focus on candidates with at least 15 percent average annual sales growth over the past three years. Longer is better. Value investors don't need growth that strong. For them, 5 percent average annual sales growth is sufficient, but, as with growth investors, more is better.

Women's clothing retailer Chico's FAS looked like a prospective growth candidate in early 2002. Table 11-3 shows its recent sales in terms of year-over-year percentage growth.

The long-term trends helps you spot potential candidates, but companies don't grow at accelerated rates forever. You need to determine whether the long-term growth rate is continuing, slowing, or accelerating, to further qualify a promising candidate. You can do that by examining the most recent quarterly sales reports. Reuters is the best site for that information because its Financial Highlights report displays up to four years of quarterly sales data. Table 11-4 shows the revenue history portion of the report for Chico's as of late February 2002.

TABLE 11-3   Chico's year-over-year sales growth.

Fiscal Year	1/01	1/00	1/99	1/98	1/97
Y/Y Sales Growth	67%	45%	42%	11%	12%

TABLE 11-4   Reuters Investor Financial Highlights Report (revenue portion) for Chico's as of 2/26/02.

Quarters	1999	2000	2001	2002
April	25,896	36,425	56,692	93,233
July	27,359	36,771	60,638	89,491
October	26,754	40,009	68,990	93,978
January	26,732	41,798	73,126	

It's usually better to compare sales to the same quarter in the previous year (year-over-year), rather than comparing to the preceding quarter. For instance, compare Chico's October 2002 quarter sales to October 2001 instead of to July 2002. Many industries' sales fluctuate with the time of year. By always comparing the same time of year, you automatically eliminate the seasonal variations from your analysis.

You'll get a better perspective by computing the year-over-year (e.g., April 2001 compared to April 2000, etc.) percentage sales growth. Table 11-5 shows the sales growth percentages that I computed for Chico's.

Fiscal Years' Confusion

I downloaded Chico's sales data in February 2002, but Reuters displayed Chico's sales for April, May, and October 2002.

Was Reuters predicting the future? No! Chico's fiscal year ends in January. Each fiscal year is designated by its ending date. For instance, Chico's 1999 fiscal year ended in January 1999. So Chico's April, July, and October 2001 calendar quarters were included in its 2002 fiscal year.

TABLE 11-5 Chico's quarterly year-over-year sales growth.

Quarters	2000 (%)	2001 (%)	2002 (%)
April	38	56	65
July	36	65	48
October	41	72	36
January	52	75	

> ### Doing the Math
>
> *Calculate year-over-year growth by dividing the most recent figure by the year-ago number and subtracting 1 from the result. For instance, to calculate Chico's FY October quarter's growth, divide 93,978 by 68,990, yielding 1.36, and then subtract 1, which gives you 0.36, or 36 percent.*

Chico's most recent sales growth looked consistent with historical trends except for its October 2002 (calendar 2001) figure which was half the FY 2001 October quarter's year-over-year growth rate (36 vs. 72). Normally a growth rate falloff of that magnitude (–50%) is a red flag signaling future problems. However the events of September 11 disrupted commerce in September and October 2001, and probably accounted for much of the shortfall. Chico's performance illustrates the consistent sales growth pattern that distinguishes a promising growth candidate.

TABLE 11-6 Priceline.com quarterly sales.

Quarters	1998	1999	2000	2001
March	0	49,411	313,798	269,704
June	7022	111,564	352,095	364,746
September	9222	152,222	341,334	301,989
December	18,993	169,213	228,169	235,304

TABLE 11-7   Priceline.com's quarterly year-over-year percentage sales growth.

Quarters	1999 (%)	2000 (%)	2001 (%)
March		535	-14
June	1494	216	4
September	1554	124	-12
December	791	35	3

Online travel agency Priceline.com's sales history shown in Table 11-6 tells a different story.

Once again, calculating the year-over-year percentage sales growth (Table 11-7) gives a clearer picture.

Priceline.com's sales took off like a house afire, but by 2001 its sales growth had evaporated. Judging from its sales record, Priceline.com might be a value candidate, but it doesn't make the cut for growth investors. Here's how growth and value investors should interpret sales growth.

Growth Investors

Pick candidates with recent sales growth consistent with, or higher than, the firm's long-term historical sales growth. Look for at least 15 percent recent year-over-year growth, and higher—up to 50 percent or so—is better. Extended annual sales growth much above 50 percent is an unrealistic expectation.

Value Investors

Ignore recent sales growth figures. Declining sales probably explains why the stock is a value candidate. Focus instead on historical figures and avoid companies showing less than 5 percent average annual long-term growth.

The analysts' consensus sales growth forecasts available on Yahoo's Research report can also help you analyze sales growth trends. See Chapter 12 for details.

Analyzing Margins

You can use three different margins to gauge profitability: gross margin, operating margin, and overall profit (net income) margin. All three are computed by dividing profits by total sales:

margin = profit/total sales

Margins can be computed for any period (e.g., days, weeks, months), but for stock analysis, the only periods used are the last quarter (three months), the last four reported quarters (TTM), or a fiscal year. The only difference between the three types of margins is the profit figure that is compared to sales.

Gross Margin

Theoretically, gross income is the profit made on a product considering only the costs of materials and labor to produce the product.
Gross profit is sales less the cost of sales:

gross profit = total sales – cost of sales

Gross margin is the gross profit divided by total sales:

gross margin = gross profit/sales

When Home Depot sells a hammer, its gross profit is the difference between the sales price and the price that Home Depot paid for the item. The costs to put the hammer on the shelves, advertise it, ring up the sale and put the hammer in a bag are not considered in the gross profit calculation. The product costs are labeled cost of goods sold, or cost of sales on the company's operating statement.

The hammer example holds true for many firms. However, many others, Microsoft for instance, add depreciation and amortization (D&A) charges to the product cost. In these instances, the cost of sales listed on the company's operating statement filed with the SEC and on operating statements compiled by Reuters, includes these embedded D&A charges.

But Core Data deducts the embedded D&A charges from the cost of sales and lists them on a separate line on the income statement. Core Data determines the embedded charges by comparing the D&A listed on the cash flow statement to charges listed on the income statement.

Bottom line: MSN Money, Hoover's, and other sites displaying Core Data compiled data will show lower costs of sales, and hence, higher gross margins, than listed on the reporting firm's own financial statements and on sites using Reuters supplied data.

You will get *different answers* calculating gross margins for the same companies on sites using Core Data data than you'd get calculating gross margins on sites using Reuters data.

Core Data's approach makes sense in theory. But it makes a variety of other changes to a company's financial statements besides for the D&A adjustment, including adjustments to the reported sales total. Core Data doesn't provide any explanation of its changes, making it virtually impossible to reconcile its statements to the company's SEC filings.

Consequently, I generally use Reuters financial statements unless I'm comparing gross margins of companies with dissimilar D&A accounting practices that would affect the calculations.

Operating Margin

Operating expenses include costs of goods sold, plus sales, general and administrative (SG&A) expenses, research and development, depreciation and amortization (if not in cost of sales), and most other costs of doing business, except interest expenses and taxes.

Operating income is sales less operating expenses:

operating income = total sales – operating expenses

Because it doesn't account for interest expenses and income taxes, operating income is also called EBIT, an acronym for earnings before interest and taxes.

Operating margin is:

operating margin = operating income/total sales

Since depreciation and amortization are included in operating expenses, if not already included in cost of sales, the differences between the Reuters and Core Data totals mostly disappear by the time you calculate operating margin.

Net Profit Margin

The net profit margin calculation takes all other expenses not included in the operating margin calculation into account, namely interest expenses and income taxes.

Income before taxes is the operating income (EBIT) less interest expenses:

income before taxes = operating income – interest expense

Net income is operating income less interest expenses and income taxes.

net income = operating income – interest expense – income taxes

The net profit margin is net income divided by total sales:

net profit margin = net income/total sales

The net profit margin is often simply called the profit margin. Net income is the bottom line, and EPS is the net income divided by the number of outstanding shares.

Comparing Margins

This section describes how to use the gross, operating, and net profit margins to evaluate investment candidates.

Gross Margins

Since gross margins gauge the difference between a firm's product costs and selling price, companies with lower production costs or in-demand products that command higher prices should report higher gross margins than the competition. Table 11-8 compares software vendors Microsoft and Oracle's recent gross margins

The gross margins reflect the vastly different competitive situations facing the two firms. Microsoft sees virtually no competition since practically all personal computers come with Microsoft Windows operating system already installed. Oracle faces competition from SAG, Siebel Systems, and PeopleSoft, among others.

TABLE 11-8 Gross margins for Microsoft and Oracle.

Fiscal Year	Microsoft (%)	Oracle (%)
2001	86	74
2000	88	71
1999	88	65
1998	88	68
1997	86	73

For another example, Table 11-9 compares microprocessor makers Intel and Advanced Micro Devices' recent gross margins.

Advanced Micro produces microprocessors that are competitive with, if not better than, Intel's. Despite being technologically competitive, Advanced Micro's brand identity is inferior to Intel's. Consequently, Advanced Micro must underprice its products compared to Intel to win orders. Compounding its problems, Intel with its much larger production facilities, probably has a lower cost of production than Advanced Micro.

Higher gross profits translate to higher operating margins, and higher operating margins result in higher bottom line profit margins. Microsoft racked up a 31 percent net profit margin in its 2001 fiscal year compared to Oracle's 24 percent bottom line margin. Intel scored a 31 percent net profit margin in 2000 compared to Advanced Micro's 21 percent.

Did Advanced Micro's higher gross margin in 2000 portend better times in 2001? Nope. Advanced Micro's gross margin slipped to 33 percent in 2001, and the company ended up losing money for the year.

TABLE 11-9   Gross margins for Intel and Advanced Micro Devices.

Fiscal Year	Intel (%)	Advanced Micro (%)
2000	62	46
1999	60	32
1998	54	32
1997	61	33
1996	56	26

Operating Margins

Finding gross margin differences as pronounced as the Microsoft versus Oracle and Intel versus Advanced Micro examples are the exception rather than the rule. Typically, gross margins don't differ much among competitive firms, and normal year-to-year variations make it difficult to discern a meaningful difference.

On the other hand, operating margins often do tell a story and can convey important information pointing to the eventual dominator of a heretofore competitive industry.

Two firms, Bed Bath & Beyond and Linens 'n Things, pioneered the linen retail superstore category in the 1990s. Table 11-10 illustrates how you could have used operating margins to pick the eventual winner.

Linens 'n Things was the sales leader in the early 1990s, but it seemingly couldn't figure out how to consistently run its business profitably. Meanwhile, Bed Bath & Beyond chugged along year after year reliably recording 12 percent operating margins. Linens 'n Things profit margins took a big hit in 1995, the year that Bed Bath & Beyond surpassed the former market leader in sales. Linens' 1995 margins probably reflect price cutting on its part to maintain market share.

By 2000, Bed Bath and Beyond was the clear leader with 60 percent market share. In 2001, Linens faltered, taking a big charge or restructuring, including among other items, closing unprofitable stores.

TABLE 11-10 Operating margins and sales for Bed, Bath and Beyond (BBBY) and Linens 'n' Things (LIN).

Year	Sales (millions)	Operating Margin (%)
2000		
BBBY	2400	11%
LIN	1573	7%
1999		
BBBY	1858	11%
LIN	1300	7%
1998		
BBBY	1382	11%
LIN	1067	6%
1997		
BBBY	1067	11%
LIN	874	5%
1996		
BBBY	823	11%
LIN	696	4%
1995		
BBBY	601	11%
LIN	555	2%
1994		
BBBY	440	12%
LIN	440	7%
1993		
BBBY	306	12%

TABLE 11-10   Operating margins and
sales for Bed, Bath and Beyond (BBBY)
and Linens 'n' Things (LIN). *(continued)*

Year	Sales (millions)	Operating Margin (%)
LIN	331	7%
1992		
BBBY	217	12%
LIN	271	0%
1991		
BBBY	168	12%
LIN	221	3%

There could be many reasons why Bed Bath & Beyond came from behind to overtake Linens 'n Things. But one reason is apparent. Bed Bath & Beyond was more profitable, so it had more money to expand. For instance, Bed Bath & Beyond generated $598 million in cash from operations in 1993 though 2000. Linens' operations garnered only $242 million in the same period. Bed Bath & Beyond had $356 million more than Linens did to spend on new stores or on operational improvements during that timeframe.

You would have made a respectable 246 percent return on your investment if you had purchased Linens 'n Things shares when it went public in November 1996 and sold on February 15, 2002. But you would have made 419 percent making those same trades buying Bed Bath and Beyond instead.

Analyzing Margins

While gross margins can be useful for detecting deterioration in a company's competitive position, and profit margins are a key ingredient in the target price calculation, I've found operating margins the most useful of the three measures for evaluating a company's profitability trends.

TABLE 11-11 Black Box Corporation's operating margin.

Period	Q 3/00	Q 3/99	FY 3/00	FY 3/99	FY 3/98	FY 3/97
Operating margin	15.8%	20.5%	16%	19%	19%	19%

For instance, Table 11-11 shows communications equipment provider Black Box Corporation's operating margin history, as it appeared in May 2000.

Black Box's operating margin held at a steady 19 percent through fiscal 1999. However, it dropped to 16 percent in its fiscal year ending March 1999. That amounts to a 16 percent year-over-year decline (16 vs. 19). I've found operating margin percentage declines as little as 5 percent (e.g., 19 vs. 20) to be significant. Comparing the most recent data is especially significant. The 23 percent decline in operating margin (15.8 vs. 20.5) from March 1999 to March 2000 showed that the problem was worsening.

Black Box's March 2000 results served as a warning to astute investors. Its June quarter results came in below forecasts, driving its share price down more than 30 percent on announcement day.

The Black Box example illustrates the importance of analyzing the most recent quarter's margins to spot signals pointing to future shortfalls. Compare the quarterly margins to the year-ago number, not the annual data, to allow for seasonal variations. However allow for more volatility in the quarterly data.

Growth Investors

Observe trends in annual operating margins and avoid companies with a decline of 5 percent or more (e.g., 19 vs. 20) year-over-year decline. Compare the most recent quarter's margin to year-ago and avoid if the latest operating margin declined 10 percent or more (e.g., 18 vs. 20).

Value Investors

Value candidate's margins are typically depressed compared to historical levels. But the historical margins are useful for estimating earnings when the company recovers.

High vs. Low Margins

Intuitively, you'd surmise that it's a good idea to pick the most profitable company in an industry. That strategy works for growth investors, especially when analyzing competing firms in fast-growing emerging markets. But value investors should take the opposite view, that is, seek out companies with margins below industry, or better yet, their own historical averages.

For instance, Albertsons, Kroger, and Safeway are the three major U.S. nationwide grocery chains, and they compete head-on in many markets. Table 11-12 shows each firm's operating margins for 1992 through 2000. The table also lists each company's average price/sales ratio to show how the market valued their shares over the years shown.

In the early 1990s, the market valued each dollar of Albertsons' sales higher, in fact, six times higher, than Kroger or Safeway's. The market valued Albertsons higher because Albertsons was percolating, with operating margins roughly double Safeway's.

TABLE 11-12   Historical operating margins and price/sales ratios for major U.S. grocery chains.

	2000	1999	1998	1997	1996	1995	1994	1993	1992
Albertson's	4.8%	3.6%	4.8%	5.3%	7.0%	6.8%	7.2%	6.6%	5.9%
Avg. P/S	0.3	0.4	0.9	0.8	0.6	0.7	0.6	0.6	0.6
Kroger	4.7%	4.1%	2.6%	3.9%	4.3%	3.7%	3.9%	3.6%	3.1%
Avg. P/S	0.4	0.3	0.6	0.4	0.2	0.2	0.1	0.1	0.1
Safeway	7.2%	6.9%	6.6%	5.7%	5.5%	3.8%	4.0%	2.7%	2.7%
Avg. P/S	1.1	0.6	1.2	0.7	0.6	0.3	0.2	0.1	0.1

But Safeway's valuation caught up with Albertsons when the operating margins equalized in the mid-1990s. By 2000, Safeway and Albertsons had reversed positions with the market giving each dollar of Safeway's sales almost four times the value of a dollar of Albertsons' sales. Not coincidently, by that time, Safeway's operating margins were 50 percent higher than Albertsons'.

Safeway's and Albertsons' valuations reversed because the market's perceptions of winners versus losers reversed, at least partly based on profit margins. You can capitalize on the market's propensity to value winners so much higher than also-rans. Here's an example.

Suppose a company in an industry with 7 percent average net profit margins (net income divided by sales) is underperforming its peers:

Sales	$1000
Net Profit Margin	3%
Net Income	30

To keep it simple, assume that the company has only one share of stock outstanding. Further assume that this firm's P/E ratio is only 10, compared to the industry's average 20 P/E. The low P/E assumption is realistic because the company's subpar margins would have labeled it a loser, hammering its stock price.

If you do the algebra, you'll see that a company's stock price is equal to its P/E multiplied by its earnings per share.

$P = P/E \times EPS$

In this example, I've stipulated that the P/E is 10, and EPS is 30, so the share price is $300:

$P = P/E \times EPS = 10 \times 30 = 300$

Now suppose a year goes by and the company reports that its sales have gained 25 percent, and even better, its net profit margin recovered to 5 percent, still low, but closer to the 7 percent industry average. So you have:

Sales	$1250
Net Profit Margin	5%
Net Income	62.50

The net income more than doubled, even though sales increased only 25 percent, thanks to the higher profit margin.

But that's not the whole story. The market likes the higher profit margin and sensing that it will be even better next year, rewards the company's stock with a 15 P/E. So the stock price goes up to $937.50:

$$P = P/E \ x \ EPS = 15 \ x \ 62.50 = \$937.50$$

Bottom line: a 25 percent sales increase combined with an improving profit margin tripled the share price.

Analyzing Overhead Expenses

Sales, general and administrative (SG&A) is a catch-all category that includes most of a firm's operating expenses except for cost of sales, research and development, and depreciation and amortization. SG&A expenses are, in effect, overhead.

Sometimes companies list marketing expenses on a separate line from other SG&A expenses on the income statement. Consider all operating expenses except cost of sales, research and development, and depreciation/amortization charges as SG&A for this analysis.

The lower the SG&A, the tighter the ship that management is running. Comparing competitors' SG&A expenses can give you important insight into each company's operations. The best way to compare SG&A between companies is to divide the total SG&A by sales:

SG&A % sales = SG&A/total sales

For instance, in 1999, Bed Bath & Beyond's SG&A totaled 30 percent of sales compared to Linens' 34 percent. How significant is that 4 percent difference? Linens' sales totaled $1,300 million in 1999. So a 4 percent reduction in costs would have amounted to $52 million. Linens' 1999 pretax income totaled $85 million. So saving that 4 percent would have increased pretax income by 61 percent. I'd say that's significant.

Observing trends in SG&A percentage of sales may also be useful for detecting operational problems within a company. However, out-of-control SG&A expenses will likely also be reflected in deteriorating operating margins.

Profitability Ratios

Legendary investor Warren Buffet is often quoted as advising investors to analyze purchasing a company's shares as if you were buying the whole company.

One of the items you'd probably evaluate if you were actually buying a company is your return on investment.

return on investment = annual profits/total investment

For instance, your return on investment is 10 percent if you bought a company with a $100,000 cash investment and you made $10,000 in profits annually (10,000/100,000).

Return on Equity

ROE measures a company's returns on its shareholders' investments in the same manner. ROE is a company's annual net income divided by its shareholders equity.

ROE = net income/shareholder's equity

ROE is widely reported, and many money managers rely on it as a key gauge of a company's profitability. In fact, many that I interviewed for this book would not consider buying a company with less than a 15 percent ROE.

In the example, I suggested a situation where a $100,000 investment (equity) yields a $10,000, or 10 percent annual return on your equity. Let's postulate that you could earn a 10 percent return on any additional cash you put into the business. Further assume that you are willing to invest your profits into growing the business, but you're not willing to put in additional cash or borrow more money.

Based on those assumptions, you'd invest your first year's 10 percent return ($10,000) on your equity back into the business, so the second year, the company would earn 10 percent on $110,000 equity, 10 percent more than the first year's $100,000 equity, and so on.

Your 10 percent return on equity defined the maximum annual growth that your company can achieve given the assumptions. In the same way, ROE determines the maximum achievable growth for a corporation, making similar assumptions. That is, that the company doesn't raise additional cash by borrowing or selling more stock, and that its profit margins remain constant.

Suppose in my hypothetical example that you had decided that you'd take $1,000 out of the business annually, but reinvest the balance of the profits in the business. In that instance, your $1,000 dividend would have to be subtracted from your ROE to determine the future growth. The term implied growth defines a corporation's maximum achievable growth accounting for dividends paid out by the firm.

implied growth = (net income − dividends)/shareholders' equity

Implied growth is the same as ROE if a company doesn't pay dividends.

Assuming that it doesn't raise additional cash, and profit margins remain constant, a non-dividend-paying firm's ROE defines its maximum growth rate. Applying numbers to the equation, a 15 percent ROE firm that doesn't pay dividends is limited to 15 percent long-term annual earnings growth, and less if it does pay a dividend.

Of course, companies often do raise additional funds through borrowings or stock sales, and profit margins often do increase over time, especially for newer companies. But stockholders are usually better off if a company doesn't have to resort to those measures to grow. Here's why:

Selling additional stock dilutes per-share profits. For instance, a company with one million shares outstanding, and $1 million net income earns $1 per share. However, its EPS drops to $0.67 if the company makes the same profit after selling another 500,000 shares.

The math works much the same if the firm borrows instead of selling shares. For example, say the same company had borrowed

$1 million at 8 percent interest a year earlier. In that instance, it would earn $920,000 ($1 million less $80,000 interest), bringing its EPS down to $0.92.

Despite this sensible reasoning, using ROE to evaluate a company's profitability has practical limitations.

Recall that ROE is calculated by dividing net income by shareholders' equity. Book value is another way of expressing shareholder's equity. Book value is shareholder's equity per share; that is, equity divided by shares outstanding.

The problem lies in the equity or book value calculation. From the name, you might conclude that book value represents the value of the company's hard assets, give or take asset depreciation or appreciation. There is such a balance sheet figure—total assets—but it's not the same as equity or book value.

According to accounting rules, the left-side assets column total must equal the right-side liabilities column total. Normally assets exceed liabilities, so shareholder's equity is added to the liabilities column to make them equal, giving you the basic accounting equation:

assets = total liabilities + shareholder's equity

or

shareholders' equity = assets – liabilities

Here's how it works. Say a firm has current assets such as cash and inventories totaling $1,000 and long-term assets such as plants and equipment adding up $2,000. The assets portion of the balance sheet would look like:

ASSETS

Current Assets	1000
Long-term Assets	2000
Total Assets	3000

Here's how the liabilities would be shown if the company owed $800 for accounts payable and other short-term debts and $300 for a long-term loan.

LIABILITIES

Current Liabilities	800
Long-term Liabilities	300
Total Liabilities	1100

The assets exceed the liabilities by $1,900, so that's the shareholders' equity. So the complete balance sheet is:

ASSETS

Current Assets	1000
Long-term Assets	2000
Total Assets	3000

LIABILITIES

Current Liabilities	800
Long-term Liabilities	300
Total Liabilities	1100
Shareholders' Equity	1900

If the company earned $250 last year, its ROE is 13 percent:

ROE = net income/shareholders equity = 250/1,900 = 13%

Now consider another company with a similar balance sheet except that its long-term debt totals $1,500 instead of $300.

ASSETS

Total Assets	3000

LIABILITIES

Current Liabilities	800
Long-term Liabilities	1500
Total Liabilities	2300
Shareholders' Equity	700

If the second company earned the same $250 as the first company, its ROE would be 36 percent instead of 13 percent:

ROE = net income/shareholders equity = 250/700 = 36%

All other factors being the same, the company with the most debt has the highest ROE.

For real examples, Table 11-13 compares Church & Dwight, the maker of Arm & Hammer sodium bicarbonate-based products, to communications products supplier Andrew Corporation.

TABLE 11-13   ROE calculation for Andrew vs. Church & Dwight.

Andrew (FY 9/01)	
Sales	$1.05 billion
Net Income	$61.7 million
ROE	10%
Church & Dwight (FY 12/01)	
Sales	$1.08 billion
Net Income	$50.9 million
ROE	18%

Both firms reported nearly the same sales total, but Andrew reported more than 20 percent higher income. Yet investors insisting on a 15 percent minimum ROE would reject Andrew in favor of Church & Dwight. Why? Debt! Andrew's liabilities totaled only $257 million, less than half of Church & Dwight's $667 million total.

Since other things being equal, most investors prefer a low debt company to a heavy borrower, it's clear that the ROE formula treats debt backward. It penalizes efficiently run firms that grow without borrowing and rewards companies that are hooked on debt. In fact, if a company pays down its debt, its ROE goes down—not up!

A CHECK ON ROE

Some very smart money managers believe that ROE is the best profitability measure. If you fall into that camp, you can overcome the downside of ROE regarding debt by comparing the growth in book value to ROE. That is, if management is properly reinvesting ROE, the firm's book value (shareholders equity) should be increasing at the same rate as the ROE.

Return on Capital

The return on capital (a.k.a. return on invested capital) formula takes a stab at correcting for the debt anomaly by adding long-term debt to the equity figure in the ROE equation.

return on capital = net income/(shareholders' equity + long-term debt)

Table 11-14 shows that applying the ROC formula to the Andrew and Church & Dwight analysis paints a different picture than using ROE.

TABLE 11-14   Return on capital for Andrew vs. Church & Dwight.

	ROC
Andrew	7.9%
Church & Dwight	7.4%

The ROC formula makes a big difference, but it doesn't completely solve the problem. ROC works when firms follow the intent, rather than the letter, of accounting rules:

1. They confine items listed as short-term liabilities to accounts payable, income taxes payable, and so forth.
2. They list all of their long-term debts on the balance sheet line labeled "long-term debt."

That doesn't always happen. Some firms have replaced long-term debt with continuously renewed short-term instruments, and list them on the balance sheet as short-term debt. Some list long-term obligations as other long-term liabilities instead of as long-term debt.

Bottom line: debt is debt, wherever it's listed. Barring outright fraud, all debt will be listed as a liability somewhere on the balance sheet. It's easier to count everything instead of trying to outguess the company's accountants.

Return on Assets

Let's take another look at the basic accounting equation:

total assets = total liabilities + shareholders' equity

Total liabilities is just what is says: everything that the company says it owes, regardless of where it appears on the balance sheet. The point of using an ROE-type formula is to measure a company's profitability by comparing its net income to its assets. The return on assets formula (ROA) does just that; it divides net income by total assets, which includes shareholder's equity plus all borrowings.

return on assets = net income/total assets

Table 11-15 shows that considering all debt, Andrew is more profitable than Church & Dwight.

TABLE 11-15   Return on assets for Andrew vs. Church & Dwight.

	ROA
Andrew	7.2%
Church & Dwight	5.4%

Church & Dwight had listed $64 million of long-term debt as other liabilities, a figure not picked up by the ROC formula. What's included in the $64 million? Deferred (still owed) income taxes, postretirement benefits, and other unspecified long-term liabilities. ROA measures a company's profits compared to its entire investment.

Another advantage of using ROA to gauge profitability over ROE and ROC is its stability. Also, ROA can be calculated for companies with negative shareholder's equity, a condition where liabilities exceed assets. For instance, Table 11-16 compares the three profitability ratios for Safeway.

Safeway's historical ROE ratios indicate a declining profitability trend. In fact, Safeway's ROE declined because it paid down debt. Safeway's ROA history shows that its profitability improved in the early 1990s, and then stabilized.

ROA is useful for analyzing competing companies in the same industry. For instance, Table 11-17 compares Albertsons', Kroger's, and Safeway's ROA.

TABLE 11-16   Safeway's fiscal year end profitability ratios. (%)

Fiscal Year	ROE	ROC	ROA
12/00	20	10	7
12/99	24	9	7
12/98	26	10	7
12/97	29	12	7
12/96	39	16	8
12/95	41	12	6
12/94	39	9	5
12/93	32	4	2
12/91	37	3	2
12/90	neg.	3	2

TABLE 11-17   Historical return on assets (ROA) for major grocery chains (%).

	'00	'99	'98	'97	'96	'95	'94	'93	'92	'91
Albertson's	5	3	5	15	11	11	12	10	10	12
Kroger	5	4	3	9	6	6	6	4	2	3
Safeway	7	7	7	7	8	6	5	2	2	2

Albertsons was the profit king until its ill-fated 1998 acquisition of American Stores. Safeway was taken public in 1990 after an earlier leveraged buyout. Safeway's low ratios in the early 1990s reflect the debt that the company was saddled with after its IPO.

Besides for comparing competitive firms, ROA is useful for gauging the profitability of a company on an absolute basis. High ROA firms are more profitable than low ROA firms and the implied growth limitation described in the ROE section applies to ROA as well. High ROA firms can grow faster than low ROA firms without borrowing or selling additional shares to raise capital.

What's a satisfactory return on assets? I ran a screen in early 2002 that listed the five-year average annual ROA for all companies that met the following requirements:

1. The companies were not in the utility, mining, real estate or oil exploration or oil-production industries. I excluded these because many firms in these industries report unusually high ROAs.

2. The market capitalization had to be greater than $500 million, the share price over $5, the trailing twelve months' sales over $80 million and the after-tax TTM net income greater than $1 million. These requirements screened out very small companies, or companies without significant sales or earnings.

Only 1,339 companies passed those tests. Of the survivors, 543 reported five-year average ROAs of 7 percent or higher, 305 had ROAs of 10 percent or more, and only 144 showed 15 percent or higher ROAs.

Because ROA takes liabilities into account, and ROE doesn't, a company's ROE will always be higher than its ROA. The amount of debt and other liabilities determines the difference. Of the 1,339 companies checked, 616 sported ROEs of 15 percent or higher, and 338 reported ROEs of at least 20 percent.

Most money managers that I interviewed for this book said that they required minimum 15 percent ROEs. You'd have to accept ROAs of less than 7 percent to choose from an equal size universe.

Based on preliminary research, 7 percent ROA is acceptable, but 10 percent is desirable, and higher is better.

Marginal Return on Assets

Profitability margins reflect the returns on a company's total investments without regard to the investment date. Some money managers gain insight by measuring the returns on the most recent investments. They do that by computing marginal return on equity, capital, or assets.

TABLE 11-18   Marginal ROA for Safeway.

Year	Marginal ROA (%)
2000	5
1999	-8
1998	0
1997	-10
1996	27
1995	30
1994	100
1993	10
1992	20
1991	-23

You can calculate the marginal return on assets by dividing the change in net income by the change in asset value over the period. To calculate the marginal ROA for the past year, calculate the year-over-year change in net income and divide it by the asset growth over the year. Despite the logic, I found the results too volatile to be of value, as Table 11-18, showing Safeway's marginal ROA return history illustrates.

Table 11-18 illustrates, that at least for Safeway, you would have drawn drastically different conclusions from the marginal ROA data, depending on the year.

Cash Flow Analysis

Cash flow is easy to understand. If you had $5,000 in your bank account on January 1, and only $1,000 on December 31, your cash flow for the year was a negative $4,000, regardless of how much income you reported to the IRS. Corporate accounting follows the same rules; only the numbers are bigger.

Interestingly, companies have been required to include cash flow statements with their financial reports only since 1987.

Accountants construct the cash flow statement by starting with reported earnings and then adding back noncash items that were subtracted from earnings to figure income, but did not actually result in cash moving out of the firm's bank accounts.

Expenses such as depreciation and amortization, for example, represent a reduction in the book value of capital equipment and other assets, but require no actual cash outlays.

Working Capital Changes

Another operating cash flow category, changes in working capital, represents real cash outflows and inflows that are not reported on the income statement.

For instance, cash used to buy raw materials isn't charged against income until the goods are incorporated into finished products and sold. The net change in cost of *inventories* during the reporting period *subtract* from cash flow because the monies were spent, but not deducted from reported income.

Accounts receivables, the money owed the company by its customers, is recorded as income when it's billed, usually long before the actual cash is received from the customer. Since the company doesn't really have the cash, net increases in accounts *receivables subtract* from operating cash flow.

Accounts payables are monies owed to suppliers and service providers. Those charges are deducted from income when the company is billed (or the items are billable), not when it's actually paid. Since the firm didn't pay out the cash, increases in accounts *payables* (unpaid bills) add to the firm's bank balance, and thus, *add* to operating cash flow.

Cash Tells the Story

While corporations can do all sorts of things to manipulate their reported earnings, outside of outright fraud, there's little they can do to fudge their bank balances.

Lucent Technologies reported making $4.8 billion net income in its September 1999 fiscal year, but even after adding back $1.3 billion in noncash depreciation and amortization charges, its bank balances actually shrunk by $1.8 billion during the year. What accounted for the discrepancies? Ballooning accounts receivables and inventories together sopped up $4.8 billion, and other unspecified changes in operating assets and liabilities accounted for a cool $2.3 billion cash drain. Investors had seven months after Lucent released that report to react before Lucent began its dive from its $60 July 2001 trading range down to $7 by year's end.

ACT Manufacturing provides an even more flagrant example. The contract manufacturer reported $6.2 million net income in 1999, but it actually lost $49 million in real cash. What did it do with the money? Again, bulging accounts receivables and inventories were the main culprit, absorbing $133 million of the hard-pressed firm's cash. It was even worse in 2000 when ACT reported $29 million net income but lost $62 million when you counted the cash. Obviously they couldn't continue at that rate, and ACT filed bankruptcy in 2001.

Creative executives have some room to fudge the operating cash flow numbers, but all inflows and outflows have to show up somewhere on the cash flow statement. Otherwise the cash flow total won't balance to the bank account totals.

Because the cash flow statement must balance to real cash, savvy investors pay more attention to cash flows than to reported net income. The cash flow statement consists of three sections: operating, investing, and financing activities.

- Operating cash flow, in theory, includes all items related to operating the firm's main business.

- Investing cash flows are supposed to be restricted to capital expenditures and other investments.

- Financing activities theoretically include cash flows from stock sales or buybacks, and changes in debt levels.

However accounting rules require that certain items end up in funny places on the cash flow statement, as you'll see in the next section.

Dubious Allocations

Deferred taxes, that is, income taxes that were deducted from income but not actually paid, logically a financing item, are added to operating cash flow.

Accounting rules give companies the option of capitalizing most software development expenses. The capitalized software development costs are treated similarly to capital expenses, that is, they are depreciated over time rather than being charged against income in the year the money was spent. Since some firms capitalize software development and others don't, software development cash flows listed in the investing section should be deducted from operating cash flow, when you're comparing different companies' operating cash flows.

At this writing, companies that pay their employees with stock options in lieu of higher salaries are not required to deduct the cost of those options as expenses on the income statement. But the firm does get to deduct the entire cost from its income tax bill, and that credit adds to the operating cash flow. It's possible that the rules regarding treatment of employee stock option expenses will have been changed by the time that you read this. But currently, the stock option credit can substantially inflate the reported cash flow. For example, Cisco System's reported $6.1 billion operating cash flow on its July 2000 fiscal year cash flow statement. But of that total, $2.5 billion, or 41 percent, came from employee stock option related income tax benefits.

You'll have to refer to each company's original SEC filed cash flow statement to find employee stock option related credits to operating cash flow. Most Web sites don't show it as a separate line item on their financial statements, instead including in a catch-all "other operating" category.

Using Operating Cash Flow

Operating cash flow offers a better picture of a company's profitability than reported earnings. In most instances, the dubious allocations mentioned earlier will not significantly affect your analysis.

However, it's best to use SEC Info or a similar site to download detailed cash flow statements if you do want to perform a thorough analysis and check for dubious items. Subtract dubious items, such as deferred income taxes, employee stock option benefits, and others that you may discover from the reported operating cash flow, before performing your analysis.

Several academic studies found that stocks of companies with positive operating cash flow outperform those with negative cash flow. However, negative operating cash flow doesn't always signal problems. Small, fast growing firms often absorb lots of cash to finance burgeoning, but necessary, inventories and receivables. However, slower growers, say firms growing sales less than 30 percent annually, should be generating positive operating cash flow. Mature companies, those growing sales in the 10 percent to 20 percent range, should be generating large operating cash flows. Many investors consider positive operating cash flow a prerequisite for considering a stock.

How much operating cash flow (OCF) is enough? Table 11-19 shows a few examples of strong cash flow generators.

Recent academic research found that observing the relationship between operating cash flow and net income can help pinpoint stocks with potential earnings quality issues. Normally, operating cash flow should exceed net income because noncash depreciation and amortization charges that were deducted from net income are added back to operating cash flow. Operating cash flow less than net income signals possible inflated accounts receivables or inventory levels, both indicators of potential future earnings disappointments. Rising net income accompanied by declining operating cash flow was found to be the most dangerous signal. This subject is covered in detail in Chapter 12.

Still, OCF doesn't tell the whole story. Depreciation accounts for the aging of previous capital expenditures. The OCF formula adds back the depreciation deducted from net income, but doesn't account for new capital spending.

TABLE 11-19   Operating cash flow examples.

Company	Fiscal Year	OCF (in millions)	% of Sales
Bed, Bath, and Beyond	3/01	$198	8
Dell	2/01	$4200	13
Safeway	12/00	$1901	6
Starbucks	9/01	$461	17
Wal-Mart	1/01	$9600	5

Free Cash Flow

Free cash flow is the cash left over after accounting for capital spending on plants and equipment, software development, and similar items. Despite its wide use, free cash flow is not shown on cash flow statements; you have to calculate it.

free cash flow = operating cash flow – capital spending

For this analysis, capital spending includes the capital spending line item plus all of its variants including capitalized software expenses, cost of acquisitions, and so forth.

Free cash flow is the bottom line for many investors, and some want to see large positive numbers in that category. However, many firms spend almost all of their free cash flow expanding their businesses. Table 11-20 lists the free cash flow for the same companies listed in Table 11-19.

Of those listed, Dell is the only firm that didn't allocate most of its operating cash profits to expanding its business. You'll often see firms go in the hole occasionally in terms of free cash flow. That shouldn't influence your analysis unless it becomes a habit.

Is it difficult to combine positive cash flows and fast growth? Yes, but not impossible. Table 11-21 lists a sampling of recent fast growers reporting positive operating cash flow.

Penn National's free cash flow shortfall was due to a $203 million payout for an acquisition.

The table illustrates that it is possible to find fast growers that still mange to produce not only positive operating cash flow, but positive free cash flow as well.

TABLE 11-20   Free cash flow examples.

Company	Fiscal Year	OCF (in millions)	Free Cash Flow (in millions)
Bed, Bath, and Beyond	3/01	$198	$58
Dell	2/01	$4200	$3713
Safeway	12/00	$1901	$488
Starbucks	9/01	$461	$77
Wal-Mart	1/01	$9600	$935

Cash burners have to regularly raise more cash, either by selling stock or borrowing. Either alternative diminishes existing shareholders' earnings. Positive cash flow is how small companies become large. There are more than 9,000 stocks trading on U.S. exchanges. Why not put the wind at your back and require positive operating cash flow at a minimum, and at least close to breakeven free cash flow?

That said, sometimes fast growers temporarily burn cash for justifiable reasons, such as to build a new plant, or acquire a needed technology. The management discussion in a firm's SEC reports should explain why cash is flowing out rather than in.

TABLE 11-21   Fast-growing companies reporting positive operating cash flow.

Company	Fiscal Year	Revenue Growth (%)	OCF (in millions)	Free Cash Flow (in millions)
Chico's FAS	2/01	67	$39	-$1
Christopher & Banks	3/01	60	$27	$10
Escalade	12/00	35	$12	$10
Nvidia	1/01	96	$68	$32
Penn National Gaming	12/00	72	$42	-$188

Quarterly Cash Flow Reports

Unlike income statements that show each quarter's results separately, cash flow statements show only year-to-date numbers. So the second quarter's cash flow statement shows the combined first and second quarter totals, and the third quarter's statement shows the totals for the first three quarters, and so on.

The only way to see the third quarter results is to subtract the second quarter year-to-date figures from the third quarter totals. That's a pain, but it is doable using sites such as MSN Money or Reuters that show the five most recent quarter's data side by side. It's much harder using the company's SEC reports, because the cash flow statements in those reports do not show the previous quarter's year-to-date totals.

EBITDA vs. Operating Cash Flow

EBITDA stands for earnings before interest, taxes, depreciation and amortization. EBITDA offers an alternative to operating cash flow for evaluating a company's performance. EBITDA is similar in purpose to OCF in that it attempts to describe the actual cash generated by a company's main business, but it is calculated differently.

Where the OCF calculation starts with net income, the EBITDA calculation starts with operating income, which is also described as EBIT, earnings before interest and taxes. EBITDA is calculated by adding back depreciation and amortization expenses to operating income.

EBITDA is not defined by generally accepted accounting practices (GAAP), and it is not listed on most financial statements. In fact, MSN Money is the only site I've found that displays EBITDA as a separate line item on its income statements.

Calculating EBITDA is not difficult because operating income (EBIT) is listed on most income statements. You can compute EBITDA by adding depreciation and amortization charges to operating income.

EBITDA = operating income (EBIT) + depreciation + amortization

Depreciation and amortization charges are listed on the cash flow statement, on the income statement, or both.

Many companies report a figure that they call EBITDA in their earnings report press releases. However, since EBITDA isn't an officially defined term, they often change the definition to make their numbers look better. If you want to use EBITDA, ignore the press release figure and look it up on MSN Money or calculate it yourself.

EBITDA does not account for changes in working capital, as does operating cash flow. That's both a disadvantage and an advantage.

Recall that comparing operating cash flow to net income helps to identify potential earnings quality issues, namely abnormal increases in accounts receivable and inventory levels. So using EBITDA in place of operating cash flows requires that you do the math and compare accounts receivables and inventory levels to sales to warn of earnings quality issues as described in Chapter 12.

Some analysts ignore working capital changes believing that receivables and inventories often change in response to short-term market conditions, but end up pretty much where they started in the long run. For them, EBITDA is a better measure than operating cash flow.

A major advantage of using EBITDA is that it isn't inflated with dubious entries such as deferred income taxes and employee stock option income tax benefits. Watching EBITDA instead of operating cash flow also avoids being misled by unusual working capital changes.

Dell Computer provides a good example of how EBITDA can give you a better reading than cash flow. Table 11-22 shows Dell's EBITDA and operating cash flows for its February 1999 and February 2000 fiscal years.

Dell Computer's OCF increased $1,490 million in fiscal year 2000, while EBITDA rose only $270 million. What accounted for the difference?

TABLE 11-22   Comparison of Dell Computer's EBITDA vs. operating cash flow.

Fiscal Year	EBITDA (in millions)	Operating Cash Flow (in millions)
2/99	$2149	$2436
2/00	$2419	$3926

TABLE 11-23   Dell Computer's changes in working capital between FY 1999 and FY 2000.

Inventory	+ $118 million
Accounts Receivable	+ $514 million
Accounts Payable	+ $1.14 billion
Change in Working Capital	+ $509 million

Table 11-23 lists the changes in Dell's working capital accounts between FY 1999 and FY 2000.

Dell increased its accounts payable account, the money owed to suppliers, by $1.1 billion in the year. Recalling the math, increases in accounts payables add to working capital while additions to inventory levels and accounts receivables subtract. By taking longer to pay its suppliers, Dell was able to report a $509 million increase in operating cash flow based solely on changes in its working capital.

Table 11-24 shows that dubious OCF entries accounted for another $790 million or so of Dell's operating cash flow increases in FY 2000 compared to 1999.

Many pundits pooh-pooh EBITDA as a self-serving standard devised by company executives to improve the appearance of their operating results. You be the judge.

TABLE 11-24   Dell's FY 2000 dubious operating cash flow entries.

Employee Stock Option Tax Benefit	$596 million
Purchased R & D	$194 million

Free EBITDA

Just as subtracting capital expenditures from operating cash flow gives you free cash flow, you can calculate the EBTIDA equivalent of free cash flow; call it free EBITDA, by subtracting capital expenditures from EBITDA:

free EBITDA = EBITDA − capital spending

Since using EBITDA in place of operating cash flow smoothes out the volatility caused by dubious operating cash flow entries and by short-term working capital changes, free EBITDA should give a better picture of a firm's cash flow after accounting for capital expenses than the traditional free cash flow measure.

As an example, Table 11-25 compares Chico's fiscal year free EBITDA and free cash flow numbers over recent years.

Although both figures increased over the years, Chico's free EBITDA reflected a steadier growth path. Chico's relatively weak 2001/ 2002 free cash flow probably reflects inventory buildups to support store expansions.

TABLE 11-25   Comparison of free EBITDA vs. free cash flow for Chico's.

Year	Free EBITDA (in millions)	Free Cash Flow (in millions)
1997	$1.3	$0.3
1998	$4.3	$1.6
1999	$12.2	$7.2
2000	$13.3	$0.8
2001	$11.4	-$1.3
2002	$41.1	$28.0
2003	$58.9	$44.1
2004	$131.4	$93.1
2005	$168.5	$130.6

Summary

Sales growth, operating margins, profitability ratios, and cash flows all figure into the profitability equation. Many of the analysis tools described in this chapter can serve a dual purpose: (1) determine a company's absolute profitability, and (2) help pinpoint the most profitable players in a market sector. Analyzing an investing candidate's profitability is something that professionals almost always do, but it is something individual investors often overlook.

12

ANALYSIS TOOL #9:
DETECTING RED FLAGS

Stock prices, in the end, reflect the markets' earnings growth expectations for the underlying company, and all goes well as long as the firm continues to meet or beat expectations. But company executives face an impossible task. It's mathematically impossible to maintain early-stage growth rates after sales reach a certain level. For example, Table 12-1 shows year-over-year sales growth rates for some recent super-growers.

TABLE 12-1   Year-over-year sales growth for recent high flyers (%).

Company	2001	2000	1999	1998	1997
Amazon.com	13	68	169	312	825
eBay	74	92	161	108	
Priceline.com	-5	156	1300		

The funny part is, regardless of whether it is a single company or an entire industry experiencing super-fast growth, everybody involved, especially company executives and the analysts covering their stocks, believes that the fast growth will continue for the foreseeable future. In fact, company executives envision even higher growth in future quarters, and the analysts happily go along.

However, the law of gravity still applies, and as time goes on, meeting earnings forecasts becomes harder as company executives struggle to maintain growth. Ultimately it ends. The company reduces guidance and/or misses earnings forecasts, and everything, especially the stock price, comes crashing down.

Occasionally these disasters appear out of the blue, and there wasn't any way to see them coming. But by and large, that is not the case. There is usually more than one signal that, had they been noticed, would have warned shareholders of the forthcoming disaster.

Chapter 4 showed you how to detect clues to disaster embedded in analysts' earnings forecasts. Here, you'll learn how to detect the disaster clues embedded in financial statements. This analysis focuses on two issues: slowing sales growth and creative accounting that management employs to mask slowing growth. I call the clues found by this analysis red flags because they warn of earnings shortfalls that could come as soon as the next earnings report, or even earlier in the form of reduced guidance from company management.

You can detect the red flags warning of future disasters by analyzing:

- Sales growth trends

- Accounts receivable and inventory levels

- Pension plan income

You'll also learn how to detect yellow flags, that is, conditions pointing to potential shortfalls that are of a less urgent nature. You'll find them by evaluating:

- Capital expenditures

- Income tax rates

Sales Growth Trends

Although mentioned before, it's worth repeating that while the market prices stocks based on earnings expectations—earnings come from sales. That's important because a slowdown in sales growth often precedes an earnings disappointment.

Zoll Medical provides a good example. Zoll makes defibrillators, devices used to resuscitate heart attack victims. Table 12-2 shows Zoll's sales and earnings from 1998 through 2000, as displayed on Reuters Investor's Highlights report.

It's best to compare Zoll's sales or earnings to the same year-ago quarter, rather than to the previous quarter to eliminate seasonal variations. For instance, compare the December 2000 quarter results to December 1999, not to September 2000.

The numbers show that Zoll was reporting reasonably consistent earnings growth. However, you see a different story when you compute the year-over-year growth percentages (Table 12-3).

TABLE 12-2   Reuters reports quarterly sales and earnings data for Zoll Medical.

Quarter	1998	1999	2000
Quarterly sales (in millions)			
March	13.6	17.9	25.7
June	12.9	20.8	27.4
September	16.2	23.9	28.8
December	16.1	24.4	28.6
Quarterly EPS			
March	0.05	0.14	0.23
June	-0.13	0.22	0.28
September	0.06	0.32	0.34
December	0.10	0.19	0.26

TABLE 12-3   Zoll Medical year-over-year quarterly sales and earnings growth percentages.

Quarter	1999	2000
Quarterly year-over-year sales growth (%)		
March	32	43
June	62	32
September	47	21
December	52	17
Quarterly year-over-year earnings growth (%)		
March	180	64
June	nm	27
September	433	6
December	90	37

Zoll's March through September 1999 quarter's earnings growth figures reflect that Zoll reported little or no earnings in the corresponding 1998 quarters. However starting with December 1999, its numbers generally reflect reasonably solid earnings growth.

But the sales growth figures tell a different story. Zoll's March 2000 quarter's 43 percent sales growth exceeded March 1999's growth rate. But June shows the opposite picture. The June 2000 quarter's sales growth was about half the June 1999 growth rate. That trend accelerated in Zoll's September 2000 quarter, and December's growth was far below the year-ago growth rate.

You wouldn't have seen the slowdown by looking at earnings. Zoll's December 2000 earnings still showed strong growth.

Slowing year-over-year sales growth is a red flag, especially when earnings growth doesn't reflect the same trend. Revenue growth tends to move in steadier and smoother trends than earnings growth, and a slowdown in sales growth warns of a coming earnings shortfall.

Table 12-4 shows the year-over-year growth figures again, only this time with the March 2001 quarter's results added.

TABLE 12-4 Zoll Medical year-over-year quarterly sales and earnings growth percentages including March 2001.

Quarter	1999	2000	2001
Quarterly year-over-year sales growth (%)			
March	32	43	-2
June	62	32	
September	47	21	
December	52	17	
Quarterly year-over-year earnings growth (%)			
March	180	64	-65
June	nm	27	
September	433	6	
December	90	37	

The sales growth decline continued with March sales coming in slightly below year-ago, but March earnings took a much larger hit, and the share price dropped accordingly.

Sales growth naturally varies somewhat from quarter to quarter, so don't be alarmed at relatively small changes. It usually takes a slowdown approaching 50 percent (e.g., from 80 percent to 40 percent) to qualify as a red flag. The 50 percent guideline applies to the latest growth rate compared to the year-ago number. The absolute value of the growth rate doesn't matter. For instance a drop from 30 percent to 15 percent is just as significant as a drop from 200 percent to 100 percent.

It's natural to accept a drop from, say, 150 percent to 75 percent as understandable because everybody recognizes that 150 percent growth is unsustainable. Besides, 75 percent year-over-year growth is plenty. That's all true, but it doesn't matter—the sales growth slowdown still signals a forthcoming earnings disappointment.

Yahoo's recent addition of revenue forecasts to its Analyst Estimate report makes sales growth analysis even more powerful.

TABLE 12-5   Scientific Atlanta's year-over-year historical
quarterly sales and earnings growth percentages.

Quarter	1999	2000	2001
Quarterly year-over-year sales growth (%)			
March	11	38	51
June	17	56	
September	36	71	
December	20	69	
Quarterly year-over-year earnings growth (%)			
March	18	77	100
June	48	19	
September	63	332	
December	64	105	

Cable TV set-top box maker Scientific Atlanta provides a good
example. Table 12-5 shows its historical year-over-year growth figures
after the firm reported its March 2001 results.

Scientific Atlanta was showing monster year-over-year earnings
growth and strong sales growth, especially after reporting its March
2001 quarter results. There were no red flags in those numbers.

Table 12-6 shows Scientific Atlanta's year-over-year sales
growth data with its June and September 2001 analysts' consensus forecasts added.

There are those pesky red flags' again. The 24 percent sales
growth forecast for the June quarter was only half the year-earlier
growth rate, and September's forecast was much worse. Thanks to Yahoo, you get to see these red flags before disaster strikes. I originally did
this analysis in May 2001 when Scientific Atlanta's shares were trading
close to $60. By August, SA's shares were going for $21 after the company had reduced its earnings forecasts at least twice.

Ignore the next fiscal year's consensus sales forecast. I've found
that the further-out sales forecasts almost always change. In fact,

TABLE 12-6 Scientific Atlanta's historical year-over-year sales growth with June and September 2001 analysts consensus revenue forecasts.

Quarter	1999	2000	2001
Quarterly year-over-year sales growth (%)			
March	11	38	51
June	17	56	24 (est.)
September	36	71	17 (est.)
December	20	69	

analysts usually increase their next quarter's sales forecast if the company makes its current quarter numbers.

Apply the same limits to sales growth forecasts as for historical figures. That is, a 50 percent drop in forecast year-over-year growth (e.g., from 25% to 12%) is a red flag.

Accounts Receivables & Inventories

Analyzing accounts receivable and inventory levels is arguably the most widely used method for spotting red flags.

Accounts Receivables

Unlike when they sell to us, a company doesn't usually require payment in advance when it sells to another firm. Instead, it bills the customer and specifies a payment due date. Accounts receivables are the monies owed by customers for goods already shipped and billed. Normally, you'd expect the receivables total to more or less track sales. That is, if sales double, receivables should double also.

You can compare a company's accounts receivables to an earlier period, or even to a different company's receivables, by dividing the receivables by sales. You can use either the most recent quarter's sales, or the last four quarters' sales in the denominator. The result is usually expressed as a percentage; e.g., 45 percent of sales.

> ## *Days Sales Outstanding*
>
> *If you used four quarters' sales and multiplied the result by 365 instead of converting to percentage, you'd have Days Sales Outstanding (DSOs), a popular method for expressing receivables. For instance, assume receivables totaled $100, and the last four quarters totaled $500. Dividing 100 by 500 gives 0.2, and multiplying 0.2 by 365 gives you 73 DSOs. We'll stick with the percentage of sales format for our analyses.*

Every industry has its own payment customs, and you can't compare receivables percentages of companies serving different markets. Many corporations prefer to delay paying their bills for as long as they can because they view those unpaid bills as an interest-free loan. Often, companies within the same industry will exhibit differing receivables percentages due to differences in billing or collection procedures.

Accounts receivables should track sales. Something's amiss when receivables increase significantly faster than sales. It's a red flag when you detect that happening. Receivables analysis doesn't apply to retail stores or restaurants because they sell on a cash basis and they don't have significant receivables.

The reasons receivables can grow faster than sales include:

1. Accounts receivables department falling behind in billing or dunning customers
2. Unhappy customers are withholding payments
3. Channel stuffing
4. Customers cannot pay their bills

In general, the latter two reasons are the more serious, and those are the only two that we will describe in detail. But all we'll be able to determine from this analysis is that a receivables problem exists, not the cause.

CHANNEL STUFFING

Channel stuffing occurs when a company realizes that it will not meet its sales goals by following its normal practices. At that point, the company devises incentives to spur sales. One approach is to offer customers better terms. For example, it could offer them six months to pay instead of the usual 60 days. If that doesn't work, the company might offer customers even longer terms, and even better, allow them to return the goods with no penalty if, in the end, the customer decides that it doesn't need the product.

That's a deal that's hard to refuse. If accepted, the company ships the goods and the transaction appears on the income statement the same as any other sale, helping the firm meet its sales and earnings numbers for the quarter.

A more extreme example of channel stuffing involves shipping goods that customers didn't order or even recording nonexistent shipments.

CUSTOMERS CAN'T PAY

The telecommunication equipment industry's experiences in 2000 and 2001 illustrate a situation where customers wanted the products, but they couldn't pay for the goods.

In 1998 and 1999, a new breed of telephone companies appeared on the scene. They intended to compete with the entrenched Baby Bell incumbents, and thought that they could teach the old fogies a thing or two about the telephone business. By mid-2000, the young upstarts ran out of cash, and most eventually folded. That left equipment suppliers such as Lucent and Nortel stuck with receivables that would never be paid.

CALCULATE RECEIVABLES/SALES PERCENTAGE

Regardless of the cause, inflated receivables can be easily detected by comparing the most recent receivables/sales percentage to an earlier figure.

Start by dividing the accounts receivables (A/R) total from the most recent balance sheet by the last quarter's sales, or by the last four quarter's sales.

receivables percentage of sales = accounts receivables/total sales

Use the most recent quarter's sales unless there is an overriding reason to use 12 months' sales. For instance, a full year's sales might be the best choice for industries with strong seasonal variations, such as patio furniture. Using the last quarter's sales is easier, and that's what I usually do.

TABLE 12-7   Amkor Technology's March
quarter sales and accounts receivables.

	2000	1999
Sales	554,811	419,957
Receivables	195,871	120,754

Except in the healthcare field, accounts receivables typically run
between 40 percent and 80 percent of one quarter's sales, and a number
in excess of 100 percent is cause for concern by itself. Firms selling to
hospitals and other healthcare providers typically show receivables running as high as 150 percent of quarterly sales.

Always compare the current A/R to sales percentage to the year-
ago figure. There is no red flag if the current receivables percentage is
equal to, or less than the year-ago figure. Variations of 5 percent (e.g.,
52 vs. 50) or so are common and not a cause for concern. It's a red flag
if the current quarter's A/R to sales percentage exceeds the year-ago ratio by 20 percent (e.g., 60 vs. 50), and a potential red flag if the current
figure exceeds the year-ago number by 10 percent or higher.

Semiconductor chip fabricator Amkor Technology illustrates
the principle. Amkor released its March 2000 quarter results in May
when its shares were trading in the low $40 range. Amkor reported that
its March quarter sales gained 32 percent and its earnings per share increased 69 percent in March 2000 compared to March 1999.

Table 12-7 shows Amkor's March quarter sales and accounts receivables for 2000 compared to 1999.

Amkor's receivables had increased 62 percent year-over-year
compared to a 32 percent gain in sales. Table 12-8 shows Amkor's accounts receivables expressed as a percentage of sales.

TABLE 12-8   Amkor's March quarter
accounts receivables divided by sales.

	2000	1999
Rec'v/Sales	35.3%	28.8%

Amkor's receivables percentage of sales increased 23 percent (35.3 percent vs. 28.8 percent) in the year, triggering a red flag. In late June, Amkor's announcement that it wouldn't meet its June quarter forecasts took its share price down to the low $20s.

If the increase of A/R percentage of sales falls into the 10 percent to 20 percent gray area, compare the A/R percentage to the three previous quarters to get a better feel for the significance of the increase. It's not a red flag if the latest percentage falls within the range defined by the last four quarters.

The company will often discuss reasons for the increase in receivables in the management's discussion section of its SEC report. Also, the topic is often raised in the question-and-answer portion of the company's conference call with analysts following the earnings report. Management always presents a plausible reason for increasing receivables. One common excuse is that a new product line sells to a slower paying industry than existing products. I've found that it's usually a mistake to ignore a receivables red flag.

Inventory Analysis

INFLATED INVENTORIES EQUAL HIGHER PROFITS

Motivated management can manipulate inventory values to artificially boost reported earnings. You have to understand the gross profit calculation to see how that works. The formula for gross margin is:

$GM = gross\ profit/sales$

where

$gross\ profit = sales - cost\ of\ sales$

Assume that there's no labor involved in producing a product, only raw materials. Accountants don't calculate the cost of sales by adding up the cost of the raw materials used to build the products. Instead, they total the value of the inventory on hand at the beginning and at the end of the period. To keep it simple, assume that the firm didn't buy any raw materials during the period. Then:

$cost\ of\ sales = beginning\ inventory - ending\ inventory$

where beginning inventory is the total value of all inventories at the beginning of the quarter (or fiscal year), and the ending inventory is the value at the end of the period.

If the beginning inventory was $100 and the ending inventory was $50, the cost of sales would be:

cost of sales = $100 – $50 = $50

If the firm sold its products for $75, its gross profit is $25 (75-50). But if the ending inventory is $75 instead of $50:

cost of sales = $100 – $75 = $25

If the firm again sold its products for $75, its gross profit would now be $50 (75-25) instead of $25. You can see that increasing the value of the ending inventory figure on the books can be a tempting way of boosting profits.

INFLATED INVENTORIES CAN MEAN SLOWER SALES

Rising inventory levels (compared to sales) doesn't necessarily imply creative accounting. Inventory levels can increase simply because the company is producing more than its customers want to buy, causing finished products to pile up. If that were the case, you'd probably see slowing sales growth along with the higher inventory levels.

You can analyze inventories by comparing inventory levels to sales, exactly the same as described for accounts receivables.

Flash memory maker SanDisk provides an example. In October 2000, with its stock trading around $60, SanDisk reported its September quarter sales up 153 percent year-over-year, and that earnings more than tripled compared to September 1999.

Table 12-9 shows SanDisk's September quarter sales and inventories for 2000 compared to 1999, including the end-of-quarter inventory percentage of sales for each period.

SanDisk's inventory percentage of sales increased 31 percent (39.4/30.1) year-over-year, solidly in red flag territory. SanDisk's December quarter results fell short of expectations, and by February, SanDisk's shares were changing hands in mid-$20 territory.

Manufacturing company inventories are usually subdivided into three categories: raw materials, goods in process, and finished goods. A company may stock up on hard-to-get parts in times of shortages,

TABLE 12-9 SanDisk's September 2000 and September 1999 quarterly sales, inventory levels, and inventory expressed as a percentage of sales. Sales and inventories are in millions.

	2000	1999
Sales	170.8	67.5
Inventories	67.3	20.7
Inventory % Sales	39.4%	30.1%

inflating raw materials levels. If that's the case, it will probably be noted in the management's discussion. Most companies report just a single combined total for inventory, but you can often find a table showing the category breakdown in the SEC report. I rarely look for that data, relying instead on the management's discussion to point out reasons why I should ignore this red flag.

RETAIL STORES

Retail stores usually don't have significant accounts receivables. But inventory analysis is equally, if not more, important for retail stores than it is for industrials.

Regardless of whether a store sells clothing or hard goods, much of retail is about fad and fashion. Hot items come and go, and inventory levels increase when customers lose enthusiasm for the stores' wares. When measured as a percentage of sales, growing retail inventory levels often signal problems.

Most retail store sales are strongly seasonal. Retail store fiscal years typically end on January 31, and January quarter sales are usually double the next highest quarter. Retailers stock up on holiday merchandise prior to Thanksgiving, so the October quarter's ending inventory levels will always be the highest of the year.

Because retail sales are so strongly seasonal, it's logical to use TTM sales to iron out the seasonality factors. That works for looking at long-term trends and for comparing competitive chains. For instance, Table 12-10 compares Wal-Mart and Kmart over a 10-year period.

TABLE 12-10   End of fiscal year inventory percentage of TTM sales (%).

	1/01	1/00	1/99	1/98	1/97	1/96	1/95	1/94	1/93	1/92
Wal-Mart	11.3	12.2	12.7	14.2	15.2	17.1	17.1	18.0	16.8	16.8
Kmart	17.3	19.8	19.4	19.8	20.2	19.0	23.2	21.8	26.2	21.5

Wal-Mart has been the more efficient operator over the entire period, and had been steadily improving its inventory turns (sales divided by inventory) while Kmart was floundering. However, the table doesn't give you any indication that Kmart's performance was faltering. In fact, with its inventory percentage of sales at 17.3% in fiscal 2001, it looked as though Kmart was getting its act together.

Comparing inventory levels to quarterly sales makes it easier to spot trends. For example, Table 12-11 shows Kmart's inventory percentages of sales for the four quarters before the discount store filed bankruptcy in January 2002, along with the year-ago figures.

Table 12-12 shows the same data for Wal-Mart. Wal-Mart's performance faltered during the 2000 holiday season and by the end of its January 2001 quarter was stuck with inventory 22 percent above the year-ago figure, based on its percentage of January quarter sales. However, Wal-Mart quickly corrected, and outperformed for the balance of the year.

Kmart did the story in reverse. Its January 2001 quarter's inventory levels improved compared to the year-ago numbers, but Kmart's performance deteriorated from there.

Comparing inventory levels to quarterly sales gives better signals than using annual numbers, but you have to compare the results to the year-ago percentages, not to recent quarters.

TABLE 12-11   Kmart inventory compared to quarterly sales (%).

	10/01	7/01	4/01	1/01
Inv./Q Sales	104	92	103	55
Year-Ago Q	96	73	89	64

TABLE 12-12   Wal-Mart inventory compared to quarterly sales (%).

	10/01	7/01	4/01	1/01
Inventory/Q Sales	52	44	47	38
Year-Ago Q	55	46	49	31

Retail inventory levels generally run between 10 percent and 25 percent of annual sales. Retailers keep a tighter rein on inventory levels than manufacturing companies, so smaller changes constitute a danger signal or red flag. If you're using annual sales, a 5 percent increase warrants investigation, and 10 percent is a definite red flag. Double those tolerances when you use quarterly sales figures.

Statement of Cash Flows

Cash flow is the amount of actual cash that flowed in or out of a firm's bank accounts during the reporting period. Cash flow is a better gauge of a company's profitability than reported earnings because earnings reflect a myriad of arbitrary accounting decisions while cash flow reports the real change in bank balances.

Operating cash flow reports the cash generated or used by the company's basic operations. Free cash is operating cash flow minus capital expenditures. Companies can, and frequently do, report positive earnings when, in fact, they've lost money on a real cash basis.

Cash Flow Red Flags

Some companies, though cash flow positive on an annual basis, habitually burn cash during certain quarters. Therefore, it's best to look at trailing-twelve months cash flow rather than just the last quarter. Doing that requires some extra effort because the statement of cash flow shows year-to-date totals, rather than each quarter's results separately. So you have to subtract the previous quarter's totals to derive the latest quarter numbers. If you don't want to do the math, Morningstar displays the TTM operating and free cash flow totals in its Financials section.

Negative cash flow and negative free cash flow, although undesirable, do not by themselves signal creative accounting or earnings manipulation and are not necessarily red flags.

TABLE 12-13   Wal-Mart fiscal year net income and operating cash flow (in millions).

	1/01	1/00	1/99	1/98	1/97
Net Income	6295	5377	4430	3526	3056
Operating Cash Flow	9604	8194	7580	7123	5930

COMPARING OPERATING CASH FLOW TO NET INCOME

Net income or after-tax income, the bottom line on the income statement, is the top line on the cash flow statement. Cash flow from operations is usually a larger number than net income because depreciation and amortization are subtracted from net income but not from operating cash flow.

For example, Table 12-13 shows a summary of Wal-Mart's fiscal year net income and operating cash flow figures.

Wal-Mart's operating cash flow substantially exceeds its net income each year. That's the way it's supposed to happen. Operating cash flow usually increases in proportion to net income.

Accounts receivables and/or inventories increasing faster than sales are both red flags. If you recall the accounting math, increasing receivables and inventories also reduces operating cash flow. So less than expected operating cash flow could be a tip-off to accounting shenanigans.

As mentioned in Chapter 11, recent research found that operating cash flow less than net income signals future share price underperformance, and the combination of increasing net income and decreasing operating cash flow was found to be especially significant. Table 12-14 showing those figures for Motorola offers a good example.

TABLE 12-14   Motorola net income vs. operating cash flow (in millions).

	12/00	12/99	12/98	12/97
Net Income	1318	891	-907	1180
OCF	-1164	2140	1295	2596

TABLE 12-15 Examples of firms reporting annual net income (NI) exceeding operating cash flow (OCF).

	2001	2000	1999	1998	1997	1996
Strouds						
Net Income (000s)		1303	214	-3798	-21,968	2570
OCF (000s)		-6931	5616	2197	-4686	-5171
PolyMedica						
Net Income (millions)	22.7	15.1	7.6	7.6	2.3	.3
OCF (millionss)	14.6	10.1	0.5	-9.9	-0.1	4.8
ACT Manufacturing						
Net Income (millions)		28.9	6.2	3.1	-2.4	10.2
OCF (millionss)		-62.4	-48.9	11.7	-5.4	-26.0

Motorola managed to record 48 percent year-over-year income growth in fiscal 2000, but its operating cash flow told a different story. As of this writing, the company hasn't seen a profitable quarter since the 2000 report.

While the research showed that the combination of increasing earnings and decreasing cash flow was especially significant, it makes sense that any company that habitually reports more net income than operating cash flow is problematic. Table 12-15 shows some examples.

PolyMedica and ACT Manufacturing habitually reported operating cash flows below net income. In PolyMedica's case, the shortfall came from direct advertising costs, which, according to GAAP, are not included on the income statement. Nevertheless, those costs were significant. For instance, in its March 2001 fiscal year, PolyMedica recorded a $31.5 million direct advertising charge against operating cash flow, more than wiping out its $22.7 million net income.

Contract manufacturer ACT's operating cash flow shortfalls related to buildups in receivables and inventories. ACT filed bankruptcy in 2001.

Strouds had a spotty record but usually recorded cash flows higher than earnings. Strouds reported impressive earnings growth in its

February 2000 fiscal year report, but it also reported its biggest ever operating cash flow deficit. Strouds filed bankruptcy in September 2000.

Comparing net income to operating cash flow is faster and easier than computing accounts receivables and inventory percentages of sales. It may not be as effective as analyzing receivables and inventories, but it looks like an efficient method for spotlighting stocks requiring detailed examination. Specifically, net income greater than operating cash flow, or net income increasing faster than operating cash flow, signals the need to analyze receivables and inventories.

Pension Plan Income

Most corporations establish pension plans for employees. Older corporations maintain defined-benefit plans, meaning that the company funds the plans with cash that the plan invests in stocks and other assets. Theoretically, the plan's assets should approximate its future obligations, that is, the money it will be required to pay out to its retired employees.

The defined-benefit's pension plan's assets depend, however, on the returns it receives from investing the assets. The assets total will not necessarily match the plan's liabilities at any given time. If assets exceed liabilities, the plan is said to be over-funded. It's under-funded if its assets fall short of liabilities.

If the plan is over-funded, the company can count the plan's annual returns (income less costs) on its income statement, thereby increasing reported income. These pension plan credits can be substantial. For instance IBM added $1.3 billion to its reported income in 2000.

The SEC doesn't require firms to show pension plan credits as separate line items on their income statements, so they are frequently buried in other income. The SEC does require companies to detail pension plan benefits in the footnotes to their annual reports, so you can find them by searching (Ctrl-F on a PC; Cmd-F on a Mac) for "pension" or "retirement."

There's an easier way, however. The pension plan's contribution to reported income is an accounting entry; it's not real money, and no cash moves anywhere. That brings us back to operating cash flow. IBM's reported net income increased from $7.7 billion in 1999 to $8.1 billion in 2000, but its operating cash flow dropped from $10.1 billion to $9.8 billion in the same period. The divergence between reported net income and operating cash flow signaled earnings quality issues.

By the way, newer companies offer 401k type defined-contribution plans instead of defined-benefit plans. The sponsoring company's contributions to defined-contribution plans are deducted from its profits each year, and there is no ongoing interaction as with defined-benefit plans.

Yellow Flags

Yellow flags are danger signals warning of long-term problems, but not necessarily in the next quarter.

Capital Expenditures

Depreciation accounts for the deterioration and obsolescence of buildings and capital equipment. To remain viable, a company must be continuously upgrading and replacing its aging equipment.

You can tell if that's happening by comparing the depreciation credit in the operating cash flows section to the capital equipment expenditures listed in the investing section of the cash flow statement. At a minimum, capital expenditures should equal the depreciation charge, and ideally capital expenditures should exceed depreciation.

Table 12-16 shows how Intel and Xerox did in that category. After looking at that data, it's no mystery why Intel dominates its industry while Xerox struggles to survive.

TABLE 12-16 Depreciation charges vs. capital expenditures.

	2000	1999	1998	1997	1996
Intel					
Depreciation (billions)	3.2	3.2	2.8	2.2	1.9
Cap. Expenditures (billions)	6.7	3.4	3.6	4.5	3.0

TABLE 12-16   Depreciation charges vs. capital expenditures. *(continued)*

	2000	**1999**	**1998**	**1997**	**1996**
Xerox					
Depreciation (millions)	948	779	727	739	715
Cap Expenditures (millions)	452	594	566	520	510

Income Tax Rates

The income before taxes entry on a corporation's income statement reflects what the firm's profits would be if it paid no income taxes. Then the company subtracts income taxes to compute the bottom line net income. It's the net income that's divided by the number of outstanding shares to determine the make-or-break earnings per share.

Most corporations pay income taxes in the range of 35 percent to 40 percent of before-tax earnings. Of course, since the goal of individuals and corporations alike is to minimize taxes, the rate can vary widely.

Let's consider a hypothetical example to illustrate the significance of income taxes on reported earnings. Assume that a company earned $1,000 before taxes and has 1,000 shares outstanding. Table 12-17 shows how the reported EPS varies with the income tax rate.

It's clear that the tax rate has a huge impact on EPS, and even a small change can mean the difference between a positive or negative earnings surprise.

TABLE 12-17   Reported EPS vs. income tax rate.

Before Tax Inc.	1000	1000	1000	1000
Tax Rate	0%	20%	38%	40%
After Tax Inc.	1000	800	620	600
EPS	1.00	0.80	0.62	0.60

TABLE 12-18 Tyco International's net profit margins vs. income tax rate.

FY Year	Tax Rate (%)	Net Profit Margin (%)
6/01	23.9	13.7
6/00	29.8	15.6
6/99	37.6	4.6
6/98	31.5	9.6
6/97	39.1	6.4
6/96	40.8	6.1
6/95	43.7	4.8
6/94	38.0	3.8
6/93	43.8	2.3
6/92	27.5	3.1

For a real-life example, Table 12-18 shows the relationship between Tyco International's income tax rate and its net profit margin.

Tyco's tax rate dropped 45 percent (23.9 vs. 43.7) from 1995 to 2001, helping to increase its profit margins from 4.8 percent to 13.7 percent.

Low tax rates are great as long as they stay low. If a company reports losses, it can apply its losses to future profits, thereby paying reduced taxes until its loss carry-forwards are depleted. The problem arises when they are used up, and then the reversion to the normal tax rate unexpectedly reduces earnings.

Some companies always pay lower taxes because of conditions particular to the company and/or its industry. The best way to get a handle on a company's income tax situation is to compare its current and historical rates. You can calculate the income tax rate by dividing the income tax by the before tax income, but it's easier to look it up on MSN Money. Figure 12-1 shows MSN Money's history for Tyco.

Total Net Income	EPS	Tax Rate (%)
4671.1	2.55	23.90
4520.1	2.64	29.80
1031.0	0.62	37.60
1177.1	1.01	31.50
419.0	0.66	39.10
310.1	0.51	40.80
216.6	0.36	43.70
124.6	0.34	38.00
72.4	0.20	43.80
95.3	0.26	27.50

FIGURE 12-1   MSN Money's Financial Statements 10-Year Summary shows Tyco's annual income tax rates for 1993-2001 (top) fiscal years.

Summary

Detecting the red and yellow flags will often be your first clue that a company's growth rate is peaking. Getting out before the news becomes common knowledge can help you avert big losses. These red flags warn of potential reduction in the company's sales and earnings forecasts in the coming weeks or a negative report at report time.

Red Flags

■ Slowing sales growth

■ Accounts receivables increasing faster than sales

■ Inventory levels increasing faster than sales

■ Reported net income increased by pension plan income

Watch out for these yellow flags warning of potential problems down the road, but not necessarily by the next earnings report.

Yellow Flags

■ Capital expenditure lagging depreciation write-offs

■ Temporarily low income tax rates

Nothing is for sure in the stock market, and none of the red or yellow flags described here guarantees that the offending company will report a negative surprise with its next earnings report. However the existence of each flag signals added risk.

Many market experts advise that the key to making money in the market is to avoid disastrous losses. Reducing your risks by heeding these risk flags will help you achieve that goal.

13

STEP 10: OWNERSHIP CONSIDERATIONS

Examining the percentage of outstanding shares held by institutions and by insiders can help you avoid risky stocks.

Institutional Ownership

Institutions are mutual funds, pension plans, trust funds, and other large investors, and account for roughly 50 percent of all stockholdings. The presence of strong institutional sponsorship (large holdings) verifies that a stock is a viable growth candidate.

Institutional Percentage of Shares Outstanding

Institutions trade stocks frequently and in large quantities. By virtue of the large commissions their trades generate, institutional money managers are more wired into the market than individual investors can ever hope to be. Consequently, few public companies exist that they haven't encountered.

High institutional sponsorship (ownership) means these tuned-in investors have analyzed the company and liked what they saw. Conversely, low institutional ownership means that institutions have analyzed the company and passed.

Institutions are required to report their holdings to the SEC only twice yearly. Most report more often, usually quarterly, and a few monthly. While the timeliness issue diminishes the value of institutional holdings data (see Figure 13-1), it is still worthwhile, especially for growth investors, to evaluate the information.

Institutions, especially mutual funds, are most often growth investors and typically hold at least 40 percent of the outstanding shares of growth stocks. In many instances, institutional ownership runs as high as 95 percent of the outstanding shares. Growth investors should view candidates with less than 30 percent institutional ownership with caution. It could very well be that institutional buyers are shunning the stock for good reason.

It's a different story for value candidates. Mutual funds and other institutional holders are inclined to dump their holdings when a stock tanks so big losers won't show up on their quarterly reports. In theory then, low institutional holdings should signal an out of favor value candidate. But because of the reporting time lag, it could take several months for institutional selling to be reflected in the holdings data. Consequently, institutional holdings data is unlikely to be helpful to value investors.

Ownership Summary			
% Shares Owned:	66.40	Price Range Quarter:	$35 - $45.24
% Change in Ownership:	-1.45	# New Buyers:	34
# Institutions:	271	# Closed Positions:	18
Total Shares Held:	114,932,419		
3 Mo. Shares Purchased:	14,892,796	# Buyers:	140
3 Mo. Shares Sold:	(16,580,179)	# Sellers	115
3 Mo. Net Change:	(1,687,383)	# Net Buyers:	25

FIGURE 13-1 A portion of Reuters Institutional Holders report for Apollo Group. The report also lists the top holders in terms of shares held, and the largest institutional buyers and sellers.

Judging a Stock by the Company it Keeps

Checking the names of the funds holding large positions of a stock offers additional insight. Figure 13-2 shows Morningstar's Top Fund Owners report listing the mutual funds with the largest holdings. Many sites report similar information, but I prefer this one because it lists Morningstar's Star rating of each fund (Morningstar rates funds from one to five stars, where five is best). That's good information because I'd rather buy stocks held mostly by five-star funds than those owned mainly by two-star funds.

The investing style of the funds with large holdings is also significant. Stocks mostly held by momentum style funds are riskier than those held mostly by buy-and-hold style managers because the momentum managers will dump their holdings at the first sign of trouble. You can tell which is which by looking up the fund's portfolio turnover on Morningstar's Portfolio report for the fund. Turnover measures the percentage of the fund's trading activity. A 100 percent turnover means that, on average, the fund replaces its entire portfolio every year. Buy-and-hold style funds have turnovers below 40 percent, and momentum fund's turnovers typically run above 150 percent.

Insider Ownership

Insiders are key officers, members of the board, and others holding at least 10 percent of the outstanding shares.

Insider ownership is usually expressed as the percentage of the firm's outstanding shares held by insiders. Institutions holding 10 percent of a company's shares are considered insiders, so the total of insider plus institutional holdings can exceed 100 percent of outstanding shares.

Float

Insider holdings are not considered as available for daily trading, because insiders are restricted as to when and how often they can trade their shares. Float is defined as the shares not held by insiders and thus available for daily trading.

| Major Fund Owners | | | | | |
Fund Name	% of Shares Held	% of Fund Assets	Change (000) in Ownership	Star Rating	Date of Portfolio
Vanguard 500 Index	0.82	3.39	328	4	12-31-01
Fidelity Magellan	0.68	2.64	9,000	3	09-30-01
Fidelity OTC	0.39	16.00	1,400	2	07-31-01
Fidelity Growth & Income	0.38	3.72	2,276	4	07-31-01
Fidelity Growth Company	0.36	5.55	320	3	11-30-01
Vanguard Institutional Index	0.33	3.36	401	4	12-31-01
Putnam Voyager A	0.32	4.48	-148	3	12-31-01
Janus Twenty	0.32	6.90	12,805	3	10-31-01
Fidelity Blue Chip Growth	0.30	4.68	1,826	3	07-31-01
AXP New Dimensions A	0.22	3.56	0	3	12-31-01
Fidelity Advisor Equity Growth Instl	0.22	6.30	164	4	11-30-01
Vanguard Growth Index	0.20	6.87	676	3	12-31-01
Vanguard Total Stock Mkt Idx	0.18	2.90	346	3	06-30-01
American Century Ultra Inv	0.18	2.27	1,230	2	12-31-01
Fidelity Advisor Growth Opport T	0.16	5.66	1,890	2	11-30-01
Vanguard Primecap	0.15	2.77	0	5	12-31-01
Fidelity Spartan U.S. Equity Index	0.15	2.97	236	4	08-31-01
American Funds Growth Fund of Amer A	0.14	1.23	0	4	12-31-01
AIM Constellation A	0.14	3.98	0	2	10-31-01
American Funds Investment Co Amer A	0.14	0.89	0	4	12-31-01

FIGURE 13-2 Morningstar's Top Fund Owners report shows the funds with the largest holdings in a company, in this case, Microsoft.

Insider Holdings

Reuters Profile & Snapshot report lists the number of shares outstanding and the float. You can compute the number of shares held by insiders by subtracting the float from the shares outstanding:

insider owned shares = shares outstanding − float

Once you have the number of insider owned shares, the insider ownership percentage is the number of insider owned shares divided by the number of shares outstanding:

insider ownership percentage = insider owned shares / shares outstanding

Avoid Very High Ownership

In the past, market gurus advised avoiding stocks with low insider ownership, reasoning that company executives holding big stakes in their firm have a stronger interest in seeing the share price increase than those without big holdings. That makes sense, but these days many corporations couple their executive's pay to stock performance. Further, many grant key executives huge stock options that give them plenty of incentive to hype their stock prices. These realities of modern day corporate life make insider ownership irrelevant in terms of executive's motivation to keep the share price up.

In fact, high insider ownership (e.g., 55 percent or more) signals risk because the insiders may be large investors who are waiting for the opportune time to sell their holdings. It's no fun owning a stock when large shareholders dump a few million shares onto the market. These situations most often occur when a company was spun off from a larger corporation or was recently taken public following an earlier leveraged buyout.

In other instances, high insider ownership may reflect holdings owned by the founding family or by descendants of the founder. Such family owners may not see an advantage to higher share prices.

Avoid companies with 55 percent or more insider ownership without further researching these issues.

Insider Trading

Insider buying or selling can be a tip-off to key executives expectations for their company's stock price. But interpreting the information requires some care. Insiders often exercise stock options and then sell their shares on the same day. Such transactions are normal and do not necessarily reflect a negative opinion about the stock.

Pay most attention to transactions by the chief executive officer, or the chief financial officer. The only significant transactions are large open market purchases or sales that are unrelated to option exercises. The significance of a trade depends on the trade size compared to the insider's total holdings. It's not significant if an insider sells 20,000 shares, but still holds 2 million shares. It is significant, however, if the insider sells 1.5 million of the 2 million shares owned.

Often, an insider trade may not be as significant as it appears. Some companies loan money to executives to finance purchasing the company's shares. In these instances, their buying reflects the deal they're getting, rather than their view of the stock's appreciation prospects. Also, key insiders, especially the CEO, often have rights to shares that do not appear on their listed holdings. It may appear that they are selling all their holdings, but they actually control, or have rights to, millions of additional shares.

Insiders are supposed to report their trades by the 10th of the following month. So trades made on September 20, for instance should be reported by October 10. However, trades made on October 9, need not be reported until November 10. Late reporting is common, and I'm not aware of an insider ever going to jail for late reporting of their trades.

The financial news media as well as investors, both professional and amateur, monitor insider trading reports filed with the SEC. So it should come as no surprise that insiders are getting more creative about how they do their trades. It recently came to light that some insiders have sold shares back to their company, rather than selling on the open market. By doing so, they avoided having to report their sales in a timely manner.

Summary

Despite the timeliness issue, growth investors should be cautious about investing in stocks with less than 30 percent institutional ownership because it's likely that these savvy investors are avoiding the stock for good reason.

Avoid stocks with very high insider ownership, as that signals that big shareholders may be waiting for the opportune time to reduce their holders, among other potential problems.

The close attention given to insider trading reports in recent years has made that data less significant as insiders learned how to game the insider trading reports.

14 ⸻⸻⸻⸻⸻⸻⸻⸻

TOOL # 11:
PRICE CHARTS

Even if you do a thorough fundamental analysis, there will be
times when you're wrong. Perhaps there is bad news brewing that insiders know, but haven't made public. Maybe your candidate is about to be
blindsided by a competitor's superior product. It's possible that you've
overlooked an economic trend, such as changing interest rates, that will
adversely affect your candidate's market.

Whatever the reason, you can often avoid unnecessary losses by
looking at a company's stock price chart before you buy. You don't have
to be a charting maven to get useful information from a chart.

Trends

Stock prices tend to move in trends. A stock price moving ever
higher is in an uptrend (Figure 14-1). Stocks moving relentlessly lower

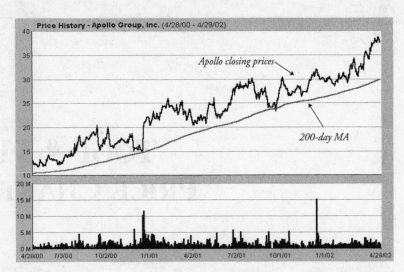

FIGURE 14-1 Apollo Group with 200 day simple moving average.
As of April 2002, Apollo had been in an uptrend for more than
two years. (MSN Money chart.)

are in downtrends (Figure 14-2). Stocks moving in a directionless pattern are in consolidation, or no trend.

Stocks in uptrends don't move up in price every single day. Instead they zigzag, some days moving up and other days moving lower. What identifies an uptrend is that each major up zigzag peak is higher than the previous peak, and each major low is higher than the previous low.

Downtrends have the opposite characteristics. Each major high is lower than the previous peak, and each major low is lower than the previous low.

If you can't see a pattern, the stock is probably consolidating, meaning that it's not trending up or down.

You can usually see which way a stock is moving by looking at a one- or two-year chart. The stock is in an uptrend if the price on the right side of the chart is much higher than the price on the left. It's in a downtrend if the right side is lower than the left. These are generalizations of course; a trend can end at any time.

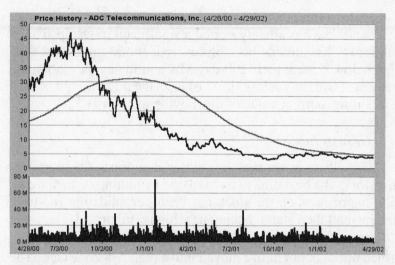

FIGURE 14-2 ADC Telecommunications with its 200-day simple moving average. ADC reversed its uptrend and started down in mid-2000. (MSN Money chart.)

Moving Averages

The moving average (MA) is the average closing price of the stock over a specified period. For instance, the current value of the 200-day moving average is the stock's average closing price over the past 200 trading days.

There are two types of moving averages: simple (SMA) and exponential (EMA). SMAs give equal weight to each day in the period averaged, while exponential averages put more emphasis on the most recent closing prices. Each version has its advocates, but I've found little advantage in using one over the other, and I usually use the SMA.

A stock is considered in an uptrend if it's above its MA. The distance between the stock price and its moving average indicates the trend strength. That is, the higher a stock is above its average, the stronger the trend. It's probably in a consolidation pattern if it's crisscrossing its MA.

Value Investors

Value investors' target price analysis will yield better buy and sell points than the price charts. Value investors should nevertheless look at a chart before buying, and avoid buying while their candidate is in a steep downtrend. On the other hand, it's too late for value investors if their candidate has already started a significant move up. That means that the stock has already been discovered. Value candidates should be trading below or near their 200-day MA and in any case not more than 10 percent above the average. For instance, the price should be no higher than $22 if the current value of the moving average is $20.

Growth Investors

Growth investors must pay closer attention to the charts than value investors. The best time to buy is at the beginning of an uptrend. That usually happens when the stock has been consolidating (no trend) for some time and then starts making new highs (Figure 14-3).

The second best time to buy a growth stock is when it's in an established uptrend, but hasn't moved into a high risk zone (see "The Risk Zone" later in this chapter).

It's okay to buy a stock when it's consolidating, but only when you're confident about your fundamental analysis, and you're sure that its next move is up.

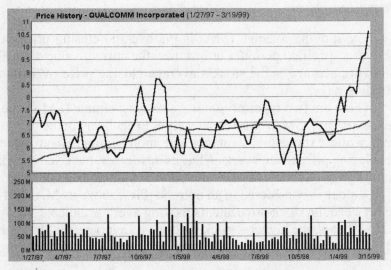

FIGURE 14-3 Qualcomm had been consolidating for more than two years before starting its 2,000 percent run-up in March 1999. The frequent crossing over and under its 200-day moving average are known as "whipsaws" and are indicative of a consolidation pattern. (MSN Money chart.)

Avoid Downtrends

No matter what, *never* buy a stock when it's in a downtrend. A downtrend signals that the stock is likely to move lower rather than higher. The only exception would be when the downtrend is induced by events unrelated to the company, such as an overall market overreaction to an external event, such as the September 11 attacks.

Don't be in a rush to jump on downtrending stocks when you think you've spotted a reversal. Most stocks consolidate for months before recovering from a significant downtrend, so you usually have plenty of time.

Another way to determine a stock's overall direction is by comparing the stock's current price to its 200-day and to its 50-day moving averages (Figure 14-4)

The 200-day moving average gives you a longer-term perspective than the 50-day moving average. The stock is probably in an uptrend if it's trading above both MAs.

If it's above its 200-day MA, but below its 50-day moving average, it's probably in a short-term downtrend of a long-term uptrend—in other words, a dip. Conversely, consider it a short-term spike if it's above its 50-day MA, but below its 200-day moving average.

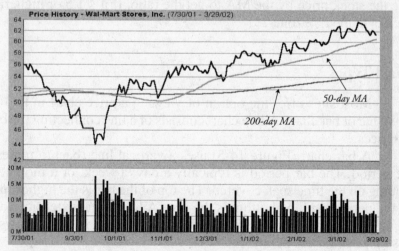

FIGURE 14-4 Wal-Mart moved above both its 50-day and 200-day moving averages in September 2001. (MSN Money chart.)

Don't use the moving averages to override what you can see by visually inspecting the chart. That is, don't interpret a stock above both of its moving averages as being in an uptrend if a visual inspection of the chart clearly shows that it's heading down.

The Risk Zone

If you're a growth investor, you often won't be the first to discover a hot prospect. Growth stocks often experience strong price run-ups, then falter, often retracing much of their recent progress. Jumping on a fast-moving stock after it has already made a big move adds risk.

I've settled on an unscientific rule of thumb for determining when a stock is in that condition. I measure the difference between the stock's closing price and its 200-day moving average. It's in the risk zone when the stock price is 50 percent greater than the moving average.

Being in the risk zone doesn't mean that the stock isn't going higher. Qualcomm moved into the risk zone when it crossed $10 in March 1999, on its way to $180.

I haven't found a site that displays that ratio directly, but it's easy to compute. The best place to get the needed data is on sites that offer Java charts such as MSN Money. The beauty of a Java chart is that you can place your cursor on the moving average, and its value pops up. Divide the stock price by the MA to get the ratio. If it's 1.5 or higher, the stock is in the risk zone.

Chart Types

Most sites offer the option of viewing a price chart in two formats: line or bar chart. A line chart consists of a line connecting the closing prices.

A bar chart (Figure 14-5) uses a vertical line (bar) to represent one period. The bar period is typically a day, a week, or a month, depending on the time span covered. The top of the bar is the highest price for the period, and the bottom is the low. A horizontal extension to the left represents the opening price, and an extension to the right shows the closing price for the period.

Line charts are best for viewing long-term trends while bar charts give detailed information useful for interpreting short-term movements.

FIGURE 14-5 Jones Apparel bar chart. Each bar represents one day. Chart from BigCharts.com (www.bigcharts.com).

Trading Volume

Trading volume is usually plotted at the bottom of a price chart. Volume is the number of shares traded during the period. A stock is said to have high volume if the current level is at least 50 percent higher than the volume over the past 10 or 20 periods. A stock is said to have low volume when the volume looks like it's petering out.

Many charting experts consider volume an important consideration when a stock starts a new uptrend after consolidating. New uptrends on low volume are considered more likely to fail than those accompanied by high volume. In general, increasing volume is considered a bullish factor during uptrends.

Summary

All investors should look at a price chart before buying and should avoid stocks in strong downtrends. Growth stocks should be in an uptrend when you buy, and value stocks should be consolidating.

PART THREE

THE ANALYSIS PROCESS

15

QUICK PREQUALIFY

COSC: Concentrate On the Strongest Candidates

The best way to analyze stocks is to start with a large group of candidates and then eliminate the weakest contenders as soon as possible so that you can spend most of your time evaluating the strongest candidates.

In this chapter you'll learn how to weed out the obvious misfits that aren't worth considering. They may be firms that are mostly hype and don't have real sales and earnings, or they simply may not fit your requirements. You should be able to eliminate most misfits in less than five minutes once you get the hang of it.

You'll probably end up eliminating 15 out of every 20 candidates if they originated from tips from TV pundits, magazines, friends, and so forth, and fewer if they resulted from your own screens.

Comverse Technology, Inc. (NASD)
Sector: Technology Industry: Communications Equipment

Company Overview ▾

Find a financial advisor   Annual Report for CMVT

VectorVest Report   educatic

Comverse Technology, Inc., with its subsidiaries, designs,
develops, manufactures, markets and supports computer and
telecommunications systems and software for multimedia
communications and information-processing applications. The
Company's products are used in a broad range of applications
by wireless and wireline telecommunications network
operators and service providers, call centers and other public
and commercial organizations worldwide. The Company
markets other telecommunications products and services,
including products that are integrated with its systems and
products that work in combination with other systems to
provide advanced telecommunications services, such as
automatic call distribution and messaging systems for
telephone answering service bureaus, and intelligent IP
gateways for wireless roaming and voice over Internet protocol
(VoIP) applications. The Company also engages in venture
capital investment and capital market activities.

FIGURE 15-1   Reuters Profile &
Snapshot report for Comverse
Technology.

You could use many financial sites to do the analysis. I'll demonstrate using Reuters to do the research and Comverse Technology as
an example. Start with Reuters Profile & Snapshot (Figure 15-1).

Profile & Snapshot Report

Begin by determining the company's line of business. Keep in
mind that this is just a quick look, not a detailed analysis. Look first at
the sector and industry listing. If you looked up Comverse Technology,
you'd see that it's in the communications equipment industry of the
technology sector.

Below the sector and industry listing is a single paragraph describing the company's business. By reading that you'd learn that Comverse sells systems and software to the telecommunications industry.

At this writing, the telecommunications industry is in the dumps
and it's expected to remain depressed for at least another year. Value investors might be intrigued by the market's pessimistic view of the telecom
equipment business and consider Comverse worth a look. However, its
dismal industry outlook would make it uninteresting to growth investors.

Discard candidates that don't interest you and continue on with
the survivors.

Market Capitalization

Market capitalization, computed by multiplying the number of shares outstanding by its recent share price, describes the company's size or market value. You won't have to do that calculation because most financial sites list each stock's market capitalization. The market capitalization categorizes a company as micro-cap, small-cap, mid-cap, or large-cap. There's no hard and fast rule that defines those categories, but here are my rules of thumb:

- Micro-cap: below $100 million

- Small-cap: $100 million to $2 billion

- Mid-cap: $2 billion to $8 billion

- Large-cap: $8 billion plus

To put the numbers in perspective, Table 15-1 lists some familiar names in each category.

When I looked up the market cap for Comverse, I found that it was $3.9 billion, in the mid-cap category.

There are no good and bad market caps. Large-cap companies are usually considered the safest category because they've generally been in business for years, are financially solid, and have survived a variety of economic ups and downs. Micro-caps and small-caps usually have the greatest growth potential because they are typically emerging companies introducing new products or entering new markets. However, micro-caps are usually too small to interest mutual funds and other institutional investors and consequently won't have much analyst coverage, making them difficult to research. Large-caps generally outperformed the overall market in the 1995-1998 timeframe until tech and Internet firms took the spotlight. Small- and mid-cap firms shined after the tech bust in 2000 and were still outperforming in early 2002.

Avoid firms with market caps below $50 million because they're too risky, and evaluate all micro-caps with caution. Otherwise, the choice of firms size to eliminate at this stage, if any, depends upon your preferences.

TABLE 15-1   Examples of well-known firms in each market-cap category.

Company	Market Cap
Large-Cap	(in billions)
Microsoft	330
Pfizer	250
Costco	20
Mid-Cap	(in billions)
BEA Systems	7
Office Depot	5
Outback Steakhouse	3
Abercrombie & Fitch	3
Small-Cap	(in millions)
Alaksa Airlines	800
Beazer Homes	700
California Pizza Kitchen	400
Micro-Cap	(in millions)
Bassett Furniture	180
Stanley Furniture	180
Gadzooks	140

Valuation Ratios

Valuation ratios tell you something about whether the market is pricing your candidate as a value, growth, or momentum stock. In this context, value stocks are out of favor; that is, they are of no interest to most market participants who prefer growth stocks. Momentum-priced stocks are not really a separate category; rather they are the most in-favor subset of the growth category. They have already substantially moved up in price, outrunning their fundamentals, and hence represent higher risk than growth-priced stocks.

Reuters displays four valuation ratios: price/earnings (P/E), price/sales (P/S), price/book (P/B) and price/cash flow (P/CF). Each valuation ratio has its pluses and minuses. Your goal at this point, how-ever, is simply to determine you candidate's category. The P/S ratio is, in my view, best suited to the task. Again, there's no universal standard, but here are some guidelines for using the P/S ratio:

P/S	Category
less than 2.5	value
3.0 to 9	growth
10 +	momentum

Use these guidelines to rule out stocks that clearly don't fit your investing style, but since they're arbitrary, don't take them too lit-erally. For instance, a value investor shouldn't reject a stock because its P/S is 2.6. Nevertheless, it would be unusual to find a worthwhile value candidate with a P/S ratio of 5, for instance. Conversely, it's un-likely that a growth investor would find a stock with a P/S of 0.5 that had sufficient earnings growth potential to qualify as growth candi-date. Growth investors will find momentum-priced stocks interesting, but caution is advised. Use these guidelines to avoid obvious misfits, not as a final arbiter of value.

Trading Volume

Trading volume, also referred to as liquidity, is the number of shares traded daily, on average. When considering trading volumes, higher is usually better. Stock message boards on Yahoo and other sites are filled with postings intended to move a stock price up or down. It's not hard, with a well-crafted message, to motivate gullible investors to buy or sell enough shares to move a stock's price if only 10,000 shares trade daily. It's another story if, say, a million shares trade every day.

There's another equally important reason to prefer high trading volume stocks. You want mutual funds and other institutional buyers to buy stocks that you own, because it's their buying pressure that usually moves a stock price up.

Institutions have hundreds of millions, if not billions, of dollars to invest. They must buy many thousands of shares to take a meaningful position. These large buyers prefer stocks that trade enough shares daily to enable the institution to move into or out of positions without disrupting the market for the stock. Obviously, they can't do that if only a few thousand shares trade daily.

As a rule of thumb, avoid stocks with daily trading volumes below 50,000 shares, and higher is better. When I looked, Comverse Technology's 5 million share trading volume easily qualified.

Float

Stock prices, like the prices of so many things, respond to the laws of supply and demand. Stock prices move up if buyers want to buy more shares than sellers want to sell, and vice versa. Ideally, when good news hits the wires for a stock you own, you'd like to see buying demand overwhelm the supply. It stands to reason then, in terms of supply, smaller is better, at least up to a point.

The supply side of the equation starts with the number of shares outstanding; that is, the number of shares issued by the corporation. But that's not the total story. Insiders such as key executives, directors, and other large shareholders hold some of those shares. Insiders can't freely trade their shares. They can only trade at certain times, they must notify the SEC of their trades, and there are other limitations on their trading. So shares owned by insiders are not considered available for daily trading. The number of shares that are available for trading, which is the total shares outstanding less the insiders' holdings, is termed the float.

Reuters lists the float as well as the total number of shares outstanding. By the way, you can determine the shares held by insiders by subtracting the float from the number of shares outstanding.

While in terms of supply and demand, smaller is better, a too small float would dissuade institutional investors. As a rule of thumb, below 5 million shares is too small, and a 10 million to 25 million-share float is ideal. However most stocks won't fit that criterion. For instance, Microsoft's float exceeds 5 billion shares.

Reuters listed Comverse Technology's float as 186 million shares, about typical for a mid-cap stock.

Cash Flow

Cash flow is the amount of cash moving into, or out of a company's bank account generated by its basic business. Very fast-growing companies often burn cash (negative cash flow) in their early stages. However companies growing sales 30 percent or less annually should be generating positive cash flow. Growth investors should require positive cash flow of candidates in that category and would be well served by avoiding cash burners entirely.

Value investors need candidates capable of producing large cash flows, but they may not be doing so now, due to their current problems. Therefore, value investors should not eliminate cash burners at this stage.

You can tell if a company is burning cash by looking at its TTM (trailing twelve months) cash flow per share listed on the Snapshot report. The TTM cash flow will be negative if the company is a cash burner. Reuters listed Comverse Technology's cash flow as $0.29 per share, indicating that its trailing 12-months cash flow was positive.

Financial Highlights Report

Reuters Financial Highlights report lists the company's quarterly sales and earnings for up to four years. Use this data to assure yourself that you're researching a real company with real sales and real earnings. Avoid companies with sales (revenues) totaling less than $40 million or so during the most recent four quarters. It's unlikely that consistent money losers will survive your detailed analysis, so, using the earnings per share history, disqualify firms showing more money losing than profitable quarters.

When I looked, Reuters showed that Comverse Technology had racked up sales totaling more than $1 billion in its last four quarters and had reported positive earnings in each of the 19 quarters listed. So Comverse easily qualified as a real company with real sales and real earnings.

Ratio Comparison

Next, switch to Reuters Ratio report to review your candidate's historical sales and earnings growth.

TABLE 15-2   A portion of Reuters Ratio report for Comverse
Technology. (MRQ is most recent quarter, and TTM is the trailing
twelve months [last four quarters]).

Sales (MRQ) vs. Qtr. 1 Year Ago: -7.2 %
Sales (TTM) vs. TTM 1 Year Ago: 19.6%
Sales – 5 Year Growth Rate: 25.7 %
EPS (MRQ) vs. Qtr. 1 Year Ago: -97.5 %
EPS (TTM) vs. TTM 1 Year Ago: 20.0%
EPS – 5 Year Growth Rate: 32.8 %

Historical Growth Rates

Table 15-2 shows the sales and earnings growth data I found for
Comverse Technology.

Comverse's sales grew, on average, almost 26 percent annually
over the past five years. Its earnings grew 33 percent annually, even faster than the sales growth rate, indicating that its overall profit margin increased during the period.

However, the most recent results are the most important, and that
data tells a different story. Comverse's sales growth slowed to 20 percent in its four most recent quarters, compared to the year-ago period,
and worse, sales actually dropped 7 percent in its last quarter. Under-
standably, considering the sales results, TTM earnings fell 20 percent
year-over-year, and collapsed 97 percent in its most recent quarter.

Bottom line: as surmised in the beginning, Comverse is a busted
growth stock and thus a potential value candidate. Its negative recent
earnings growth makes it an unsuitable candidate for growth investors.

ONE VERY HANDY REPORT

Reuters Ratio report provides considerably more information
than I described here and is a handy resource for a variety of needs. It
lists a wide assortment of valuation ratios, growth rates, financial ratios,
profitability ratios, and much more. What's really helpful is that it displays each data point for a specific stock, its industry (e.g., software), its
sector (e.g., technology) and for all of the stocks making up the S&P
500 index.

Check the Buzz

By early 2001, Steven Madden, Limited, was a rising star in the shoe business. Madden manufactured shoes, mostly targeted to young women, and sold them to major department and specialty stores, as well as in its own Steve Madden retail stores.

The company was hot. Earnings soared 41 percent in 2000 on a 26 percent increase in sales. The company owed its success to founder Steven Madden's ability to tune in to the tastes of the fashion conscious junior marketplace. Also, the company had an advantage over the competition because Madden had devised a method of cutting the development time for new shoe styles down from many months to 60 to 90 days.

The only fly in the ointment was that, as the story shown in Figure 15-2 tells it, founder Steve Madden, in May 2001, pleaded guilty to charges of stock fraud.

Would you want to spend time researching a company if the person responsible for its success was facing a prison term? Me neither!

There's no point in digging into a firm's financial statements and figuring out target prices if the competition just announced a new widget that obsoletes one of your candidate's major products, a rating service just downgraded its bonds to junk status, or the FBI is investigating the company for Medicare fraud.

Madden to pay $10.8m stock fraud penalties
By John Labate in New York
Published: May 23 2001 19:57 | Last Updated: May 24 2001 04:45

Steven Madden, founder of the eponymous New York shoe designer and retailer, pleaded guilty to securities fraud and money laundering charges on Wednesday and agreed to pay more than $10.8m (E12.5m) in fines and other penalties.

Mr Madden faces a potential prison term of 41 to 51 months. On the criminal charges filed by the US Attorney's Office, he will repay $3m of illegal profits. In a separate settlement with the Securities and Excange Commission, he has agreed to pay $7.8m and has been barred for seven years from serving as officer or director of any public company. His company trades on the Nasdaq stock market.

Mr Madden was arrested in June and charged with multiple counts of conspiracy, securities fraud and money laundering relating to his role in an alleged stock manipulation scheme involving 23 initial public offerings.

FIGURE 15-2 Financial Times story found on MarketWatch gives you news that you can use.

On the other hand, you'd probably redouble your research efforts if you knew that the firm had a hot new product that was stealing market share from the competition.

In 2000, word spread that telecom equipment makers such as Cisco Systems, Nortel Networks, and Lucent Technologies had loaned billions to startup telecoms, by then on shaky ground, to finance equipment purchases. Wouldn't that information influence your decision to buy Cisco, Nortel, or Lucent?

Finding out the buzz could determine how you analyze a company and ought to be an early step in your research.

News Sites

Yahoo and MarketWatch are the two best sites for company news. Both display headlines from a variety of sources. Yahoo probably has the most sources, but it archives most of them for only a few months. MarketWatch, on the other hand, archives some stories for three years or longer. Also, you can search for stories by date on MarketWatch, a handy feature when you're trying to figure out why a year ago a firm's stock dived 50 percent in one day.

Summary

Your time is your most valuable asset. Don't waste time doing in-depth analyses of stocks that aren't worthwhile candidates. Concentrate on your strongest candidates by eliminating bad ideas as soon as possible. This chapter described a few simple checks. You'll probably add some of your own ideas as you gain experience.

16

VALUE INVESTING: THE PROCESS

COSC: Concentrate On the Strongest Candidates

By March 2001, the market, especially for tech stocks, was in the pits. But graphics chip maker Nvidia was riding high. Microsoft had selected its new chip for its Xbox video game machine, which was expected to be a blockbuster. Nvidia had just penetrated the Mac market for the first time. Nvidia reported January quarter sales up 70 percent, and its January fiscal year earnings had soared 137 percent. With a P/E of only 29, Nvidia's shares were undervalued by growth standards.

Much of Nvidia's success had come at the expense of competitor ATI Technologies. Although still outselling Nvidia, ATI's sales slumped 15 percent in its November 2000 quarter, and the company expected worse, a stunning 40 percent drop in its not yet reported February 2001 quarter. ATI was losing money and wasn't expected to turn a profit anytime soon. By mid-March 2001, its shares were trading in the low $4 range, an all-time low.

Nvidia was cleaning ATI's clock, so picking the winner between those two was a no-brainer. Nvidia's investors were richly rewarded for their astute stock picking. Nvidia returned 39 percent between mid-March 2001 and mid-March 2002. But ATI was the Cinderella of this story. Its investors enjoyed a 200 percent return in the same period.

Value investing works because the market overreacts to news. Good news drives stock prices into the stratosphere, creating valuations far surpassing underlying fundamentals. Conversely, news of a temporary setback or an adverse economic cycle can drive a good company's stock price into the ground.

However a beaten down stock price per se doesn't equate to a worthwhile value candidate. Value investors must understand how the company can recover from the setback that drove it into the value category.

Value investors and growth investors would never own the same stocks at the same time. Value candidates are reporting sinking profit margins—growth investors prefer healthy and rising margins. Value candidate's earnings are down or nonexistent—growth investors look for accelerating earnings growth. Value candidate's last earnings report probably disappointed the market—growth investors search out companies with recent positive surprises.

Cycles

Value investors view the economy and all industries as cyclical. They know that there are times when each industry shines and analysts predict continuing strong growth for the foreseeable future. Then, as sure as night follows day, the industry overexpands, growth falters, profit margins contract, and stock prices plunge. Eventually weaker players drop out, the excess capacity is absorbed, demand picks up, and the cycle repeats.

Value investors don't try to predict the timing of these cycles. They don't know whether the market is heading up or down. They don't know which way interest rates are heading, and they ignore analysts' buy/sell ratings. They don't know if all of the bad news is already built into a stock price, or if further disappointments will drive the share price down even further.

Rather than trying to predict the unpredictable, value investors employ a target price approach to time their trades. They calculate sell target prices and buy when and if the firm's shares trade sufficiently below the sell targets to justify the risk. They close their positions when the price moves up into the sell range. They don't know when that will happen and must be prepared to hold as long as it takes, typically two to five years. Value investors employ a process called normalizing to develop their sell targets.

Normalizing

The bad news that dropped a company's stock into the value category probably also killed its profit margins, profitability ratios, and its bottom line earnings. Consequently, value investors must look beyond the current problems and evaluate its performance after its underlying problems are fixed. They do that by analyzing historical patterns.

The process of using historical performance to look beyond current difficulties is termed "normalizing." A normalized operating margin for instance, is the expected margin, when the company has recovered, say two or three years down the road.

You can't normalize a company's performance if it's only been in business for two or three years. You need at least five years, and 10 years is best. Normalizing also requires reasonably consistent performance. Companies with erratic historical margins, cash flows, and profitability ratios do not lend themselves to the process.

Value Analysis Process

Although different in detail, the value and growth analyses processes follow the same 11 steps.

1. Analyze analysts' data
2. Examine current valuation
3. Set target prices
4. Evaluate industry
5. Analyze business plan
6. Assess management quality
7. Gauge financial health
8. Analyze profitability and growth trends

9. Search for red flags

10. Examine ownership

11. Check the price chart

Each step employs a corresponding analysis tool explained in detail in Part 2. The procedures described in this chapter assume that you're already familiar with the analyses tools.

The chapter concludes with deciding when to sell, a key decision for value investors.

Start with at least 10 and preferably 20 candidates so that you can compare them and eliminate the weakest contenders as you progress through the analysis steps. Be sure to run your candidates through the quick prequalify analysis (Chapter 15) to eliminate the obvious misfits before you begin this process.

Remember; COSC: Concentrate on the strongest candidates. Eliminate candidates as soon as you find that they don't meet a requirement. Don't waste time analyzing weak candidates.

Step 1: Analysts' Ratings & Forecasts

Start by analyzing the analysts' ratings and forecasts.

Sentiment Index

The sentiment index gauges the market's enthusiasm by compiling the number of analysts rating the stock strong buy versus hold, sell, or strong sell. Negative sentiment scores mean that most analysts are recommending selling, and stocks with negative scores make the best value candidates. Boeing, for instance, trading in the $30 range, hit sentiment scores as low as –14 in late 1999 before starting its run to $70.

Stocks scoring as high as one or two could also be value candidates, but scores of three and above reflect positive analysts' sentiment, which is inconsistent with value stocks.

Table 16-1 shows ATI Technologies' analysts recommendations in mid-March 2000.

Calculate the sentiment index by adding one point for each strong buy and subtracting one point for each hold, sell, or strong sell recommendation. Buy recommendations are not considered. ATI's Sentiment Index score was –4 (+2–4–2), qualifying it as a value candidate.

TABLE 16-1   Distribution of
analysts' buy/sell recommendations for ATI Technologies.

Strong Buy	2
Buy	7
Hold	4
Sell	2
Strong Sell	0

Earnings Growth Forecasts and Trends

Analysts' earnings growth forecasts and recent forecast changes
will give you further insight as to whether your candidate qualifies as a
value prospect.

FORECAST EARNINGS GROWTH

Earnings forecasts predicting strong year-over-year earnings
growth connote high expectations, which are inconsistent with value investing. Value candidates should have negative, or at best, flat earnings
growth expectations, reflecting the event that propelled it into the value
category. Year-over-year earnings growth forecasts higher than 5 percent disqualify a value candidate.

In mid-March 2001, analysts were expecting ATI to report a
$0.12 per share loss in its February 2001 quarter, compared to a $0.22
profit the previous year, thus qualifying ATI as a value candidate.

EARNINGS FORECAST TRENDS

Analysts change their earnings forecasts when they receive new
information. Positive forecast trends signal improving sentiment, meaning that the market is pricing a recovery into the stock price, and it's too
late for value investors. The best value candidates will show a negative
earnings forecast trend. A flat trend, that is, less than a $0.02 change in
either direction is okay.

By mid-March 2001, ATI's February 2001 quarter's earnings
forecast had come down to -$0.12 from $0.03 just four weeks earlier. So
ATI passed the earnings forecast trend test.

Surprise History

Value candidates' recent earnings surprises are likely to be negative. Surprise history is not used in the value analysis process.

Revenue Forecasts

Analysts will have probably reduced a value candidate's revenue growth forecasts down to flat or negative. Revenue forecasts are used in the target price calculation, but not at this stage of the analysis.

Analysts Research Reports

Since many are recommending selling the stock, analysts' research reports will probably have a negative tone. Nevertheless, they contain relevant background and industry information that is otherwise hard to come by. Read all of the analysts' reports that you can find for the information that they contain, but ignore their buy/sell recommendations.

Step 2: Valuation

Gauging the expectations built into a stock's current price and determining buy and sell target prices are the linchpins of value investing. The GARP (growth at a reasonable price) strategy does not apply to the value analysis.

Implied Growth

Table 5.1 in Chapter 5 identifies the long-term earnings growth rate implied by a stock's P/E ratio. Value candidates should be priced at a minimum 50 percent discount to their normalized growth rates.

For example, suppose that you've identified a candidate that you expect to resume its earlier 15 percent average annual earnings growth rate when it recovers from its current difficulties. In that instance, you'd expect the candidate's current price to reflect no more than half the 15 percent normalized growth rate, i.e., 7.5 percent.

USING THE PRICE/SALES RATIO TO ESTIMATE IMPLIED GROWTH

Many value candidates will be reporting losses instead of earnings. So you can't use the P/E ratio to look up implied growth because there is no E. However, despite its troubles, it is still selling products and you can use its P/S ratio (share price divided by one-year's sales) in place of P/E.

P/E and P/S are related mathematically by the firm's net profit margin (net income/sales). Specifically:

$$P/E = \frac{P/S}{\text{Profit Margin}}$$

You must first determine the candidate's normalized profit margin to make use of this relationship. Estimating the normalized profit margin entails reviewing the firm's historical margins, and from that, drawing conclusions about the future.

You can look up a firm's historical profit margins on MSN Money, or you can calculate them from the income statements by dividing each year's net income by total sales. Table 16-2 shows ATI's historical annual profit margins using data that was available in March 2001.

TABLE 16-2 ATI Technologies' historical annual profit margins as of March 2001.

Fiscal Year	Profit Margin (%)
8/00	-5.4
8/99	9.0
8/98	14.6
8/97	7.9
8/96	5.9
8/95	4.4
8/94	-1.2

ATI's profit margin history is more erratic than you'd like to see. Still, it looks reasonable to expect margins in the 8 percent to 9 percent range when the company recovers.

P/S ratios are displayed on many financial sites and ATI's mid-March 2001 $4.20 share price translated to a 0.9 P/S ratio. Using the P/S to P/E translation formula yields an 11.3 P/E: :

$$P/E = \frac{P/S}{PM} = 0.9/.08 = 11.3$$

Table 16-3 contains a P/S to P/E conversion table, so you don't have to do as much math. Use it by looking up the P/S multiplier corresponding to your estimated profit margin, and then multiply the P/S by that number to convert it to P/E. For example, a 10 percent profit margin and P/S of 5 converts to a 50 P/E (5 x 10).

Using the table, you'd multiply ATI's 0.9 P/S ratio by 13 to come up with an 11.7 estimated P/E.

Using ATI's equivalent P/E of 12, Table 5.1 in Chapter 5 showed that the market was pricing ATI's shares for 4 percent to 6 percent annual earnings growth. You don't have to predict ATI's future annual earnings growth. All you must decide is whether ATI's normalized growth is at least double the 5 percent or so growth rate priced into the stock.

TABLE 16-3 Price/Sales to estimated price/earnings conversion table. (Multiply the price/sales ratio by the estimated profit margin to derive the estimated price/earnings ratio.)

Estimated Profit Margin (%)	P/S Multiplier
2	50
4	25
6	17

TABLE 16-3 Price/Sales to estimated price/earnings conversion table. (Multiply the price/sales ratio by the estimated profit margin to derive the estimated price/ earnings ratio.) *(continued)*

Estimated Profit Margin (%)	P/S Multiplier
8	13
10	10
15	6.7
20	5.0
25	4.0
30	3.3
35	2.9
40	2.5
50	2.0

If you decide that ATI's annual earnings growth will meet or exceed 10 percent, it's still a candidate. You'll be in the money whether ATI ends up growing earnings 10, 15, or 20 percent.

Price/Sales Valuation Check

Another way of confirming that a candidate has upside potential is to compare its current price/sales or price/book ratios to historical levels. You can see historical valuation ratios going back five years on Morningstar's Stock Valuation report.

Table 16-4 lists ATI's available historical price/sales ratios as of March 2001.

Comparing ATI's recent P/S ratio to historic valuations shows that ATI's share price had room to more than double, even if its revenues remained static.

TABLE 16-4   ATI Technologies historical price/sales ratios.
You can find the historical data on Morningstar's Stock
Valuation report.

	3/01	8/00	8/99	8/98
P/S	0.9	1.7	2.1	2.8

Step 3: Target Price Ranges

The implied growth calculation tells you there's money to be made owning ATI shares if the company gets its act together and returns to profitability. Now it's time to get down to brass tacks and establish viable buy and sell target price ranges.

Calculating target prices starts with the assumption that the company will return to profitability at some point. Call that the recovery year. Then calculate target prices for the date when the recovery year's results are reported. For instance, the recovery date would be early 2005 if you think the company will return to profitability in its fiscal year ending December 2004. It's not a big disaster if the company recovers a year later than you expect. That event just pushes the date back when you can take profits, but it doesn't materially affect the result.

Here's how the target price range analysis could have been applied to ATI in March 2001, if you assumed that it would return to profitability in its August 2003 fiscal year. In that instance, you'd calculate the target price range for September or October 2003, after ATI's reports its August 2003 fiscal year results.

The first step is to estimate sales in the target fiscal year, in this case August 2003.

Target Year Sales

Table 16-5 lists ATI's fiscal year sales since going public, as of March 2001. I've also listed the year-over-year sales growth expressed as a percentage and in absolute dollars.

Prior to its August 2000 fiscal year slowdown, ATI's sales growth was erratic, but totaled at least 30 percent annually. Expressed in actual dollars instead of percentage gains, ATI's annual sales growth ranged from a low of $68 million up to $458 million in fiscal 1999.

TABLE 16-5   ATI Technologies annual sales (millions), and year-over-year sales increase expressed in percentage gain and in actual dollars (millions).

Fiscal Year	Sales	% Increase	$ Increase
8/00	1283	8	97
8/99	1186	63	458
8/98	728	92	349
8/97	379	29	85
8/96	294	30	68
8/95	226	55	80
8/94	146		

On March 1, 2001, ATI said it expected its February quarter sales to come in at around $230 million compared to $368 million in February 2000. The company reported sales of $342 million in the November quarter, typically its highest sales quarter. Since ATI had dramatically reduced its guidance for 2001, you would not have found meaningful analysts consensus sales forecasts to help with the evaluation.

I assumed that ATI's May and August quarters would also come in at around $230 million. Table 16-6 summarizes my ATI's fiscal year 2001 sales estimates.

Since 2001 was looking like a disaster, I figured that 2002 would be a stabilizing year, with improving margins but flat sales. I assumed that sales growth would resume in 2003, my targeted recovery year. How much is anybody's guess, but I figured that given its historical figures 25 percent was doable. Table 16-7 summarizes my sales forecasts.

TABLE 16-6   My estimates for ATI's 2001 fiscal year sales.

November	342
February	230

TABLE 16-6   My estimates
for ATI's 2001 fiscal year sales.
(continued)

May	230
August	230
Fiscal Year	**1032**

The $258 million growth estimate for fiscal 2003 looked conservative considering ATI was adding sales in the $350 million to $450 million range before it stumbled.

Estimate Profit Margin

The next step is to estimate ATI's profit margin in its recovery year, which I forecast to be fiscal 2003.

Normally, you'd first list ATI's historical profit margins, but I had already done that in the implied growth analysis described earlier. In that section, I figured that when it recovers, ATI's profit margins should be in the 8 to 9 percent range. I'll use 8.5 percent.

TABLE 16-7   Summary of my sales forecasts for ATI
Technologies.

Fiscal Year	Sales (millions)	% Increase	$ Increase
8/03 est.	1290	25	258
8/02 est.	1032	0	0
8/01 est.	1032	-20	-251
8/00	1283	8	97
8/99	1186	63	458
8/98	728	92	349

Estimate Net Income

Once you have forecast sales and profit margin, you can compute estimated net income:

net income = sales x profit margin = $1,290 million x 8.5% = $109.7 million

My income estimate for ATI's August 2003 fiscal year is $109.7 million; call it $110 million.

Estimate Outstanding Shares

You first have to estimate the number of shares outstanding at the end of ATI's 2003 fiscal year before you can convert the estimated net income to the all-important earnings per share. You can do that by starting with the current number of outstanding shares and estimating the likely share inflation from ATI's past performance shown in Table 16-8.

It looked as though ATI had been liberally printing new shares, probably for acquisitions. The company probably won't repeat its 2000 fiscal year mistakes, so I estimated that it would add five million shares annually in fiscal 2001, 2002, and 2003, yielding a total of 244 million shares outstanding as of August 2003.

TABLE 16-8   ATI Technologies shares outstanding (in millions).

Fiscal Year	Shares Out	$ Increase	% Increase
8/00	229.4	24	12
8/99	205.0	6	3
8/98	199.2	5	3
8/97	194.0	4	2
8/96	190.0		

Estimate Earnings Per Share

The formula for converting net income to earnings per share is:

EPS = net income /shares outstanding = \$110/244 = \$.45 per share

The final step, figuring what the market will pay for ATI's \$0.45 per share earnings in the autumn of 2003 requires estimating its probable P/E range at that time.

Forecast P/E Range

Reviewing its own history is the best way to estimate ATI's P/E in 2003. ATI, a Canadian firm, only started trading on Nasdaq in 1988, so the P/E data was sparse, especially since ATI lost money in fiscal 2000. Table 16-9 shows the available P/E data.

TABLE 16-9   ATI's historical average P/Es.

Fiscal Year	P/E
8/99	28
8/98	19

The data was scanty, but I figured that ATI's historical P/E range was probably representative of what I could expect after its August 2003 report came out. Consequently, my autumn 2003 forecast high and low P/E forecasts for ATI were 28 and 19, respectively.

Estimate Target Price Range

Once you have the forecast earnings per share and P/E, you can compute the target prices:

target price = forecast P/E x forecast EPS

Plugging the estimated high and low P/E and the estimated 2003 fiscal year earnings per share into the formula gives:

ATI Technologies high target forecast = 28 x \$0.45 = \$12.60

ATI Technologies low target forecast = 19 X \$0.45 = \$8.55

Average target: \$10.58

The maximum buy target is 50 percent to 55 percent of the average sell target, or $5.29 to $5.80. ATI was trading at around $4 per share in mid-March 2001, so ATI qualified as a buy according to the target price calculation.

Target prices are not cast in concrete. Adjust your targets as conditions change. The main variables are your forecast revenues and profit margins. Adjust the targets accordingly when it becomes apparent that your forecasts were too low or too high. However, do not even think about increasing the maximum P/E that you used to set the high target.

Step 4: Industry Analysis

Value investing, unlike growth, is not about picking the strongest player in hot industries. Instead, value analysis focuses primarily on the candidate, rather than its industry. Even so, there are aspects of the industry analysis that require the attention of value investors.

Industry Growth

According to MSN Money's Earnings Growth Rate report, ATI Technology is in the graphics subsector of the computer industry. Analysts had forecast 30 percent annual earnings growth for the industry in mid-March 2001. Discounting the forecast industry earnings growth by 30 percent yielded 21 percent expected average annual sales growth. High forecast industry growth implies high expectations, the bane of value investing. Nevertheless, high forecast industry growth is not a disqualifying factor. The only disqualifying industry growth factor is too slow growth, namely less than 3 percent.

Industry Concentration

Concentration refers to the number of companies competing in the same industry sector. Industries with few major competitors are said to be concentrated, as opposed to fragmented industries with many competitors. Companies in concentrated industries are usually more profitable than players in fragmented industries.

Using Hoover's Fact Sheet and checking industry reports, I found that the computer graphics industry had been fragmented until 2000 when four players left the market, and Nvidia bought the remaining contender, aside from ATI. So by March 2001, ATI and Nvidia dominated graphic chip sales. ATI's industry was fast growing and highly concentrated, a desirable combination.

Industry Scuttlebutt

Surveying trade publications, I found that industry analysts (not stock analysts) believed that despite ATI's then current problems, ATI and Nvidia were expected to remain more or less equal contenders indefinitely.

The industry analysis found that ATI has only one major competitor in a fast-growing industry, an encouraging result.

Step 5: Business Plan Analysis

The business model analysis evaluates qualities of a company's business plan that are likely to influence its success. Use the business plan scorecard to tabulate the scores for each category. Score each category one, minus one, or zero, corresponding to advantage, business plan disadvantage, or not applicable, respectively.

Brand Identity

Both ATI and Nvidia have strong brand identity with the end user. However, graphics chip consumers are fickle and wouldn't hesitate to embrace another brand if they thought that it was a better product. Thus ATI has no brand identity advantage. Score = 0.

Other Barriers to Entry

ATI and Nvidia together dominate the graphics chip industry. Their technological advantage is their main barrier to entry. Prior to March 2001, Intel had also produced graphics chips, but by that time had exited the business. I rated the barriers to entry high. Score = 1.

Distribution Model/Access to Distribution

ATI sells its products to computer and game manufacturers as well as to end users. ATI has no particular distribution advantage or disadvantage. Score = 0.

Product Useful Life/Product Price

Computers and game machines are expensive consumer products with relatively long product lives, a business plan disadvantage. Score = –1.

Access to Supply/Number of Suppliers

Obtaining materials to produce its products is not an issue for ATI's industry. Score = 0.

Predictable Revenue Stream

The computer gaming industry is highly cyclical and fad driven. Thus ATI's revenue stream is unpredictable, adding risk to ATI's business model. Score = –1.

Number of Customers

Most of ATI's revenues come from major game and computer manufacturers. In fiscal 2000, one customer accounted for 13 percent of ATI's revenues. The small number of customers adds risk to ATI's business model. Score = –1.

Product Cycle

ATI and Nvidia are constantly introducing new designs. ATI's product cycle is very short and adds risk to its business model. Score = –1.

Product & Market Diversification

ATI markets only a single product category, and its products go into only two market segments: computers and video games. ATI's lack of product and market diversification adds risk to its business model. Score = –1.

Organic Growth vs. Acquisition Growth

ATI had made several acquisitions, and its goodwill/tangibles to total assets ratio measured 37 percent, marking ATI as a serious acquirer. Score = –1.

Business Model Score

ATI's business model score was –5, low, but not unusual for a tech stock.

Step 6: Management Quality

Key Executive and Board Quality

ATI's CEO, K.Y. Ho, was one of the company's founders. The company had a small board of directors with only five members. Except for the CEO, all directors were from outside the company, and one of those was the founder of Silicon Optix, another chipmaker. The small board was a negative, and not much information was available on company officers. I rated ATI's key executive and board quality as fair.

Clean Accounting/Earnings Growth Stability

The clean accounting test totals the firm's one-time charges or nonrecurring charges found on its annual income statements and compares that total to annual sales. The test judges a firm's accounting as clean if the nonrecurring charges' percentage of sales averaged less than 3 percent over the past five years.

ATI showed no one-time or nonrecurring charges on its income statements, qualifying its accounting as clean.

The earnings growth stability test requires a visual look at the firm's quarterly earnings history to gauge its earnings volatility. Reuters Financial Highlights report displays the needed data in an ideal format for this purpose. Table 16-10 shows the quarterly earnings data for ATI as of March 2001.

ATI's quarterly earnings were reasonably stable until the company ran into trouble in May 2000. I rated ATI's earnings stability as good.

TABLE 16-10   ATI's quarterly earnings history.

Quarters	1998	1999	2000	2001
November	0.12	0.01	0.24	-0.01
February	0.13	0.18	0.22	
May	0.13	0.16	-0.78	
August	0.13	0.15	-0.13	
Total	0.50	0.50	-0.45	

Stock Ownership

ATI, a Canadian-based company, did not report detailed insider ownership data to the SEC. Consequently, I could not rate ATI's management for stock ownership.

I rated ATI's key executive and board quality fair, its accounting clean, and its earnings stability good. I couldn't rate it for stock ownership. Overall, I rated ATI's management quality as fair plus.

Step 7: Financial Health

The purpose of evaluating financial strength is not to determine if the company has the ability to develop new products and regain its market share. Rather, it's to determine if it can survive long enough to carry out a recovery strategy.

Firms running into financial difficulties fall in one of two categories: busted cash burners and overburdened debtors. Busted cash burners are typically newer companies, while overburdened debtors are usually well-established, formerly profitable firms. Value candidates are more likely to be potentially overburdened debtors than potential busted cash burners. Potential busted cash burners can be evaluated using the Busted Cash Burners analysis, while potential overburdened debtors require the Detailed Fiscal Fitness Exam.

Use the total liabilities/equity ratio (TL/E) to determine the test most appropriate for your candidate:

TL/E	Financial Health Test
Less than 0.5	Busted Cash Burners
0.5 and higher	Detailed Fiscal Fitness Exam

Busted Cash Burners

ATI's total liabilities were $184.9 million and its shareholder's equity was $722.2 million, yielding a TL/A ratio of 0.3 and qualifying ATI for the busted cash burner strategy.

The first step in the test is to evaluate ATI's operating cash flow history. Table 16-11 shows the cash flow figures that you would have seen on Morningstar's 5-yr Restated Financials report in March 2001.

TABLE 16-11   ATI's operating cash flow history.

Period	Operation Cash Flow (millions)
TTM 2/01	-158.0
FY 8/00	-17.9
FY 8/99	74.8
FY 8/98	21.8

ATI's latest trailing 12-months –$158 million operating cash flow looked scary. However, it wasn't as bad as it first appeared. I downloaded ATI's balance sheet and found that ATI had used $40 million to pay down its accounts payables during the period.

I figured that was a good thing, and I deducted the $40 million payables reduction from the $158 million outgoing cash before I calculated ATI's cash burn rate. The burn rate was $118 million ($158 million – $40 million), or roughly $10 million per month.

burn rate = $118 million/12 = $10 million/month

ATI's February 2001 current assets totaled $501 million compared to $175 million current liabilities. Subtracting the liabilities from the assets showed $326 million working capital.

working capital = current assets – current liabilities

working capital = $501 million – $175 million = $326 million

Assuming that the $10 million monthly burn rate continued unabated, ATI had enough working capital to last 32 months, above my 24-month minimum requirement. Since ATI passed the burn rate test, it was not a potential busted cash burner.

Step 8: Profitability Analysis

The value strategy requires buying stocks in the worst of times. Margins will be down, sales growth will have stalled, or even be negative, and earnings will probably have turned to losses. The value investing strategy is based on the reversion to the mean principle.

Reversion to the mean suggests that abnormally high numbers will come down, and unusually low numbers will move back up to historic values. For example, companies reporting unusually high operating margins, compared to historical values or to industry averages, will likely see those margins come down in future quarters, and vice versa. Where growth investors see above average or rising margins as good, value players interpret them as a potential sell signal.

Reversion to the mean, in terms of value investing, means that you are buying companies performing below historical ranges. With that in mind, avoid companies with a history of negative cash flow, and/or erratic operating and profit margins, and/or abnormally low ROA (less than 8 percent).

For ATI, early 2001 was the pits, as the sales growth figures and margins complied in Table 16-12 illustrate.

ATI hadn't kept up with Nvidia's technology, and it had cut prices in an attempt to gain market share until it could bring new products to market.

Table 16-13 shows that ATI's ROA profitability measure and its operating cash flow and EBITDA numbers told a similar story.

TABLE 16-12 ATI's key operating figures (%).

	Q 2/01	Q 11/00	FY 8/00	FY 8/99	FY 8/98	FY 8/96
Y/Y Sales Growth	-40	-7	8	63	92	29
Gross Margin	13.8	24.3	18.5	34.2	37.0	32.1
Operating Margin	loss	loss	loss	13.3	19.9	11.4
Net Profit Margin	loss	loss	loss	9.0	14.6	7.9
SG&A % of Sales	12	9	9	8	11	13

TABLE 16-13   ATI's profitability, operating cash flow, and EBITDA
history (%).

	Q 2/01	Q 11/00	FY 8/00	FY 8/99	FY 8/98	FY 8/96
ROA	loss	loss	-7	19	28	16
Operating Cash Flow	-42	8	-18	75	22	18
EBITDA	-15	57	6	223	151	47

Positive operating cash flow is an especially important consideration for value investors. ATI reported positive cash flow in four of the five years preceding its current problems. It looked to me as though ATI would probably generate at least $20 million operating cash flow annually when it recovers. ATI's pre-problem return on asset ratios were impressive, and I saw no reason that ATI wouldn't again produce 15 percent-plus ROA.

From a value perspective, ATI's numbers reflect opportunity. Although ATI was taking a whipping from Nvidia, the two rivals' sales were still running neck and neck. ATI had slipped technologically, but there was no clear reason why it couldn't recover. Nvidia's advantage was one of timing, rather than fundamental. It didn't have patents, better manufacturing techniques, or any other important sustainable advantage. There was nothing fundamentally different about ATI from two years earlier when it was on top of the heap. Its founder was still at the helm, and there was no evidence that it had lost personnel crucial to its operations. ATI had no long-term debt, so there are no complications lurking from that angle.

Once ATI stabilized, its gross margin would probably recover to the 30 percent range, its SG&A percentage of sales would likely drop back to 9 percent, and its operating margin would likely be in the low to mid-teens.

What level of earnings can you expect if all goes well? In Step 3 (price targets), I postulated that ATI's sales would recover to $1,290 million in its August 2003 fiscal year. Table 16-14 shows ATI's estimated net income assuming that that happens, the operating margin returns to 14 percent, and the company's income tax rate returns to 33 percent.

TABLE 16-14   ATI's estimated 2003
fiscal year net income based on forecast
sales and operating margin (in millions).

Sales	$1,290
Operating Income (14%)	181
Interest Expense	0
Before Tax Income	181
Income Tax (33%)	-60
Net Income	121

The $121 million forecast net income is consistent with the $110 net income forecast for the target price calculation.

Step 9: Red Flags

Value investors don't have to look for red flags pointing to future disaster, because usually the disaster has already happened. However, there is still one earnings quality issue that should be assessed.

Capital Expenses vs. Depreciation

Smart managers know that they must continue to invest in new capital equipment, even when times are tough. Generally, capital expenditures should at least equal depreciation charges. Table 16-15 shows ATI's record on that score.

The data shows that despite its temporary setbacks, ATI continued to invest in new capital equipment, a positive sign.

TABLE 16-15   ATI's depreciation and capital expenses (in millions). The February 2001 and November 2000 column represents the first two quarters of fiscal 2001.

	11/00 & 2/01	FY 8/00	FY 8/99	FY 8/98	FY 8/97
Depreciation	10	18	14	7	4
Capital Expend	15	26	31	22	22

Step 10: Ownership

Total insider holdings is the only significant ownership factor for value investors.

Institutional ownership data is not a factor in the analysis because of its lack of timeliness. Institutional ownership will generally be less than 50 percent of outstanding shares if the company has been in the market's doghouse for six months or longer. However, at best, the institutional ownership data will only confirm what you've already determined.

Insider ownership levels exceeding 55 percent of shares outstanding signals potential problems. You can compute insider ownership by subtracting the float from the total shares outstanding. Both figures are shown on Reuters Profile & Snapshot report. ATI's insider ownership totaled only 2 percent and thus did not signify a problem.

Large stock purchases by key insiders such as the CEO or CFO after a big selloff in a stock may indicate that these insiders have confidence in the company's future. However, insider buying is a secondary signal and is not as relevant as other factors.

Step 11: Charts

The stock price versus its 200-day moving average is the only relevant price chart factor because value investors should give primary weight to their calculated buy and sell target prices to establish entry and sell points. Typically, a value stock's trading price will be below or near its MA. ATI was trading below its 200-day MA in March 2001.

Value investors should be wary of stocks trading more than 10 percent above their 200-day MAs. It usually means that you are too late to the party.

When to Sell

Deciding when to sell is just as important as analyzing purchase candidates. Here are suggested selling rules for value investors.

Target P/E Achieved

Your best sell signal is when earnings have recovered and the stock's P/E is between the high and low estimates you used to calculate your target sell prices. If all went well, sales and earnings roughly tracked your targets, and the stock price is within your target range. You will be selling when analysts are increasing their earnings forecasts and growth investors are buying.

You Realize That Your Estimates Won't Happen

Your biggest risk is that the company does not achieve your estimated sales and/or earnings goals. Your first clue will be when you realize that the company is continuing to lose ground to competitors or that its market sector is not as robust as you originally thought. Sell as soon as it becomes apparent that your targets won't be met.

Acquisitions

Sell if your company acquires another business that is at least 25 percent (sales or market capitalization) as large as the acquiring company. Also sell if the company makes a series of smaller acquisitions that taken together add up to 25 percent of the company's original size.

Deteriorating Fundamentals

Sell if the firm's return on assets (ROA), operating cash flow, or operating margins continue to deteriorate two or three quarters after you own the stock.

Restates Earlier Financials

Restating previously reported results increases the likelihood of future problems. Unless the firm has new management at the helm, sell when it significantly restates downward previously reported sales or earnings.

Increased Borrowings

Ballooning debt signals that the company isn't generating sufficient cash flow to solve its problems. Sell if the company significantly increases borrowings.

Share Price 50 Percent Above Moving Average

Stocks in this territory have already made a big move in a relatively short time. It's time for you to move on, rather than hold out for the stock to hit your sell target.

Red Flags

Our buy analysis didn't check for red flags because most value companies' financial statements are in disarray when you find them. Check for inventory and receivables red flags in its quarterly reports after the company stabilizes. Don't worry about revenue growth but look for earnings quality factors such as pension plan income included in operating cash flow or employee stock option income included in operating earnings. You can expect the company to pay a lower income tax rate if it suffered earlier losses, but be wary of how future tax rate increases could depress net income.

Summary

Value investors sell for one of two reasons: (1) the stock has reached your price targets, or (2) something has gone wrong and the company is unlikely to produce your predicted sales and/or profit margins in anywhere near the timeframe you originally envisioned. Procrastination is the enemy in both situations. Waiting for more information in the face of solid sell signals will likely diminish your profits and turn small losses into big ones.

17

GROWTH INVESTING: THE PROCESS

COSC: Concentrate On the Strongest Candidates

Every generation has its success stories: the Microsofts, Intels, and Wal-Marts that seemingly came out of nowhere to become mammoth enterprises and make their shareholders rich.

Finding the next Microsoft is the Holy Grail for growth investors. But you don't have to find the next Microsoft to be successful at growth investing.

In the end, share prices follow earnings. If you can find a company growing earnings, and hence share price, 15 percent annually, you'll turn $1,000 into more than $4,000 in 10 years. Find a stock growing 20 percent annually and you'll grow $1,000 into more than $6,000; 25 percent annual growth turns $1,000 into more than $9,000 in 10 years.

Despite the 2000/2001 downturn, as of early 2002, 140 U.S. listed stocks had averaged more than 15 percent compounded average annual earnings growth over 10 years, 84 firms grew their earnings more than 20 percent annually, and 61 exceeded 25 percent average annual earnings growth. Looking back five years, 149 firms grew their annual earnings faster than 20 percent annually, and 116 exceeded 25 percent average annual earnings growth.

Growth investing is about finding companies with exciting new products and services that are capable of growing at above-average rates. It isn't even necessary to find a single company that will sustain above-average growth for extended periods. You can start with one firm and switch to another when your first pick's growth falters. The trick is, you have to detect sputtering growth early and switch horses before it becomes common knowledge and sinks the stock price.

In the late 1990s, growth was synonymous with tech investing, but growth is everywhere. Companies with better than 25 percent average annual growth could have also been found in the banking, broadcasting and cable TV, consumer financials, electric utilities, food processing, healthcare, homebuilding, hotel, household products, insurance, natural gas, oil, pharmaceuticals, and retail industries.

Growth investors enjoy the process. They relish the excitement of spotting the next high flyer ahead of the crowd. Some follow a top down strategy, that is, they try to pinpoint a strong industry and then pick the best candidates from the leading players in the group. Others follow a bottom up approach, searching out fast growers regardless of industry.

Growth Candidates

The ideal growth candidates are most often found in emerging markets. The rewards can be enormous for investors able to pinpoint the eventual winner in a growing but still-fragmented industry, such as early investors in Dell Computer, Microsoft or Wal-Mart were able to do.

Those opportunities are hard to find, and the next best growth candidates are firms offering unique products or services to existing markets, with a history of consistent earnings growth and expanding profit margins.

The worst growth candidates are those selling into markets where price is the main differentiator between competitors' products or firms that are not the number one or number two players in their market.

Growth investing is not about buying low. Prime candidates will likely be well off their lows when you discover them. Growth stocks often rise to values unsupported by their fundamentals. They crash when their growth rate slows, rarely simply because they're overvalued. Spotting the red flags pointing to slowing growth before the crowd notices is crucial to successful growth investing.

The Process

The growth analysis process consists of 11 steps:

1. Analyze analysts' data
2. Examine current valuation
3. Set target prices
4. Evaluate industry
5. Analyze business plan
6. Assess management quality
7. Gauge financial health
8. Analyze profitability and growth trends
9. Search for red flags
10. Examine ownership
11. Check the price chart

Each step employs a corresponding analysis tool explained in detail in Part 2. The procedures described in this chapter assume that you're already familiar with the analyses tools.

The chapter concludes with deciding when to sell, for many investors the most difficult step of the investing process.

It's best to research several stocks at the same time. The process of comparing competing candidates forces you to be more analytical and to make better decisions. Be sure to run your candidates through the quick prequalify analysis (Chapter 15) to eliminate the obvious misfits before you begin this process.

Remember COSC: Concentrate on the strongest candidates. Eliminate weak candidates as soon as you identify them.

I'll use cancer diagnostic services provider Impath, Inc., to illustrate the analysis process. Impath first came to my attention when it turned up in a growth screen in 1999. At that time, fast-growing growth candidates were a dime a dozen. I didn't give Impath serious consideration until June 2000 when it became apparent that the tech sector was in trouble.

Step 1: Analysts' Ratings & Forecasts

Growth investing works best when you find stocks garnering increasing interest from market participants. Analysts' buy/sell ratings and earnings forecasts are a key indicator of market enthusiasm.

Sentiment Index

Use the sentiment index to confirm that you have a viable growth candidate. Strong negative scores such as –4 or lower typically identify value rather than growth candidates. Index scores of nine or higher mark growth stocks with unusually high market expectations, hence, higher than usual risk.

Qualified growth candidates with low sentiment index values (e.g., –2 to +2) often have the strongest upside potential. Increasing sentiment index values, say from 1 to 4, signal growing expectations, which is good as long as the fundamentals continue to support those expectations.

Cancer lab Impath never generated much market enthusiasm. In June 2002, when its stock was trading at $24, six analysts covered Impath. Two of them rated Impath a strong buy, two said buy, and two said hold (sell). Impath's sentiment scores ranged from 0 in June 2000 to a maximum of 3 in February 2001, when its shares were changing hands in the low $50 range.

Earnings Forecasts and Trends

Analyst's earnings growth forecasts, and more specifically changes in earnings forecasts, are the primary driver of growth stock prices and consequently should be weighted accordingly in your analysis.

For instance, in June 2000, as its 0 sentiment score showed, Impath had lackluster support from the analyst community. But Impath's share price almost tripled in five months, soaring to $59 by October.

Why? Impath's share price took off after the company reported that its March quarter earnings surpassed the year-ago figure by 63 percent.

Even better, its March earnings beat forecasts by $0.03, prompting analysts to increase their forecasts for the balance of 2000 and for 2001 as well. The forecast increases didn't come all at once. Table 17-1 shows the analysts' consensus forecast history as of mid-June 2000.

Consensus forecasts for Impath's 2000 fiscal year increased from $1.52 per share in April to $1.57 in June. The $1.57 June forecast for fiscal year 2000 represented a 41 percent earnings increase over 1999. Similarly, analysts' fiscal 2001 forecasts moved up from $1.97 to $2.06 per share in the same period.

On a percentage basis, the increases in forecasts from April to June didn't amount to much. But the market pays more attention to the number of pennies than it does to percentage changes. What also worked to Impath's advantage was that the forecast changes didn't come all at once. They moved up in May and then again in June. Many investors screen specifically for just that sort of positive momentum trend in earnings forecasts, believing that it portends a positive surprise at report time. What's interesting is that, according to my notes, none of the analysts changed their buy/sell ratings between April and June.

By mid-October 2000, when Impath's share price peaked, the analysts' FY 2001 consensus forecast had further moved up to $2.10.

That was as good as it got. Nothing bad happened. Impath didn't reduce its guidance or miss forecasts until early 2002. Its December 2000 results came in $0.01 above forecasts. It's just that consensus earnings forecasts stopped going up. By March 2001, Impath's share price had drifted down to the low $40 range, where it would languish for at least another year.

TABLE 17-1 Impath analysts' earnings forecasts in June 2000.

	FY 2000 EPS	FY 2001 EPS
June 6	1.57	2.06
May 6	1.55	2.04
April 6	1.52	1.97

FORECAST EARNINGS GROWTH

Pay most attention to the current and the next fiscal year's earnings forecast earnings growth rate. Usually stocks with the highest year-over-year growth forecasts get the most attention.

However, that doesn't apply if the year-ago earnings figure is very small, say 10 cents or less. Require consistency between the current and next fiscal year's forecast growth to preclude that anomaly. The next fiscal year's forecast growth should be in the same ballpark as the current year's forecast, or better.

Although earnings growth in the 10 to 15 percent range technically qualifies for the growth category, you'll do best sticking with companies growing earnings at least 20 percent annually, and higher is better, up to a point. Forecast annual earnings growth rates much above 50 percent are not sustainable.

Compare the earnings and sales growth forecasts for the same period. Higher growth forecasts for earnings than sales is a potential red flag. It means that the earnings forecasts assume improving profit margins. That may, or may not, be realistic.

EARNINGS FORECAST TRENDS

Evaluate the trends in earnings forecasts for the current and next fiscal years by comparing the current forecasts to earlier forecasts for the same period. Ignore less than two-cent changes in forecasts. Eliminate all candidates with negative forecast trends because the negative trend is likely to continue and could lead to a negative surprise at report time.

Positive forecast trends are best, but don't eliminate companies with flat trends at this point. If, in the end, it comes down to choosing between two otherwise equal companies, pick the company with the strongest positive forecast trend.

Surprise History

A company's recent earnings surprise history often portends the future. Chances are, a company with a recent history of positive surprises will continue to produce positive surprises, and vice versa. Avoid companies with a history of recent negative surprises. The amount of the negative surprise doesn't matter. A one-cent negative surprise is just as significant as a 50-cent shortfall.

On the other hand, the positive surprise amount is significant. Many firms manage earnings expectations so that if all goes as planned, they will report a positive one- or two-cent surprise. Thus a one- or two-cent surprise is not a surprise. It would be a surprise if a company with a history of positive two-cent surprises reports earnings even with forecasts. That event would likely drive its share price down.

A consistent history of large surprises, say 15 cents and up, can be dangerous because the market expects more of the same, and will be disappointed if next time the company only surpasses forecasts by five cents.

The optimum surprise history is a consistent trail of positive surprises in the four- to nine-cent range. Those are sufficient to move the stock price up on report day without creating abnormal expectations. A history of small (e.g., 0.01 or 0.02) positive surprises or of zero surprises is okay. The only surprise danger signal is a history of persistent negative surprises.

If the last four quarter's surprise history is mixed, pay the most attention to the latest quarter. Table 17-2 shows Impath's surprise history as of mid-June 2000.

Impath's surprise history showed no trend and would not have influenced the analysis one way or the other.

Revenue Forecasts

Slowing sales growth is usually bad news for growth stocks and eventually leads to earnings disappointments. However, the slower sales growth expectations don't always show up in the earnings forecasts because analysts sometimes compensate by forecasting higher profit margins.

You'll compare the revenue growth forecasts to the historical growth in Step 8 (profitability and growth) of the analysis, so for now, simply note the forecast revenues for the current and next quarters.

TABLE 17-2   Impath's earnings surprise history.

	May '99	June '99	Sept. '99	Dec. '99	March '00
Estimate	0.22	0.28	0.30	0.35	0.33
Actual	0.22	0.28	0.30	0.32	0.03
Surprise	0.00	0.00	0.00	-0.03	0.03

Research Reports

Analysts' research reports contain valuable background information about a company and its industry. Sometimes the information
detailed in the report contradicts the analysts' buy/sell rating for the
company. Try to find at least two research reports for each candidate.

Step 2: Valuation

In the late 1990s, growth investors didn't spend much time worrying about valuation. That's not as ridiculous as it sounds because
growth stocks often trade at levels unjustified by their fundamentals during their glamour phase. It's usually slowing growth rather then valuation that knocks them off their pedestal.

For instance nobody cared much when Cisco Systems's share
price reached absurd valuations in 1999 and early 2000. It was the
news that Cisco couldn't achieve its expected growth rates that brought
its share price down from $70 to the mid-teens. Step 9 (red flags) de-
scribes strategies for detecting slowing growth before the news sinks
the stock price.

That said, no glamour stock levitates forever, and eventually
share prices reflect the fundamentals. So, as a growth investor you must
assess how the market is valuing your candidate.

Growth at a Reasonable Price

Historically, GARP has been the growth investor's valuation
measure of choice. GARP's biggest attraction is its simplicity. You can
value a stock using GARP without ever looking at a financial statement.

Basically, GARP comes down to another acronym, PEG, which
stands for the P/E ratio compared to forecast earnings growth.

$$PEG = \frac{P/E}{Earnings\ Growth}$$

The E of the P/E is typically the current year's consensus earnings forecast, but sometimes the trailing twelve months' (TTM) per
share earnings is used instead.

The earnings growth or *G* can be historical earnings growth, but it's usually based on earnings growth forecasts. Most often, especially on financial Web sites, analysts' five-year estimated earnings growth is used for *G*, but others define it as the current or next fiscal year's earnings growth.

You can read the PEG value right off of Yahoo's Research report if you want to use the TTM earnings for *E* and the five-year analysts consensus annual earnings growth forecast for *G*.

The PEG determines a stock's fair value. Growth investors consider a stock overpriced if it trades above its fair value, and underpriced if it trades below.

Originally, fair value was defined as PEG =1, meaning that the P/E ratio equals the earnings growth rate. However in the late 1990s, nothing fit that description, so many growth investors changed their definition of fair value to PEG = 2. In that instance, the P/E ratio is twice the earnings growth rate. Doing that makes sense since stocks do in fact trade at higher valuations in exuberant markets.

Using the current fiscal year's expected earnings and analysts long-term consensus growth forecasts, Impath's PEG was 1.0 in June 2000 and 2.4 in October.

Implied Growth

Implied growth gives you another, and in my view better, way of looking at a stock's valuation.

The implied growth rate table (Chapter 5/Table 5-1) uses Benjamin Graham's intrinsic value formula to determine the long-term earnings growth implied by a stock's P/E. The only variable is the current corporate AAA-rated bond interest rate, which you can easily look up at the Financial Forecast Center (www.neatideas.com/aaabonds.htm).

Impath's 42 P/E in June 2000 implied about 28 percent average annual earnings growth. At the time, analysts were forecasting more than 30 percent growth, so Impath was fairly valued, if not undervalued.

By October 2000, however, Impath's shares were trading at a 96 P/E based on trailing earnings, or a 79 P/E based on fiscal year 2000 forecast earnings. By then, analysts were forecasting 33 percent average annual earnings growth, but the growth implied by Impath's valuations were in the 60 percent to 70 percent range.

So by October, Impath was gauged overvalued by both the PEG and implied growth valuation methods.

Step 3: Target Prices

It's more work, but the target price method gives you the best insight into a stock's valuation. The strategy involves forecasting EPS for the target year by estimating sales and the profit margin, which gives you net income, and then dividing by the expected number of shares outstanding to get estimated earnings per share. Once you know the EPS, you can establish target prices by estimating the likely P/E range for the stock after its target year earnings have been announced. Here's how I would have done it for Impath in June 2000.

I'd typically held growth stocks for 12 to 18 months, so I would have calculated Impath's target prices for early 2002, after its 2001 fiscal year results had been reported. The numbers used in this analysis are as of June 2000, before Impath's stock 2-for-1 stock split in August 2000.

Target Year Sales

The first step in the target price analysis is to forecast the target year's (2001) sales. Table 17-3 shows Impath's sales figures and its year-over-year sales growth rates for its 1996–1999 fiscal years, as well as for its March 2000 quarter.

Impath was going gangbusters in 2000, but I doubted it could keep up the pace in 2001. So I estimated that while Impath's sales would soar 60 percent in 2000, it would gain only 50 percent in 2001. Table 17-4 shows Impath's historical sales with my forecasts for Impath's 2000 and 2001 fiscal year sales added.

TABLE 17-3   Impath's sales and year-over-year growth.

Period	Sales (millions)	% Y/Y Growth Rate
Q 3/00	31	80
FY '99	85	52
FY '98	56	52
FY '97	37	69
FY '96	22	49

TABLE 17-4 Impath's historical sales growth with my forecasts for fiscal years 2000 and 2001 added. (*Indicates my estimates.)

Period	Sales (millions)	% Y/Y Growth Rate
FY '01	*205	*50
FY '00	*137	*60
Q 3/00	31	80
FY '99	85	52
FY '98	56	52
FY '97	37	69
FY '96	22	49

The next step is to estimate Impath's profit margin in 2001. MSN Money's Key Ratio 10-Year Summary report showed that Impath's historical profit margins were mostly in the 9.3 percent to 9.8 percent range. I figured its margins would stay in that range, and I estimated Impath's margin at 9.5 percent for 2001.

Estimate Net Income

Once you've estimated sales and profit margin, you can calculate your net income forecast for the target year, which is 2001:

NI = sales x profit margin

NI = $205 million x 9.5% = $19.5 million

Estimate Outstanding Shares

You must estimate the number of shares outstanding at the end of 2001 before you can calculate your estimated EPS. Table 17-5 summarizes my forecasts to this point and also shows the number of shares outstanding at the end of Impath's last four reported fiscal years. The table also lists my forecasts of shares outstanding for 2000 and 2001.

TABLE 17-5   Summary of estimates for Impath. (*Indicates my estimates.)

Period	Sales (millions)	Net Profit Margin (%)	Net Income	Shares Out
FY '01	*205	*9.5	*19.5	*7.9
FY '00	*137			*7.8
FY '99		9.6		7.7
FY '98		12.4		8.2
FY '97		9.8		5.5
FY '96		9.3		5.3

Impath's number of shares outstanding took a big jump in 1998 but decreased in 1999. The 1998 increase was probably acquisition related. I figured that Impath would probably make additional small acquisitions and estimated that it would have 7.9 million shares outstanding at the end of 2001.

Estimate Earnings Per Share

Once you've estimated net income and estimated shares outstanding, you can compute EPS by dividing the two:

EPS = net income / shares outstanding

EPS = $19.5 million / 7.9 million = $2.47

My forecast for Impath's earnings per share in fiscal 2001 is $2.47.

Forecast P/E Range

The best way to estimate Impath's future P/E is to review its historical trading range. Table 17-6 shows Impath's average P/Es for each of the past four years, plus its P/E in June 2000.

TABLE 17-6   Impath's P/E
ratio history as of June 2000.

Period	Average P/E
June '00	42 (actual)
FY '99	26
FY '98	34
FY '97	40
FY '96	39

Based on its history, I figured that Impath's shares would likely be trading at a P/E between 34 and 42 in early 2002. That gives me the target price forecasts for early 2002:

target price = P/E x EPS

Impath high target forecast = 42 x $2.47 = $104

Impath low target forecast = 34 x $2.47 = $84

average of high and low targets: $94

The maximum buy price range, according the target price strategy, is 50 percent to 55 percent of the average target, or $47 to $52. Impath closed at $48 on June 12, the day I did my analysis.

Taking Impath's August 2-for-1 price split into account, the low and high target prices became $42 and $52, respectively. By October 2000, Impath was trading in the $60 range, well above the target range.

How close were my targets? Table 17-7 compares my hypothetical estimates to what actually happened.

Impath's reported sales about 7 percent below my forecasts but its profit margin fell far short of my estimate. Impath blamed its profit margin drop on the September 11 terrorists' attack and on acquisition-related costs.

TABLE 17-7   Impath's 2001 fiscal year estimated vs.
actual performance.

	Estimated	Actual
Sales (millions)	$205	$190
Net Profit Margin	9.5%	5.8%
Net Income (millions)	$19.5	$11
Shares Out (millions)	15.8	16.7
EPS	2.47	0.66
P/E	34 to 42	58
Feb. '02 Share Price	$44 to $52	$38

Step 4: Industry Analysis

Understanding your candidate's industry prospects and its competitive position is an important part of the growth stock analysis process.

The Industry

According to Reuters Profile & Snapshot report, Impath provided patient-specific diagnostic and treatment information to physicians treating cancer. Pathology departments of small- to medium-sized community hospitals, where most cancer is diagnosed, were its primary customers. Reuters's description, which is pulled from the company's own SEC filings, also noted that these smaller hospitals generally are not equipped to perform their own sophisticated cancer analysis.

Industry Growth

MSN Money's Earnings Growth Rate report noted that Impath was part of the Medical-Outpatient/Homecare industry, which was expected to grow earnings 22 percent annually over the next five years. Discounting the analysts' earnings projections by 30 percent, I came up with 15 percent expected sales growth for Impath's industry. So its industry growth rate qualified as fast growth.

TABLE 17-8 Sales growth figures for Impath and its two most significant competitors.

	1999 Revenue (in millions)	% Y/Y Revenue Growth
Impath	84	52
Lab. Corp.	1699	5
Dianon Systems	76	22

Industry Concentration

The laboratory testing industry was highly fragmented with dozens of competitors. However, none that I found specialized in cancer diagnostic tests, which was Impath's specialty. Table 17-8 provides a breakdown of Impath and its two most significant competitors' sales and sales growth.

Picking Industry Winners

With 1999 annual sales of $1.7 billion, Laboratory Corporation of America was the biggest player in the clinical laboratory services industry. Impath's sales, by contrast, totaled only $84 million in 1999. LCA provided a wide spectrum of tests however, and it wasn't a cancer specialist. Further, LCA was hardly a growth prospect; its sales increased only 5 percent in 1999 compared to Impath's 52 percent sales growth in the same period. Dianon Systems was about Impath's size but was a slower grower and wasn't a cancer specialist.

I found no competitor that offered Impath's combination of rapid growth and specialization in oncology testing.

Industry Scuttlebutt

I couldn't find much industry trade news on Impath, other than reprints of its own press releases when I researched Impath in June 2000, so I called a practicing oncologist who confirmed that Impath was a leader in the cancer-testing field. A few months later, *In Vivo*, an industry trade magazine, described Impath and confirmed that it was the largest provider of cancer-testing services.

Industry Summary

Impath was operating in a fragmented industry, but it was specializing in a relatively narrow market niche, cancer testing, and was the dominant player in its segment.

Step 5: Business Plan Analysis

Business Plan Scorecard

The business model analysis evaluates qualities of a company's business plan that are likely to influence its success. Use the business plan scorecard to tabulate the scores for each category. Score each category one, minus one, or zero, corresponding to advantage, business plan disadvantage, or not applicable, respectively.

BRAND IDENTITY

Impath had a strong reputation among professionals. But results are the bottom line in a highly technical field such as oncology, and Impath's name recognition would not serve as an effective barrier to entry if a competitor offering better service entered the field. Score = 0.

OTHER BARRIERS TO ENTRY

The clinical analysis field per se is an easy business to enter. Any enterprise with sufficient backing could open a laboratory. However Impath had amassed a database of more than 500,000 analyzed cancer cases, linking symptoms with outcomes. That database afforded Impath a significant competitive advantage, and served as an effective barrier to new competition. Score = 1.

DISTRIBUTION MODEL/ACCESS TO DISTRIBUTION

Impath customers are hospitals and medical clinics, and distribution is not a factor. Score = 0.

PRODUCT USEFUL LIFE/PRODUCT PRICE

Each Impath sale applies to only one patient test. Impath's hospital and clinical clients are continuously conducting tests that require new analyses. In effect, Impath's services have very short product life and must be continuously repurchased, a business plan advantage. Score = 1.

ACCESS TO SUPPLY/NUMBER OF SUPPLIERS
Obtaining materials to perform its tests is not an issue for Impath. Score = 0.

PREDICTABLE REVENUE STREAM
Impath has contractual relationships with its client hospitals and clinics, and the resulting revenue streams are highly predictable. Score =1.

NUMBER OF CUSTOMERS
In June 2000, Impath provided services to more than 7,400 physicians at more than 1,700 hospitals and 400 oncology clinics. Clearly, a small number of customers did *not* account for a significant percentage of Impath's sales. Score = 1.

PRODUCT CYCLE
Impath provides services, and product cycle risk is not relevant to its business. Score = 0.

PRODUCT & MARKET DIVERSIFICATION
Impath serves only the oncology testing market sector with what is in essence a single product. Impath's lack of product and market diversification adds risk to its business model. Score = –1.

ORGANIC GROWTH VS. ACQUISITION GROWTH
Much of Impath's growth had come by way of acquisition. Impath's 24 percent goodwill/intangibles to total assets ratio labeled it as a serial acquirer. Score = –1.

BUSINESS MODEL SCORE
Impath's business model score of 2 equates to average.

Step 6: Management Quality

Key Executive and Board Quality
Impath's CEO had been with the company since 1990, and prior to that was a prominent academic researcher in the same field. Two other key officers had been with the company since the early 1990s.

Impath's CEO was board chairman. One Impath board member was a former vice chairman of the board of Johnson & Johnson, and had held numerous other prestigious positions. Another board member was an Impath cofounder and is a prominent pathologist. The third board member was the dean of an applied life sciences school and a cofounder and CEO of a biological life sciences firm. The fourth board member was the CEO of a medical research firm. The fifth board member was vice president of a unit of Bristol-Meyers Squibb. Only one board member, an attorney, was not actively involved in the medical profession.

Instead of investment bankers and venture capitalists, Impath's board was packed with top-notch movers and doers in Impath's industry. I ranked Impath's key executive and board quality as excellent.

CLEAN ACCOUNTING/EARNINGS GROWTH STABILITY

The clean accounting test totals the firm's one-time charges consisting of (1) unusual expenses, (2) restructuring charges, (3) purchased R&D, (4) extraordinary items, (5) accounting changes, and (6) discontinued operations found on its annual income statements, and compares that total to annual sales. Persistent one-time charges exceeding 3 percent of sales define a firm's accounting practices as unclean.

Impath's total one-time charges versus sales amounted to zero percent in its 1997, 1998, and 1999 fiscal years, qualifying Impath's accounting as clean.

The earnings growth stability test requires a visual look at the firm's quarterly earnings history to gauge its earnings volatility. Table 17-9 shows Impath's quarterly earnings history as found on Reuters Investor's Highlights report.

TABLE 17-9   Impath's quarterly earnings.

Quarters	1997	1998	1999	2000
March	0.10	0.17	0.22	0.36
June	0.16	0.22	0.28	
September	0.16	0.25	0.30	
December	0.22	0.23	0.21	
Total	0.64	0.87	1.01	

Impath's quarterly earnings record is very stable. There were no negative earnings quarters. Looking horizontally at the same quarter of each year, only one quarter (December 1999) showed earnings below the year-ago quarter.

STOCK OWNERSHIP

Impath's CEO owned around 125,000 shares and held options for another 270,000 shares. No other key officer held at least 100,000 shares, but several held options amounting for 40,000 to 100,000 or so shares.

Impath's key officers' commitment as expressed by their holdings was unimpressive.

SUMMARY

I judged Impath's key executive and board quality excellent, its accounting was clean, and its earnings stability was good. The only negative was the apparent lack of significant stock holdings by key officers, except the CEO. Overall, I rated Impath's management quality as very good.

Step 7: Financial Health

Ensuring that your candidate is not a bankruptcy candidate is a critical factor in your analysis. Different financial health tests are required depending on whether your candidate is a low- or high-debt firm. Many growth candidates are younger companies that haven't been in business long enough to acquire much debt, and thus qualify for the quick Busted Cash Burner test. High-debt firms require the Detailed Fiscal Fitness Exam.

Use the total liabilities/equity ratio (TL/E) to determine the appropriate financial test. The TL/E ratio results from dividing a firm's total liabilities by shareholders equity. The ratio is not calculated on any financial site, but both figures can be found near the bottom of the most recent balance sheet on either MSN Money or Reuters.

TL/E	Financial Health Test
less than 0.5	Busted Cash Burners
0.5 and higher	Detailed Fiscal Fitness Exam

Impath's March 2000 quarter balance sheet listed these values for the TL/E components:

Total Liabilities	$37.1 million
Shareholders' Equity	$120.1 million

Calculating TL/E:

TL/E = 37.1/120.1 = 0.3

As is the case for most growth stocks, Impath's 0.3 TL/E ratio qualified it for the busted cash burner test.

Busted Cash Burners

The first step evaluates Impath's operating cash flow history. Table 17-10 shows the cash flow figures that you would have seen on Morningstar's Financials report for Impath in June 2000.

Impath's TTM operating cash flow was negative, making it necessary to compare its burn rate to its working capital. Impath's current assets totaled $77.6 million compared to $20.3 million current liabilities. Its working capital was:

working capital = current assets – current liabilities = $57.3 million

With $57 million in working capital, and considering that Impath was not a habitual cash burner, its $0.1 million trailing twelve-month (TTM) burn rate was insignificant. Impath easily passed the busted cash burner financial strength test.

TABLE 17-10   Impath's operating cash flow history.

Period	Operating Cash Flow (millions)
TTM	-0.1
FY 12/99	1.6
FY 12/98	1.7
FY 12/97	0.8

Step 8: Profitability

Successful growth investing hinges on identifying candidates that will meet, and hopefully beat, the market's earnings growth expectations for the company. Step 7 stressed mostly balance sheet factors to ensure that your candidate is financially sound. In this step, you will analyze factors that will help you assess your candidate's earnings prospects.

When you research a stock, everything about the company's past performance—sales growth, earnings growth, earnings per share, profit margins, earnings surprises, and so forth—has already been factored into earnings growth expectations.

Those expectations are probably wrong! Your job is to figure out which way. If the expectations are too low, the stock price will rise when the market realizes its mistake, and vice versa.

The Trend Is Your Friend

Analyzing historical profitability factors representing a single point in time won't tell you much about the future. Instead, you must analyze everything from the perspective of trends. Are the profitability factors trending in a direction that foretells improving or deteriorating future results?

Sales Growth

Since sales and margins determine earnings, and earnings drive share prices, all other things being equal, faster sales growth should translate to faster share price appreciation. That relationship holds up reasonably well.

Dell Computer's 41 percent average annual sales growth translated to 56 percent average annual stock price appreciation between January 1993 and January 2001.

Bed Bath & Beyond's 35 percent average annual sales growth converted to 38 percent average annual stock price appreciation during the same period.

Alberto Culver's 10 percent average annual sales growth translated to 13 percent annual stock price appreciation between September 1992 and September 2000.

TABLE 17-11   Impath annual and year-over-year percentage sales growth.

Fiscal Year End:	12/99	12/98	12/97	12/96	12/95	12/94
FY Sales (millions)	85.4	56.3	37.1	22.0	14.7	10.0
Y/Y Sales Growth (%)	52	52	69	49	47	42

Obviously, glomming onto fast growers such as Dell and Bed Bath & Beyond pays big returns, but companies capable of producing those growth levels year-after-year are hard to come by.

Impath, however, looked promising, as Table 17-11 listing its historical fiscal year sales and sales growth rate figures as of June 2000 illustrates.

Impath was averaging more than 50 percent average annual sales growth in recent years, an impressive number. But we need to know what happens next. Is Impath's long-term growth trend faltering, maintaining, or accelerating? That requires examining its most recent quarterly sales data. Table 17-12 shows the data that you would have seen on Reuters Financial Highlights report in June 2000.

It's easier to analyze Impath's sales growth by converting its sales figures to year-over-year percentage sales growth as shown in Table 17-13.

Based on the sales growth figures available in June 2000, Impath's robust sales growth trend was still very much intact.

TABLE 17-12   Impath's quarterly sales.

Quarters	1997	1998	1999	2000
March	7845	11,713	16,970	30,563
June	9285	13,435	20,846	
September	9328	14,571	21,543	
December	10,606	16,540	26,007	

TABLE 17-13 Impath's year-over-year quarterly sales growth (%).

Quarters	1998	1999	2000
March	49	45	80
June	44	55	
September	57	48	
December	56	57	

Margin Analysis

Deteriorating margins can trigger a negative surprise, even if the company meets its sales goals. Conversely, improving margins lead to positive surprises. Analyzing margin and overhead (SG&A) trends can help you determine if margins are more likely to improve or deteriorate in upcoming quarters. Table 17-14 shows Impath's gross margin, operating margin, and SG&A history as of June 2000.

Operating margin is the most important of the three because it includes the effects of gross margin and SG&A changes. Compare the most recent quarter's operating margin to the year-ago quarter and also to the historical annual operating margins.

Impath's March 2000 quarter's operating margin increased 5 percent (15.7 vs. 14.9) compared to March 1999. Its March 2000 operating margin also compared favorably to its historical figures. Impath's improving operating margins probably reflected the reduced overhead signaled by the downtrending SG&A percentage of sales.

TABLE 17-14 Impath's margins & SG&A percentage of sales.

	Q 3/00	Q 3/99	FY 12/99	FY 12/98	FY 12/97	FY 12/96
Gross Margin	60	58	62	62	59	57
Operating Margin	15.7	14.9	14.2	15.1	15.6	12.0
SG&A % of Sales	37	37	40	40	40	41

TABLE 17-15   Impath's annual return on assets (profitability) ratios.

Fiscal Year	12/99	12/98	12/97	12/96
ROA (%)	5.5	4.6	7.9	5.5

Flat operating margin trends are acceptable, and increasing trends are even better. So Impath easily passes the operating margin test. Avoid companies with declining operating margins. As a rule of thumb, consider a 5 percent decline (e.g., 9.5 down from 10.0) significant when you're comparing annual operating margins. A 10 percent decline (e.g., 9.0 down from 10.0) is significant when you're comparing quarterly figures.

Return on Assets

Most of the profitability analysis entails comparing the company's recent performance to its own history to assess trends. ROA measures Impath's profitability in absolute terms.

ROA is best measured using annual data because the quarterly figures are too volatile. Table 17-15 shows Impath's ROA data as of June 2000.

Impath's ROA improved in 1999 compared to the year before but was still relatively low, marking it as marginal at best, on a profitability basis.

Cash Flows

Many analysts consider cash flow the only true earnings measure. Table 17-16 shows what you would have seen for Impath in June 2000.

TABLE 17-16   Impath's operating and free cash flows (millions) for its March 2000 quarter and the last four fiscal years.

	Q 3/00	FY 12/99	FY 12/98	FY 12/97	FY 12/96
Operating Cash Flow	-2.7	1.6	1.7	0.8	-1.2
Acquisitions	0	-9.3	-2.8	-6.2	-0.8
Capital Expenditures	-0.8	-3.8	-9.5	-4.1	-0.4
Free Cash Flow	-3.5	-11.5	-10.6	-9.5	-2.4

Since some of Impath's growth was fueled by acquisitions, I subtracted acquisition costs as well as capital expenditures from operating cash flow to compute its free cash flow.

Impath's operating cash flow, its real bottom line earnings, is unimpressive at first glance. With over $85 million in sales, Impath was able to put only $1.6 million in the bank in 1999. But Impath's sales soared more than 50 percent in 1999. That level of growth makes achieving positive cash flow a challenging proposition because, all things being equal, the company had to fund 50 percent higher receivables and inventories.

Impath was a cash burner on a free cash flow basis. But again, considering Impath's growth rate, positive free cash flow is hard to come by.

Step 9: Red Flags

Now it's time to check for red flags signaling a potential earnings shortfall in the current or next quarter and for yellow flags warning of longer-term problems. At your option, you can compare net income to operating cash flow, and if your candidate passes that test, skip the accounts receivables and inventory tests.

Sales Growth

A slowdown in historical year-over-year sales growth rates is a red flag, but if it exists, you would have discovered it in Step 8. In this section, you'll compare forecast sales growth rates to historical trends. It's a red flag if the forecast sales growth rates are significantly below historical levels.

Table 17-17 shows the quarterly sales summary for Impath that was shown in the Step 8 (Table 17-12), except that I've added the analysts' sales forecasts for its June and September 2000 quarters. Yahoo didn't provide consensus forecasts back then, so I used forecasts from analysts' research reports.

TABLE 17-17   Impath's quarterly sales with June and September 2000 analysts' forecasts added.

Quarters	1997	1998	1999	2000
March	7845	11,713	16,970	30,563
June	9285	13,435	20,846	30,200 (est.)
September	9328	14,571	21,543	31,200 (est.)
December	10,606	16,540	26,007	

Table 17-18 shows Impath's year-over-year percentage sales growth figures including the June and September forecasts.

Impath's forecasted 45 percent June and September year-over-year sales growth is consistent with historical trends. Forecasted growth rates around 25 percent or lower would have constituted a red flag.

Net Income vs. Operating Cash Flow

Net income or after-tax income, the bottom line on the income statement, is the top line on the cash flow statement. Cash flow from operations would normally be a larger number than net income because depreciation and amortization are subtracted from net income but not from operating cash flow. Operating cash flow should increase in proportion to net income.

TABLE 17-18   Impath's year-over-year quarterly sales growth including June and September 2000 forecasts (%).

Quarters	1998	1999	2000
March	49	45	80
June	44	55	45 (est.)
September	57	48	45 (est.)
December	56	57	

TABLE 17-19   Impath NI and OCF (millions).

Period	FY 12/99	FY 12/98	FY 12/97	FY 12/96
Net Income	8.2	7.0	3.7	-2.1
Operating Cash Flow	1.6	1.7	0.8	-1.2

Table 17-19 compares Impath's historical annual net income and operating cash flows as of June 2000.

Impath's operating cash flow doesn't even come close to matching its net income. Also, Impath's net income increased from 1998 to 1999, but its operating cash flow decreased. The combination of increasing net income and decreasing operating cash flow warns of possible earnings quality problems.

The fact that net income exceeded operating cash flow, and the net income versus cash flow divergence, are not necessarily red flags, but they call for a detailed receivables and inventory analysis.

At your option, you can skip the next section if operating cash flow does exceed net income.

Accounts Receivables/Inventories

This test compares receivables growth and inventory growth to sales growth. It's a red flag if either receivables or inventories grew significantly faster than sales over the past 12 months. The easiest way to determine if that happened is to compute the ratios of receivables to sales, and inventory to sales. The ratios are expressed as percentages of sales. For instance, if the receivables were $100 and the sales $1,000, the receivables are 10 percent of sales.

Comparing the latest ratios to year-ago figures tells you if receivables and/or inventories increased faster then sales.

Table 17-20 compares Impath's March 1999 and March 2000 quarter's sales, accounts receivables and inventory numbers.

Impath had no inventories. The receivables and/or inventory ratios must increase by at least 10 percent (e.g., from 50 to 55) to be of concern. Calculate the percentage change by dividing the latest number by the year-ago figure. For instance, the ratio increased 14 percent if the latest ratio is 40 percent compared to a year-ago 35 percent number (40 divided by 35).

TABLE 17-20   Impath March 2000 A/R and inventory analysis (all figures are millions).

Quarter	March '00	%	March '99	%
Sales	30.6		17.0	
A/R	41.9	136.9%	23.2	136.4%
Inventory	0		0	

Impath's accounts receivables were in line with year-ago levels and not a red flag.

Pension Plan Income

By checking Impath's annual report on SEC Info, I determined that, typical of newer firms, Impath offered its employees a 401k defined-contribution plan and thus there was no potential for creative accounting related to pension plan income.

Yellow Flags

The next two items are potential yellow flags. They could signal long-term problems, but they're not necessarily issues that would trigger a negative surprise as soon as the next earnings report.

CAPITAL EXPENDITURES VS. DEPRECIATION

A company must keep investing in its business to remain viable. Capital expenditures measure the amount that the company is investing in new plants and equipment, while depreciation tells you how fast it's writing off its existing capital equipment. It's a yellow flag if the company's depreciation consistently exceeds its capital expenditures. Both items are found on the cash flow statement. Table 17-21 shows Impath's historical annual depreciation and capital expenditures.

Use annual figures because capital expenditures come in discreet increments and you'll see too much volatility using the quarterly numbers. On balance, Impath's capital equipment spending exceeded its depreciation deductions.

TABLE 17-21 Impath's annual depreciation and capital expenditures (millions).

Period	FY 12/99	FY 12/98	FY 12/97	FY 12/96
Depreciation	7.0	3.5	1.5	0.8
Capital Expenditures	3.8	9.5	4.5	0.7

INCOME TAX RATE

Most corporations pay income taxes amounting to between 35 percent and 40 percent of their pretax income. Unusually low income tax rates can temporarily boost a company's reported earnings. It's a potential yellow flag if the most recent year's tax rate is more than 20 percent below the preceding three years' average rate (e.g., recent 30 percent versus 40 percent three-year average). Table 17-22 shows Impath's recent annual tax rates.

Impath's most recent income tax rate was not a potential yellow flag since it was within 10 percent of the average of the prior three years.

Consult the management's discussion in the annual report if the tax rate is abnormally low. It's not a problem if it's going to permanently remain at the lower rate. However, it will adversely impact earnings if the rate returns to its former level.

Step 10: Ownership

The percentage of shares outstanding owned by institutions and by insiders are both important factors that should be considered by growth investors.

TABLE 17-22 Impath's annual income tax rates.

Period	FY 12/99	FY 12/98	FY 12/97	FY 12/96
Income Tax Rate (%)	40	40	44	44

Institutional Ownership

Strong institutional ownership means that these in-the-know investors have analyzed your candidate and liked what they saw. Conversely, low institutional sponsorship usually means that they know something that kept them from buying the stock.

Stocks with institutional ownership exceeding 40 percent of outstanding shares are your best bet. Avoid stocks if institutions hold less than 30 percent. In June 2000, institutional holdings amounted to 57 percent of Impath's outstanding shares.

Insider Ownership

Excessive insider ownership is your biggest concern related to insider ownership. Avoid companies with insider ownership levels exceeding 55 percent of shares outstanding because it could indicate that major investors with significant holdings are waiting for the opportunity to dump their shares.

It's a potential red flag if the CEO or the CFO of a company have recently sold a significant portion (25 percent) of their existing holdings. It's not a red flag if the seller has rights to significant holdings not shown in the SEC filings. You may have to call the company's investor relations representative to determine that.

Insiders held only 6 percent of Impath's outstanding shares in June 2000, and I didn't find any sign of meaningful insider selling.

Step 11: Price Chart

Check the price chart before you buy. Growth stocks should be in an uptrend, meaning the price should be above both its 50-day and 200-day moving average when you buy. The ideal buy point is when the 50-day MA has just recently moved above the 200-day MA. There is added risk if the stock has already made a big move up, that is, if the share price is more than 50 percent above its 200-day MA.

Impath was trading at $48, above its 50-day moving average and more than 60 percent above its 200-day MA in June 2000.

Impath scored high in all categories except profitability and cash flow. I didn't know about comparing net income to operating cash flow in June 2000. If I had, I probably wouldn't have bought Impath.

When to Sell

Growth stocks can drop quickly, and your first loss is often your best loss. Develop strict sell guidelines and don't procrastinate when one of your guidelines is triggered.

Target P/E or PEG Limit Exceeded

Review your target price assumptions before taking action. It may be that your original sales or profit margin assumptions are out of date and can be revised.

Exceeding your target price means that the stock has entered a higher-risk zone, not that it won't go much higher. Growth stocks often develop strong momentum and go far beyond levels justified by fundamental analysis. You should have a profit at that point. Sell some or all of your position depending on your risk tolerance and on your ability to track the stock on a daily basis.

Any Red Flag

Fast moving growth stocks crash and burn in response to any disappointment. You won't have time to react when it happens. Reanalyze the company after each quarterly report and sell on any red flag.

Lowered Sales or Earnings Forecasts

Sales or earnings forecasts reductions lead to lower share prices and are usually followed by more of the same. Sell on any significant forecast reduction.

Competitor Reduces Guidance or Misses Forecast

All industry competitors face the same market conditions. Analysts often tell you that that first disappointment was company-specific and won't affect the other industry players. If you do own one of the other players, consider it a gift that your stock wasn't hit first and sell immediately.

Consecutive Negative Surprises

Two negative surprises in a row constitute a trend, regardless of their magnitude. Sell before the next quarterly report.

Acquisitions

Sell if your company acquires another business that is at least 25 percent (sales or market capitalization) as large as the acquiring company. Also sell if the company makes a series of smaller acquisitions that, taken together, add up to 25 percent of the company's original size.

Deteriorating Fundamentals

Sell if the firm's return on assets (ROA), operating cash flow, or operating margins deteriorate in two sequential quarters.

Restates Earlier Financials

Restating previously reported results is a major red flag signaling that there is a high risk of future problems. Sell if the company significantly restates downward previously reported sales or earnings unless new management has taken over since the results were overstated.

Same Store Sales Growth Declines

Same store sales applies to retail stores and restaurants and are sales at locations that have been operating one-year or longer, as opposed to new locations. Deteriorating same store sales tells you that something is going wrong. Sell retail stores or restaurants if same store sales drop two quarters in a row.

Sequential Large One-Time Charges

Repeated instances of significant nonrecurring charges tell you that management is scrambling to meet forecasts, and disaster looms. Sell the second time that the company takes significant one-time (nonrecurring) charges.

Summary

I sold Impath in February 2001. By then, Impath was forecasting 30 percent sales growth for all of 2001, a strong number, but only half the previous year's 62 percent figure, and thus a red flag.

Two years later Impath's CEO quit in an accounting scandal and the company eventually filed for bankruptcy.

Growth stocks usually suffer big losses when current or forecast growth rates falter compared to historical values or to expectations. Successful growth investors must learn to recognize the danger signals and react before knowledge of the faltering growth becomes widespread.

PART FOUR

_____ **MORE TOOLS**

18

EARNINGS REPORTS & CONFERENCE CALLS

Most companies issue a press release reporting their last quarter's earnings within a few weeks of the quarter's end. The SEC allows firms 45 days after the quarter's end, and 90 days after the end of their fiscal year, to file their SEC reports, so the press release data could be all that you have to go on for some time.

Companies usually conduct an analysts' conference call within hours of the earnings release. Anyone can listen in on the conference call live, or listen to a recording (via your browser), for at least a month after the call. You can access the call from the investor's section of the company's We site.

All calls follow the same structure. They begin with the CEO and CFO reading the contents of the earnings report, often filling in detail not included in the press release, followed by a question-and-answer period. The Q&A session is always the most informative part of the call. Usually only analysts are allowed to ask questions, but some companies open the Q&A to everyone. Sometimes an astute question will reveal surprising information. For instance, in one call, I learned that a key employee had years earlier been CEO of a company accused of Medicare fraud. That was significant news since his current employer was then denying the same charge.

Pundits say that you can get a sense of management quality from the way that key executives handle the tough questions. That doesn't work for me. I find that I'm frequently influenced by the tone and timbre, as well as the sincerity conveyed by their voices. Then months later I realize that I've been conned by these smooth talkers.

I've learned that it's best to focus on the numbers. Analyze the reports using the strategies described in Tool 9, red flags. Here are some pointers.

Reported Earnings

Many firms report two earnings numbers: (1) pro forma, cash, operating, or some other vague term, and (2) earnings according to generally accepted accounting practices (GAAP).

Pro Forma

The reported pro forma or cash earnings typically exclude anything that the firm considers nonrecurring. Waste Management took that concept to the limit when it reported $181 million December 2000 quarter pro forma earnings. Waste Management, it turned out, had decided to ignore "$24 million of operating expense, primarily for truck painting/signage costs and loss on a construction contract," and another $49 million of SG&A costs when it calculated its pro forma earnings.

Unfortunately, market analysts play along with these shenanigans and they compare the firm's reported pro forma earnings to their forecasts when deciding whether or not the company beat estimates.

In many cases, you'll find that even though a company is said to have met or exceeded analysts' forecasts, in fact they didn't.

Nevertheless, the share price initially responds to the perceived surprise, which is the difference between the analysts consensus forecasts and the earnings headlined in the company's earnings report without regard to the validity of the assumptions used to compute the pro forma earnings.

Generally Accepted Accounting Practices

Fortunately, the companies also include their real GAAP earnings in their quarterly report. Almost all include a complete income statement and many provide at least some items from their balance sheet. Ignore the pro forma reports and focus your attention on the GAAP financial statements.

Here's a list of items that you should check, if available.

SALES

Did the reported sales meet forecasts? Compare the just reported year-over-year sales growth to the year-ago figure. A significant sales growth slowdown is a red flag.

OPERATING MARGIN

Compare the just reported quarter's operating margin to the year-ago margin. The year-ago income statement figures are always listed in a column next to the just reported quarter.

A significant decline in operating margin is a red flag. Verify management's excuses for declining performance. For instance, Boeing's December 2001 quarter's operating margin slipped to 1.6 percent from the year-ago 4.9 percent figure. Management blamed the shortfall on costs associated with the events of September 11. The company did indeed suffer costs related to those events and listed them as a separate line item on its income statement. However, Boeing's income statement also showed that its December 2001 quarter gross margins were 15.1 percent, down from the year-ago 16.8 percent. That was a significant shortfall and was unrelated to 9/11. The drop in gross margins would have impacted profits regardless of September 11.

RECEIVABLES AND INVENTORIES

Compute the accounts receivables and inventory levels percentages of sales, and compare to the year-ago figures. Either receivables or inventories increasing faster than sales is a red flag.

Guidance

Many firms now routinely include future quarter's sales and earnings forecasts in their earnings reports. Analysts will change their forecasts accordingly. Compare the company's new guidance to prior forecasts. Pay particular attention to the next two quarter's sales forecasts. Any significant reduction is a red flag.

Analysts Research

Analysts following the company usually publish their take on the company's earnings report within a day or two. Most are predictable. They'll reduce their forecasts in response to bad news and vice versa. However, some will point out information that you didn't notice or interpret the results in a way that didn't occur to you. Check out as many analysts' reports as possible before reacting to the earnings report.

Summary

Listening to the conference call, a careful analysis of the press release, and a review of analysts' interpretation of the earnings report can give you a heads up as to potential problems or improving performance weeks before the SEC reports become available.

19

DETECTING
SCAMS, FRAUDS,
AND PUMP & DUMP

I don't know about you, but I get daily email from people I don't know advising me to buy stocks that I've never heard of. These missives read like research reports from professional stock market analysts profiling companies that have just developed exciting new products or services with huge market potential.

I know that these stock-hyping emails work, because occasionally I check the touted stock's trading volume. Typically, the number of shares traded daily jumps by a factor of four or so, for days after the email.

Back in November 2001, I received a particularly enticing report from a "new financial service" that said it was "striving to find investment opportunities." I'll call this helpful adviser Ted Touter. Ted said his analyses would save me "hours of research," and that "each recommendation is extensively researched."

Opportunity Knocks

Ted was plugging a company, let's call it Miracle Tech, that was developing batteries for the automotive and electric car industries. Its mission, according to Ted, was to exploit patented and proprietary battery technology to create "the ultimate battery, characterized by superior power, higher capacity, lighter weight, and minimal acid and lead content."

You'd think that the battery project would consume the resources of most young companies, but not Miracle Tech.

The firm was concurrently developing a device to detect the presence of water in storage and fuel tanks. Wait, there's more! Evidently grain must be dried before storing, and Miracle Tech was working on a microwave device to do just that. Even that wasn't enough to satisfy the eager Miracle Tech scientists. The company was also designing equipment to join large diameter pipes together using a magnetic technology.

Ted expected Miracle Tech's earnings to grow from a loss of $0.11 per share in 2001 to a profit of $0.89 in 2005. Based on these forecasts, Ted targeted a $1.80 per share stock price by the end of 2002, and $18 by the end of 2005. That amounted to a tidy 3,000 percent gain in four years, since the stock was then trading at only $0.48 per share.

Shoestring Operation

Obviously, Miracle Tech must have employed hordes of research scientists and technicians to manage the simultaneous development of those impressive products. Here's the real miracle: Miracle Tech was doing the whole job with a staff of only 10 full-time, and two part-time employees, toiling away in a 5,000 square foot facility that it had rented for $2,000 per month.

I'm not sure how Miracle Tech managed to pay even that meager staff since, as of July 31, 2001, it had only $8,000 in the bank and its debts far exceeded its assets.

With an empty bank account, Miracle Tech must have been cranking up sales. But that wasn't happening. Miracle Tech's total sales in the previous 12 months totaled a flat zero. Nothing!

I checked up on Miracle Tech again in March 2002, when I was writing this chapter. By that time the firm's October 2001 quarterly report had been filed with the SEC. The company, with its stock now trading at 30 cents, still hadn't sold a dime's worth of products. But it had managed to burn through $767,000 in the quarter, mostly on consulting fees.

Miracle Tech may not have sold anything, but it had been busy cranking out press releases.

On November 6, 2001, Miracle Tech announced a partnership with a Chinese company based in Singapore to market Miracle Tech's products. The two companies seemed most excited about Miracle Tech's magnetic pipe joining technology.

On December 18, Miracle Tech announced the formal opening of its Beijing office, mentioned its new partnership with the Chinese company, referring to it as a "hugely significant step."

On January 30, 2002, Miracle Tech announced an agreement with a unit of the Chinese government to investigate and develop Miracle Tech's magnetic pipe joining technology.

On February 11, 2002 Miracle said that it was in discussions with a major Middle-Eastern gas producer regarding its pipe joining process.

I suppose that it's theoretically possible for Miracle Tech and its shareholders to hit the jackpot with one of their projects. However, most companies developing products as sophisticated as Miracle Tech's, spend tens of millions of dollars, and employ staffs numbering into the thousands.

Hyping Pays Well

How come Ted Touter didn't see what I saw? What about all that careful research that Ted promised in his email? Reading the disclaimer at the end of Ted's report revealed that Miracle Tech paid him to prepare and mail the report—he was paid 100,000 shares of Miracle Tech stock. It's legal for Ted to promote Miracle Tech and to get paid for it as long as he reveals the payments in the document and confesses that Miracle Tech, in truth, supplied his so-called research.

Companies like Miracle Tech hire people like Ted to create investor interest, moving the stock price up, and equally important, increasing the trading volume, thereby allowing insiders to dump their holdings. This process is known as pump & dump.

Quick Hype Checks

It's understandable that investors get taken in by promoters like Ted. It's everybody's dream to get in on the ground floor of the next big thing.

But many of the stocks you hear about from people that you don't know are not real businesses. They're just shells organized to sell stock to gullible investors.

Here are some simple checks you can run to spotlight the Miracle Techs of the world so that you don't waste time researching, or worse, buying them.

You can find everything you need on almost any major financial site. I'll use Yahoo's Key Statistics report to illustrate the process. Get a quote on Yahoo, and select Key Statistics.

PRICE

Minimum: $1

Many professional investors shun stocks trading at prices below $5 per share. However, scores of fallen angel tech stocks were still trading in the $2 to $5 range in early 2002. So $1 would have been a reasonable minimum acceptable share price in that market. Miracle Tech's $0.30 share price flunked.

MARKET CAPITALIZATION

Minimum: $50 million

Market cap is the total value of a company (shares out multiplied by the share price). Larger companies are considered safer investments than smaller companies, and those with market caps below $100 million or so are considered too risky by many investors. You will avoid most pump & dump stocks by staying above $50 million. Miracle Tech's $9 million market cap would have easily disqualified it in that category.

PRICE/BOOK RATIO

Maximum: 25

P/B (share price divided by stockholders' equity) is the appropriate value gauge when a company has neither sales nor earnings.

P/B ratios range from below 1 for value-priced companies to 20 or so for fast-growing startups. Avoid companies with ratios exceeding 25. Miracle Tech flunked because its book value was negative, thus making its P/B not measurable.

TTM REVENUE

Minimum: $40 million

A hallmark of pump & dump stocks is little or no sales (revenue). Most companies worth considering rack up annual sales exceeding $40 million, so avoid companies below that level. As mentioned earlier, Miracle Tech's annual sales totaled zero.

CURRENT RATIO

Minimum: 0.6

Current ratio, a comparison of a company's assets to its current debts, is a good measure of a company's financial condition. A current ratio of 1.0 or higher is considered safe, but some very solid companies operate with lower ratios in the 0.7 to 1.0 range. Avoid companies with current ratios below 0.6. When I checked, Miracle Tech's current ratio was 0.3.

Summary

Thousands of U.S.-traded companies meet all five of these requirements. You can avoid these risky bets by requiring your candidates to meet at least four of the five.

HOW TO READ
FINANCIAL STATEMENTS

The SEC requires that public corporations submit financial statements four times a year (quarterly). Quarterly reports (10Q) must be filed within 45 days of the end of each quarter, and a 10K (annual) report is required within 90 days of the end of the company's fiscal year.

The SEC reports are filed in electronic format and are immediately available on the SEC's EDGAR database (www.sec.gov). Anyone can access the SEC database directly, but it's easier to use a third-party site such as SEC Info.

Data services such as Core Data and Reuters compile the EDGAR data into more user-friendly formats for display on major financial sites. These reports typically display the five most recent quarters or years on one page to facilitate comparisons.

There is usually several days' delay after a report is filed with the SEC before it appears on the compiled reports. However, Core Data and Reuters update their financial statements using data from each company's quarterly report press release. So that preliminary data is often available weeks before the firm files its SEC report.

The SEC requires three financial statements in each quarterly and annual report.

- **Income statement:** Shows a company's sales and expenses for a quarter or for a year.

- **Balance sheet:** A snapshot showing the company's financial condition as of the last business day of the reporting period.

- **Cash flow statement:** Shows the change in the company's cash position from the beginning to the end of the reporting period.

Income Statement

The income statement, sometimes called the profit and loss statement, shows the firm's sales and expenses, for the quarter or fiscal year, and for the year-ago period. Here are terms which typically appear on the income statement.

- **Revenues:** The company's total sales for the period. Sometimes another revenue figure is included showing sales unrelated to its main business.

- **Cost of sales:** The direct material and labor costs of making or acquiring the products sold. Cost of sales often includes depreciation and amortization, but it doesn't include marketing, R&D, or other indirect costs.

- **Gross profit:** Revenues minus cost of sales.

- **Research and development:** Costs of developing new products and services.

- **Sales and marketing:** Often combined with general and administrative costs.

- **General and administrative:** All other expenses that are not listed separately.

- **Depreciation and amortization:** A noncash accounting entry. *Depreciation* represents the loss in value of hard assets such as buildings and machinery over the reporting period. When a company makes an acquisition, the excess paid over the acquired firm's book value is termed goodwill. Until recently, the acquiring company was required to *amortize* the goodwill over a specified period. That requirement was changed in 2002, and firms are no longer required to amortize goodwill. Note: some companies include D&A in the cost of sales.

- **Interest expense:** Interest on loans acquired to finance the firm's main business.

- **Total operating expenses:** The total of all expenses listed above including cost of sales.

- **Operating income:** Revenues less operating expenses, also known as EBIT.

- **Interest income/expense:** Interest income or expenses not associated with the company's main business.

- **Income before tax:** Operating income less interest expense.

- **Income tax:** Taxes due for period.

- **Net income:** Income before tax less income tax. This is the bottom line net profit.

- **Average number of shares:** The average number of shares outstanding during the period.

- **Earnings per share:** Net income divided by average number of shares.

Balance Sheet

The balance sheet lists a firm's assets and liabilities as of the last day of the reporting period. On traditional balance sheets, assets are listed in a column on the left and liabilities on the right. Accounting rules require that the sum of those two columns match. Since assets usually exceed liabilities, another entry, called shareholders equity, is added to the right column to make the column totals match. The shareholders equity is negative when liabilities exceed assets. Nowadays, balance sheets list everything in a single column, but the same principles apply.

Assets and liabilities are divided into two sections: current and long-term.

Current assets typically include cash, accounts receivable, inventories and prepaid expenses. Long-term assets include buildings, equipment, long-term investments, and goodwill.

Current liabilities are short-term debts such as accounts payable, short-term loans, the current portion (due this year) of long-term debts, lease obligations, and the like. Long-term debt includes lease obligations as well as bond obligations and other long-term loans.

Current Assets

- **Cash and equivalents:** Cash and highly liquid fixed income investments with maturities of three months or less.

- **Short-term investments:** Stocks and other liquid securities.

- **Accounts receivable:** Money owed to the company by customers for products received.

- **Inventory:** Raw materials, work in process, and finished products.

Long-Term Assets

- **Property, plant, and equipment:** All hard assets such as buildings, airplanes, machinery, and so forth.

- **Goodwill:** A product of an acquisition. Goodwill is the difference between the purchase price and the book value of the acquired company.

- **Intangibles:** Patents, trademarks, and so forth.

- **Long-term investments:** Investment in other companies, and so forth.

Current Liabilities

- **Accounts payable:** Amounts owed to suppliers, consultants, contractors, and so forth.

- **Accrued expenses:** Similar to accounts payable.

- **Short-term debt:** Any borrowings that must be repaid within one year.

- **Current portion LT debt:** The portion of long-term debt principal and interest due within one year.

- **Capital leases:** Lease payments due within one year.

Long Term Debt

- **Long-term debt:** Bonds and other long-term credit.

- **Capital lease obligations:** If a company signs a 10-year lease, the entire 10-years' payments are considered a long-term debt. This entry covers the lease payments due beyond 12 months.

- **Deferred income tax:** Taxes due, but not yet paid.

- **Deferred anything:** Any income statement expense that hasn't been paid can go here.

- **Other liabilities:** Other long-term obligations.

- **Total liabilities:** Total of all short- and long-term liabilities.

Shareholders Equity

A variety of accounting entries go in this section to make the total liabilities plus shareholders equity equal the total assets.

Statement of Cash Flows

Shows the cash generated or consumed by the company's business operations, and investing and financing activities. The cash flow statement consists of three sections:

- Operating
- Investing
- Financing activities

Unlike the quarterly income statement that shows each quarter's results separately, the quarterly cash flow statement shows fiscal year-to-date totals for each line item.

Operating Activities

The operating cash flows can be shown in one of two formats. The direct method lists the cash received and disbursed by line item. The more widely used indirect method starts with the net income and adds back the noncash deductions that reduced reported earnings, and subtracts real cash expenses that, according to accounting rules, weren't deducted from earnings.

- **Net income:** Reported after-tax income.

- **Depreciation and amortization:** Reverses noncash D&A added to operating costs on the income statement. If the D&A charge wasn't listed as a separate line item on the income statement, it was added to cost of sales, thereby reducing the reported gross profit by the D&A amount.

- **Deferred taxes:** Taxes deducted from income that have not yet been paid.

- **Tax benefits from employee stock options:** When an employee exercises an option to buy stock, the difference between market price at the time of exercise, and the price the employee pays, is taxable income for the employee. However, the employer is allowed to deduct the same amount from its income taxes for the period. The tax credit shows up as positive cash flow since it was deducted from income, but not paid. Most Websites do not list stock option benefits as a separate line item on their cash flow statements. It is shown separately, however, on the company's SEC reports.

■ **Deferred revenue:** Revenues received that have not as yet appeared on the income statement, usually because they are for services not yet provided.

■ **Accounts receivables and inventories:** These working capital items are shown as negative numbers (subtracted) if their value increased during the period, and vice versa. If a company sells its receivables to a third party, a process call "factoring," the amount received from the third party increases cash from operations.

■ **Accounts payable:** Added to operating cash flow if the monies owed increased, and subtracted if the accounts payable decreased during the period.

■ **Cash from operations:** Reported net income adjusted for operating cash flow line items.

Investing Activities

Investing cash flow includes capital expenditures and other investments.

■ **Capital expenditures:** Net investments in buildings and equipment. Operating cash flow less capital expenditures is typically defined as free cash flow.

Software development costs are frequently capitalized instead of appearing as a charge on the income statement. In those instances, the capitalized software expenditures are listed in investing activities. Companies capitalizing on software development will report higher operating cash flow than if they hadn't capitalized those costs.

■ **Acquisitions:** Cash flows resulting from the acquisition or sale of a subsidiary, partnership, and so forth.

■ **Purchase license:** Cisco Systems and probably others list a separate purchase license line item. Consider these and similar entries the same as capital expenditures when computing free cash flow.

- **Purchase and sales of investments:** Investments not directly related to the company's main business.

- **Change in long-term receivables:** Changes in working capital (inventories, receivables, and accounts payable) are typically included in the operating cash flow total. However, Nortel Networks, and possibly others, lists changes in long-term receivables in the investing section.

Financing Activities

Money raised from the sale of the company's own stock as well as the net of new debt versus paid-down debts and dividends paid out.

Net Change in Cash

The net effect of operating, investing, and financing activities to the company's total cash position is listed on this line.

Finding the Data

The financial statements included with the SEC reports provide more detail than the statements provided by most Websites. But the financial sites usually present the data in a format better suited to analysis. For instance, most display several quarters, or years, side by side, making it easier to spot trends.

Reuters and MSN Money both provide easily readable financial statements. Reuters reports the numbers exactly as reported to the SEC, while MSN Money subtracts D&A from cost of sales before computing gross margin.

MSN Money lists EBITDA as a separate line item, a big help when you're analyzing financial strength (see Chapter 10). Unfortunately, MSN Money's income statements combine R&D and SG&A expenses into one SG&A line item, making the statements unsuitable for many analyses. On the other hand, MSN Money's key ratios and financial statements 10-year summaries are essential tools for calculating target prices (Chapter 6).

Hoover's simplifies margin analysis by calculating gross margins, operating margins, and profit margins for you. Hoover's calculates its gross margins excluding D&A, making them usable for comparing gross margins between companies. Hoover's combines the income statement and balance sheet on the same page, making it easier to calculate receivables and inventory percentages of sales. Like MSN Money, Hoover's doesn't separate SG&A and R&D expenses on its income statements, even on their premium in-depth financials. Hoover's free service doesn't provide cash flow statements.

Morningstar is the only site I've found that displays TTM operating cash flow, making its Financials report a huge timesaver for our busted cash burner analysis (Chapter 10).

Pro Forma Accounting vs. GAAP

During the 1990s, many firms, especially techs, emphasized pro forma results in their earnings reports over the numbers resulting from generally accepted accounting practices (GAAP). Originally pro forma meant "as if" and was mainly employed to present the results of recently merged companies as if they had always been a single company. Lately company managements gloomed onto pro forma as a way of inflating their reported earnings by designating a variety of loss items as nonoperating or nonrecurring, and simply not counting them when computing earnings. Unfortunately, the analyst community decided that was a good idea and based their published earnings forecasts on pro forma instead of GAAP results.

However the SEC requires companies to report their results in GAAP format. So at least one of the detailed financial statements included in quarterly report press releases, and all financial statements filed with the SEC and compiled on financial Websites do follow GAAP standards. Since the analysts' earnings forecasts don't match GAAP earnings, you can't compare forecast EPS to historical values found on the company's financial statements.

The entire pro forma issue is in the spotlight at this writing, and it's possible that its use will have diminished by the time you read this.

B

ANALYSIS SCORECARDS

The value and growth analyses scorecards follow the same steps as the corresponding analysis chapters. Use the scorecards to document your conclusions while you are analyzing a candidate. You'll find both, for ease of photocopying, at the end of the appendix.

A single analysis step could involve multiple scorecard tests. For instance, Scorecard Step 4, Industry Analysis, includes two tests described in the corresponding analysis chapter: Industry Growth, and Industry Concentration. The scorecard tests award points for desirable characteristics and vice versa. Each test is worth a single point, but some tests can add or subtract the point, while others can only add points, and still others can only deduct a point. Some tests can disqualify a candidate from further consideration.

Generally, positive totals reflect strong candidates. But the scorecard is a guide, not the final answer. It can't cover all the nuances of your research and common sense should prevail over the numerical scores.

After you've analyzed a firm, examine where your candidate lost points and try to find similar companies without those weaknesses. For instance, look for a prospect with clean accounting if your candidate lost points in that area.

Save the scorecards whether or not you decide to buy the stock. You'll be amazed at how much you'll learn by reviewing your scorecards months later in light of the company's subsequent stock price performance.

Value Stock Analysis Scorecard

I'll use ATI Technologies, the same company I used to illustrate the value analysis process, to explain how to score a value candidate.

Step 1. Analysts' Ratings and Forecasts

The best value prospects are stocks that market analysts don't like much. The Sentiment Index reflects analysts' buy/sell ratings and the scorecard rewards low sentiment scores. It penalizes firms with high earnings growth forecasts and/or positive earnings growth forecast trends. ATI scored one Sentiment Index point and no earnings growth penalty points.

Step 2. Valuation

Value candidate's share prices should reflect low growth expectations. The score rewards candidates with implied average annual earnings growth below five percent and penalizes those with implied growth exceeding 10 percent.

ATI's 5 percent implied growth scored zero.

Step 3. Target Price

Buying at the right price is critical for successful value investing. The target price formula establishes both a low- and high-target buy price and it's okay to buy within or below that range. The scorecard rewards candidates with share prices trading below the buy range, and penalizes those trading above.

ATI was trading below its low buy target, and thus earned one point.

Step 4. Industry Analysis

It isn't necessary that value candidates be in a high-growth industry, but stagnant or declining industries are bad news. Consequently, the scorecard penalizes firms in industries growing less than 3 percent annually. Participating in a fast-growing industry increases your chances of success, and the scorecard rewards firms in industries growing faster than 15 percent.

I forecast ATI's industry growth at 21 percent; therefore it earned one point.

The scorecard awards one point for candidates in concentrated industries. ATI had only one major competitor, thus earning it one point.

Step 5. Business Plan

Transfer the business plan score computed during your analysis to the scorecard. ATI's business plan score totaled minus five. Typical of many tech firms, ATI's score suffered from short product cycles, long product lives, unpredictable revenue streams, and few barriers to entry.

Step 6. Management Quality

The right management can make a good company great, so the scorecard rewards companies with key executive and board quality that you graded as very good or excellent. Ineffective management's results will show up in other performance measures and the scorecard doesn't deduct for low grades. I had rated ATI's management as fair, so it didn't earn a point for this test.

Most firms do have clean accounting and show reasonable earnings growth stability, so the scorecard penalizes those that don't pass these tests, but doesn't reward those that do. I rated ATI's accounting as clean, and its earnings growth stability as good, so it didn't lose any points.

Step 7. Financial Health

Failing the appropriate financial health test disqualifies a candidate. ATI qualified for the busted cash burners test and passed.

Step 8. Profitability

Your best value candidates are firms that were highly profitable before they stumbled and can be expected to return to previous profitability levels. The scorecard rewards firms with expected return on assets averaging above 14 percent, and penalizes those below 6 percent. ATI's ROA averaged around 20 percent before it hit bad times in its 2000 fiscal year. I assumed it would return to that level, earning it one point.

Step 9. Red Flags

Since a value candidate's financial statements are probably already in shambles, the analysis doesn't look for red flags. However it does compare historical capital expenditures to depreciation write-offs, a yellow flag test, and deducts a point from firms failing this test. ATI's capital investments consistently exceeded its depreciation expenses, so it wasn't penalized.

Step 10. Ownership

Very high insider ownership spells risk, and this test penalizes firms in that category. ATI's insider ownership was far below the 55 percent limit, and thus wasn't penalized.

Step 11. Price Chart

A strong price chart indicates that your candidate's recovery prospects have already been recognized and it's probably too late to buy. This step penalizes firms with share prices 10 percent or more above their 200-day moving average.

ATI's share price was trading below its 200-day MA, so it wasn't penalized.

Summary

ATI's minus five business plan score drove its total down to only one point, barely in positive territory. Tech firms tend to have low scoring business plans, and ATI's unpredictable revenue stream and small number of customers exacerbated the problem.

Growth Stock Analysis Scorecard

I'll use Impath, the cancer diagnostic service provider, to demonstrate how to fill out the growth stock scorecard.

Step 1. Analysts' Ratings and Forecasts

Good growth candidates often have relatively weak, but not too weak sentiment scores, combined with strong earnings growth prospects.

The scorecard rewards firms with sentiment scores in the minus two to plus two range, and penalizes those with scores below minus two (too weak) and above plus eight (too strong). It penalizes companies with forecast annual earnings growth below 15 percent. Negative earnings forecast trends (forecast for the same period has declined from 90 days ago), or a history of negative earnings surprises (reported earnings below forecast) spell trouble and disqualify growth candidates.

Impath's zero value Sentiment Index earned it one point. Its 41 percent year-over-year forecast earnings growth was well above the minimum, so Impath was not penalized. Impath's earnings forecasts were trending up, and it did not show a persistent history of negative earnings surprises, so it was not disqualified by those tests.

Step 2. Valuation

Promising growth candidates are often richly valued, but unrealistic valuations signal high risk. This test rewards stocks priced below their expected year-over-year earnings growth rate, but penalizes those priced for more than 40 percent annual earnings growth, regardless of the analysts' forecasts.

Impath's share price reflected implied growth slightly below its forecast 30 percent earnings growth, and thus earned one point.

Step 3. Target Price

This test rewards firms trading within or below their calculated target buy range. However, since growth stocks often trade for extended periods above values dictated by their fundamentals, it doesn't penalize those trading above the target buy range until they move up into the sell target range.

Impath earned one point because it was trading within its target price buy range.

Step 4. Industry Analysis

You'll find your best growth candidates in fast-growing, concentrated industries. Consequently, this test rewards firms in industries growing faster than 20 percent and penalizes those in industries growing less than 15 percent annually. Firms in concentrated industries earn another point, but since most industries don't fit that description, firms in fragmented industries aren't penalized.

I forecast Impath's industry growth at 15 percent, so it did not earn a point for industry growth. Also, it participated in a fragmented industry, so it didn't earn a point in that category either.

Step 5. Business Plan

Transfer the business plan score computed during your analysis to the scorecard. Impath's business plan score was two, losing points for lack of market and product diversification, and for depending on acquisitions for much of its growth.

Step 6. Management Quality

Growth and value investors alike will benefit by picking firms with quality management. The scorecard rewards companies with key executive and board quality that you graded as very good or excellent. Points are not deducted for poor management. I had rated Impath's management as excellent, so it earned one point.

Since clean accounting and reasonable stabile earnings growth are the norm, firms that have those qualities aren't rewarded, but those that don't are penalized.

I rated Impath's accounting as clean, and its earnings growth stability as good, so it wasn't penalized.

Step 7. Financial Health

Failing the appropriate financial health test disqualifies a candidate. Impath qualified for the busted cash burners test and passed.

Step 8. Profitability

Strong sales growth and profit margins are hallmarks of promising growth candidates. The sales growth test rewards firms with growth exceeding 25 percent and penalizes those growing slower than 15 percent. Similarly, the return on assets test rewards firms with ROA above 14 percent and penalizes those with ROA below 6 percent.

Deteriorating operating margins warn of future problems. Significant margin declines disqualify candidates. By the same token, persistent cash burners are riskier investments than cash generators, and are also disqualified.

Impath's 50 percent plus year-over-year sales growth earned it a point in that category, but was penalized for its below-par 5 percent ROA.

Impath's operating margins were on the rise, and it was not a persistent cash burner, so it was not disqualified on those counts.

Step 9. Red Flags

Red flags signal slowing growth, a disaster for a growth company's shareholders. The discovery of any red flags disqualifies a growth candidate. Yellow flags pointing to longer-term problems signify added risk but are not necessarily disqualifying factors. The scorecard penalizes a firm for each of the two potential yellow flags found.

Impath's analysis found no red or yellow flags.

Step 10. Ownership

Mutual funds and other institutional buyers usually load up on growth stocks. Lack of institutional ownership signals that these tuned-in buyers don't think that they can make money owning your candidate. The institutional ownership test disqualifies growth candidates showing less than 30 percent institutional ownership.

Very high insider ownership may be a tip-off that big shareholders are waiting for an opportunity to unload at least a portion of their holdings, an event likely to pressure the share price. This test penalizes firms with more than 55 percent insider ownership.

Step 11. Price Chart

Growth stocks should be moving up in price, not down. However stocks well into strong uptrends are riskier than stocks that have just begun their move. This test penalizes firms with share prices trading below their 200-day moving average (downtrend), or more than 50 percent above their 200-day MA (moved up too fast).

Impath, trading 60 percent above its MA, was penalized one point.

Summary

Impath scored a respectable five points. Participating in a relatively slow growing and fragmented industry held down its total. Further, its slow industry growth rate impelled Impath to pursue a growth by acquisition strategy, further reducing its score.

VALUE STOCK ANALYSIS SCORECARD

Company:_____ Date: _____

Step 1. Analysts' Ratings & Forecasts

Sentiment Index
Add one point if the Sentiment Index score is minus 4 or below.
Subtract one point if the SI score is greater than 2.

Earnings Growth
Subtract one point if the forecast year-over-year earnings growth exceeds 4 %.

Earnings Forecast Trend
Subtract one point if the EPS forecasts increased two cents or more
during the last 90 days.

Step 2. Valuation

Implied Growth
Add one point if the implied growth is less than 5%.
Subtract one point if the implied growth exceeds 10%.

Step 3. Target Price

Current price vs. target buy price
Add one point if the current price is below the <u>low</u> target buy price.
Subtract one point if the current price exceeds the <u>high</u> target buy price.

Step 4. Industry Analysis

Industry Growth
Add one point if the industry sales growth rate exceeds 15%.
Subtract one point if the industry growth rate is less than 3%.

Industry Concentration
Add one point if the industry has less than four major competitors.

Step 5. Business Plan

Business Plan Score
Record business plan score.

Step 6. Management Quality

Key Executive & Board Quality
Add one point if you rated the Key Executive & Board Quality very good or excellent.

Clean Accounting/Earnings Growth Stability
Subtract one point if the non-recurring charges percentage of sales averaged 3% or more
over the past five years, or if you judged the earnings growth stability as poor.

Stock Ownership (not included in score)

Step 7. Financial Health
Financial health is a pass or fail test. <u>Disqualify</u> candidates that fail the appropriate test.

Step 8. Profitability

Expected Return on Assets
Expected return on assets is the ROA that you expect the firm to achieve in its recovery year.
Add one point if the expected ROA exceeds 14%. Subtracted one point if the expected
ROA is less than 6%.

Step 9. Red Flags

Historical Capital Expenses vs. Depreciation ——
> Subtract one point if recent annual depreciation charges generally exceeded
> capital expenditures in the same year.

Step 10. Ownership

Total Insider Ownership ——
> Subtract one point if insider ownership exceeds 55% of shares outstanding

Step 11. Price Chart

Share Price vs. Moving Average ——
> Subtract one point if the share price is more than 10% above its 200-day MA

TOTAL ——

GROWTH STOCK ANALYSIS SCORECARD

Company:_____ Date: _____

Step 1. Analysts' Ratings & Forecasts

Sentiment Index
_____
Add one point if the Sentiment Index score is within the range of minus two to plus two.
Subtract one point if the SI score is less than minus 2 or greater than 8.

Earnings Growth
_____
Subtract one point if the forecast year-over-year earnings growth is less than 15%.

Earnings Forecast Trend
Disqualify candidate if the current or next fiscal year EPS forecast decreased three cents or more during the last 90 days.

Earnings Surprise History
Disqualify candidate if two of the last four earnings surprises were negative.

Step 2. Valuation

Implied Growth
_____
Add one point if the implied growth is less than next fiscal year's forecast year-over-year percentage earnings growth. Subtract one point if the implied growth exceeds 40%.

Step 3. Target Price

Current price vs. target buy price
_____
Add one point if the current price is below the high target buy price.
Subtract one point if the current price exceeds the low target sell price.

Step 4. Industry Analysis

Industry Growth
_____
Add one point if the industry sales growth rate exceeds 20%.
Subtract one point if the industry growth rate is less than 15%.

Industry Concentration
_____
Add one point if the industry has less than four major competitors.

Step 5. Business Plan

Business Plan Score
_____
Record business plan score.

Step 6. Management Quality

Key Executive & Board Quality
_____
Add one point if you rated the key exec & board quality very good or excellent.

Clean Accounting/Earnings Growth Stability
_____
Subtract one point if the non-recurring charges percentage of sales averaged 3% or more over the past five years, or if you judged the earnings growth stability as poor.

Stock Ownership (not included in score)

Step 7. Financial Health

Financial health is a pass or fail test. Disqualify candidates that fail the appropriate test.
_____

Step 8. Profitability

Sales Growth   ———

> Add one point if recent historical year-over-year sales growth exceeds 25%.
> Subtract one point if recent historical year-over-year sales growth is less than 15%.

Operating Margins

> Disqualify candidate if operating margins are declining as defined in Chapter 17.

Return on Assets   ———

> Add one point if the recent annual ROA averaged higher than 14%.
> Subtract one point if the recent annual ROA averaged less than 6%.

Operating Cash Flow

> Disqualify candidate if its operating cash flow was negative in two of its last three fiscal years.

Step 9. Red Flags

Red Flags

> Disqualify candidate if any red flags are detected.

Yellow Flags   ———

> Subtract one point for each yellow flag detected.

Step 10. Ownership

Institutional Ownership

> Disqualify candidate if less than 30% institutional ownership.

Total Insider Ownership   ———

> Subtract one point if insider ownership exceeds 55% of shares outstanding.

Step 11. Price Chart

Share Price vs. Moving Average   ———

> Subtract one point if the share price is below its 200-day MA or more than 50%
> above the moving average.

TOTAL   ———

C

GLOSSARY

Accounts Receivable: Money owed by customers for received goods or services. Customers must have been billed for items to be included in receivables.

Analyst: A person who publishes buy/hold/sell recommendations and earnings forecasts for a stock. Buy-side analysts work for institutional buyers, and sell-side analysts work for brokerages or investment banking houses.

Balance Sheet: A financial statement listing a company's assets (what it owns) and liabilities (what it owes) as of a specific date, usually the last day of a company's fiscal quarter.

Bond: A long-term promissory note issued by a corporation.

Bond Rating: A grade evaluating the quality of a bond. AAA is generally the highest, or most creditworthy rating.

Book Value: Total shareholder's equity from balance sheet divided by the number of shares outstanding.

Capitalization-weighted: The largest companies in terms of market capitalization that influence an index or other calculation the most.

Capitalize: Costs of items such as buildings, equipment, and other items with a useful lifetime exceeding one year are categorized as assets to be depreciated over a number of years, rather than being expensed in the year of purchase.

Cash Burner: A firm consistently reporting negative operating cash flow.

Cash Flow: After-tax income minus preferred dividends and general partner distributions plus depreciation, depletion, and amortization (Reuters Profile & Snapshot Report definition). See Operating Cash Flow and Free Cash Flow.

Conference Call: A multiparty telephone call hosted by a company, primarily for analysts, shortly after making an earnings announcement.

Consensus Estimate or Rating: The average of analysts' individual earnings forecasts or buy/sell ratings.

Current Ratio: Current assets divided by current liabilities.

Debt to Equity (Long-Term): Total long-term debt divided by total shareholder equity.

Debt to Equity (Total): Total (short- and long-term) debt divided by total shareholder equity.

Dividends: Cash or stock paid to shareholders, usually on a quarterly schedule.

Earnings Per Share (EPS): After tax annual earnings divided by the number of shares outstanding.

EBITDA: Earnings before interest, taxes, depreciation, and amortization.

Fiscal Year: Any 12-month period designated by a corporation as its accounting year.

Float: Shares outstanding less shares held by insiders. Insiders cannot readily trade shares, so float is considered to be the number of shares available for trading.

Free Cash Flow: Operating cash flow minus amounts spent on plants and equipment and minus dividends.

GARP: Growth at a reasonable price. A method of valuing stocks by comparing their price/earnings ratio to the company's estimated annual earnings growth rate.

Generally Accepted Accounting Principles (GAAP): Accounting rules and procedures established by the Financial Accounting Standards Board, an independent self-regulating organization.

Gross Margin: Profit a company makes on goods and services considering only the direct costs of producing the goods or services.

Growth Investor: One who buys stocks of companies expected to grow sales and earnings faster than inflation.

Implied Growth: Earnings growth rate implied by a stock's price/earnings ratio.

Income Statement: A record of a company's sales and expenses over a particular year or quarter.

Initial Public Offering (IPO): First sale of stock to the public by a corporation.

Insiders: Officers, directors and anyone else owning more than 10 percent of shares outstanding.

Insider Ownership: Number of shares owned or controlled by insiders.

Insider Trading: Shares bought and sold by company insiders.

Institutional Ownership: Shares owned by pension funds, mutual funds, banks, and so forth.

Inventory: Raw materials, work in process, and finished goods that haven't been shipped to customers.

Investment Bank: An organization, usually a stock brokerage firm, involved in taking a new company public (IPO), consulting on mergers and acquisitions, handling corporate borrowing, and so forth.

Junk Bonds: Corporate bonds with less than investment grade ratings.

Large-Cap: Company with market capitalization greater than $8 billion.

Leveraged Buy Out: Take over of a public corporation using borrowed funds.

Liquidity: A measure of the number of shares, or dollar value of shares traded daily.

Market Capitalization: Latest stock price multiplied by number of shares outstanding (shares issued).

Message Board: A location on a Website dedicated to the discussion of a particular topic, usually a single stock or industry sector. Discussions are not real-time. Someone posts a message, and others respond over a period of hours or days.

Mid-Cap: Company with market capitalization between $2 billion and $7 billion.

Momentum Stocks: Highly valued growth stocks.

Most Recent Quarter (MRQ): As of the last date of the last reported fiscal quarter.

Net Income: Income after considering all costs. Earnings per share is net income divided by the number of outstanding shares.

Operating Cash Flow: Surplus cash generated from company's basic operations.

Operating Income: Sales minus all expenses except income taxes and other items not related to the firm's basic business.

Operating Margin: Operating income divided by sales.

PEG: Price to earnings ratio divided by the forecast annual earnings growth rate. Some growth investors consider a stock fairly valued when its P/E ratio and the forecast earnings growth rate are equal.

Price to Book Ratio (P/B): Latest share price divided by the book value stated in the latest report.

Price to Cash Flow (P/CF): Latest share price divided by 12 months' operating cash flow.

Price to Earnings Ratio (P/E): Latest share price divided by 12-months' earnings per share.

Price to Sales Ratio (P/S): Latest share price divided by 12-months' sales per share.

Profit Margin: Bottom-line (after-tax) net income divided by sales.

Pro Forma Earnings: (As if) earnings without considering nonrecurring or extraordinary expenses.

Receivables: See *Accounts Receivable.*

Return on Assets (ROA): Annual after-tax income divided by total assets.

Return on Equity (ROE): Annual after-tax income divided by shareholder's equity.

Return on Capital (ROC): Annual after-tax income divided by the total of shareholder's equity plus long-term debt.

Revenues: A company's sales.

Risk: The probability of losing money.

S&P 500: Capitalization weighted index of 500 of the largest U.S. corporations.

Sales: Services and products sold by a company. Sales and revenues mean the same thing.

Same Store Sales: Sales at retail stores or restaurants open at least one year. A chain's same store sales growth excludes gains due to recent new store openings.

Screening: Searching the entire universe of stocks meeting user-specified criteria, using a computer program or a Website.

SEC: The Securities and Exchange Commission, the U.S. government agency created to regulate the stock market.

Shareholders Equity: The difference between the total of assets and liabilities shown on a company's balance sheet. Book value is the shareholders equity divided by the number of outstanding shares.

Shares outstanding: The total number of shares issued by a corporation.

Small Cap: Company with market capitalization less than $2 billion.

Surprise: Difference between reported earnings and analysts' consensus forecasts. It's a positive surprise if reported earnings exceed forecasts, and a negative surprise when reported earnings come in below forecasts.

Trailing Twelve Months (TTM): The last four reported quarters.

Valuation Ratio: An expression of how the market values a stock by comparing its recent share price to per-share earnings, sales, book value, or cash flow.

Value Investor: One who looks for out of favor (value-priced) stocks.

Volume: Number of shares traded during a specified time, usually one day.

Working Capital: Current assets minus current liabilities.

INDEX

Trend Following
How Great Traders Make Millions in Up or Down Markets, New Expanded Edition
BY MICHAEL W. COVEL

For 30+ years, one trading strategy has consistently delivered extraordinary profits in bull and bear markets alike: *Trend Following.* Just ask the billionaire traders who rely on it...traders like John W. Henry, whose profits bought the Boston Red Sox! In *Trend Following,* New Expanded Edition, you'll meet them. More importantly, you'll discover how to use *Trend Following* in your own portfolio: how to limit risk, employ market discipline, and—when the moment is right—swing for the home run! Want proof it works? This New Expanded Edition includes 100+ pages of easy-to-understand performance charts. Want even more proof? You'll find comprehensive information on backtesting trend following for yourself.

ISBN 0131345508, © 2006, 448 pp., $29.99

Wealth
Grow It, Protect It, Spend It, and Share It
BY STUART E. LUCAS

Here is the first book to integrate all the essential components of wealth management into a coherent whole. Generate higher, more predictable returns...identify, retain, and coordinate the right advisors...get your family to agree on goals and priorities...intelligently manage assets received through inheritances and business sales...and much more. Stuart Lucas draws on 25 years experience managing wealth. He is CEO of Integrated Wealth Management LLC, and Principal and Investment Advisor at Cataumet Partners, his family's investment office. He is also an heir to the Carnation Company fortune after it was sold to Nestlé in 1985.

ISBN 0132366797, © 2006, 304 pp., $25.99

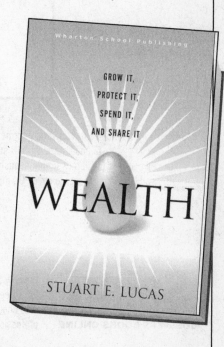